THE
OLYMPIAN

THE
OLYMPIAN

Brian Glanville

Houghton Mifflin Company
Boston

Reprinted by arrangement with
Coward, McCann & Geoghegan, Inc.

Houghton Mifflin Company paperback 1980.

Library of Congress Cataloging in Publication Data

Glanville, Brian.
  The Olympian.

  Reprint of the ed. published by Dell Pub. Co. New York.
  I. Title.
[PZ4.G546Ol 1980] [PR6057.L28] 823'.9'14 79-26550
ISBN 0-395-29086-4

Printed in the United States of America

V 10 9 8 7 6 5 4 3 2 1

FOR MARK

with thanks

There be some sports are painful, and their labour
Delight in them sets off. . .

THE TEMPEST, ACT III, Scene 1

The most beautiful actions of the human body, and
the highest results of the human intelligence, are
conditions, or achievements, of quite unlaborious—
nay, of recreative—effort. But labour is the suffering
in effort. It is the negative quantity. . . . *In brief,*
it is "that quantity of our toil which we die in."

JOHN RUSKIN, *Munera Pulveris*

THE
OLYMPIAN

I

The first time I met him, I thought he was a nut case, just a nutty old man hanging around the recreation grounds, leaning over the rails, shouting at people as they come by. Ah, shut up, shut up, you daft old bugger, that's all I thought about him, running past. Next time I come around he was still there, still shouting, and I caught a word or two, "Elbows *down!*" What the hell was it to do with *him?* Running around, I suddenly laughed, I'd suddenly remembered this old man at home that used to wander up and down the High Street, shouting at cars and waving his stick at them like they were people. When I got around, I was still laughing and that made him furious; you ought to have heard him, yelling and carrying on at me, something about "I'll bloody teach you to laugh!" and then, when I'd run past, something about I wouldn't win nothing.

I did two more laps and then I packed it in. In the showers there, in the dressing room, he come in to me. With this little white beard and this look in his eye, very pale eyes, pale blue, I'd never seen eyes like them, he was like a prophet, one of them colored pictures in the Bible at home.

He said, "What were you laughing at?" I said, "Me? I wasn't laughing at nothing." I'd have told him to fuck off, but somehow you couldn't, he was so intense. I said, "I often laugh when I train." "Well," he said, "You're not going to get much training done, not *good* training. Who's your coach?" I said, "I haven't got one. Just the club coach." He said, "Which club?" I said, "Spartacus," and he give this snort; he said, "Fifty years out of date. They couldn't teach a stag to run."

Just looking at him, listening to him, he seemed some sort of crank. In fact, it's funny the way things come full circle, because that's how I come to think of him, a crank, just like a lot of people did then; only there was the time in between, quite a long time, when I didn't think like that; and the time after. I suppose it was what Jill said; in a kind of way, he hypnotized me. There were his eyes, for a start, like I've said, so pale, like he'd spent a long time looking at the sun, and when you got to know him, you could imagine him doing that, just staring at the sun, for a challenge, not willing to be beaten by anything. He hardly ever blinked, just stared at you, almost through you, like some sort of blowtorch, burning away at anything he didn't like, any kind of disagreement with what he believed. And the hollow cheeks and his white tuft of hair and the way he shoved his face forward, into yours.

Alan, that's the sprinter, the bronze medal one, used to call him the Ancient Mariner; he'd say, "By thy long gray beard and glittering eye, now wherefore stopp'st thou me?" but not to Sam, not directly to Sam; it wasn't the kind of thing you could imagine yourself saying to him.

Then, of course, there was his rabbit. In a way, it was never so much what he said, but the tone of it, the rhythm of the words coming and coming at you, nonstop, like a torrent; you went with it, or it just swept you away, anyhow. Even now, I remember parts of.what he said, then, standing in that little, dark, cramped dressingroom, dripping water, just out of the shower, while he kept on and on at me. He asked, "What distance do you run?" I said, "Two-twenties, quarters," and he said, "You are built to run the *mile*. You are the perfect combination of ectomorph-mesomorph; long calves, lean, muscular thighs and arms, chest between thirty-seven and thirty-eight, and broad, slim shoulders. A miler is the aristocrat of running. A miler is the nearest to a thoroughbred racehorse that exists on two legs. Look at me: a natural distance runner, wiry and muscular, trained down to gristle. We are the *infantry* of running. Your four-forty and eight-eighty men, these are your cavalry. The sprinters are your shock troops, your commandos."

One of the lads changing over in the corner, someone from another club, said, "What are we, then, mate; the walkers?" and the old boy said, "The walkers are what Chesterton called the donkey; the Devil's walking parody on all two-footed things," and he give this imitation, strutting up and down the dressing room, sticking out his arse and waggling his shoulders, just like walkers do, till all of us that was in there laughed, and even the walker had to smile.

The old boy said, "I am *not* decrying walkers. Each man to the physical activity that suits him best. I would be prepared to award a gold medal even to *crawlers*. We already have hop, step and jumpers. But there must be proportion in all things. Just as a child learns to crawl, then to walk and then to run, so there is a hierarchy in athletic locomotion."

To tell the truth, I didn't know what he was on about most of the time, leaving school at fifteen like I had, dead idle, never bothering; he was using words I'd never heard of. But it held you; that was the thing about him. He could hold you.

Would you say, Ike, that you and Sam were very close?

Pretty close, yeah.

Real close? Like father and son?

Well, I don't know about that.

But he's more to you than just a coach?

I am *not* a coach. A coach is an exploiter of the young. I am an *instructor*.

An instructor of what, Sam?

An instructor of *cham*pions. Of people who de*sire* to be champions.

There's a difference?

There is no comparison. My job is not to produce runners, not to produce mere human animals; it is to produce outstanding human beings. To find these people, then to help them find themselves.

Where did he find *you*, Ike?

In a park.

In a park? You were running through a park?

I was running around a running track. *In* a park.

And Sam found you?

Yeah. He watched me training.

And you saw he had the makings of a champion, Sam?

I saw it immediately. From the way he moved, although he didn't know *how* to move. From the way he held his head.

You can tell just by how someone holds their head?

The way a man holds his head is the way a man thinks about himself.

When I was changed, we went for a cup of tea, or rather *I* had a cup of tea, he had a glass of milk. It was at Lyons, in the Edgware Road; we went and sat at one of those stone-topped tables with the tea slopped all over it and teacups everywhere. He asked me why I drank tea; he said, "An athlete is as good as his diet. Tea is bad. Coffee is bad. Alcohol is worse than either. Do you drink alcohol?" I said, "Well, yes, I have a few beers, now and again," and he slapped the table so loud everybody looked around; it was embarrassing. He said, "You are deliberately poisoning yourself. You are weakening the natural stimuli provided by the nervous system. The human body provides its own stimulant, and its own stimulant is adrenaline. This stimulant can be induced. Fear produces adrenaline. Anticipation produces adrenaline. But alcohol will clog your brain; it will dull your reflexes; it will affect your lungs; it will undermine your heart. Do you smoke?"

I wanted to say no, which was ridiculous, because who was he, I'd only known him half an hour, and whose life was it, his or mine? Which was something that I'd often find myself asking in the time to come; whose life, whose body was it, his or mine? Till I decided—mine. I said, "Well, just a little." He said, "There is no truce to be made with the cigarette. Tobacco is the body's enemy. What happens to a chimney when it's been used a long time?" I said, "Soot?" and he said, "If you smoke, your lungs are like a chimney. But you can't call the sweep. Have you any cigarettes on you now?" and, when I half nodded, held out his hand, thin with blue veins, long fingers, like a claw, and God knows why, I put my hand in my pocket and took it out, the packet, with what I had left in it, four or five cigarettes, and put them in his hand, and he crumpled them, his fingers closed around them like the grab of them mechanical cranes they have there in the arcades, in the Charing Cross Road, screwing them up; I should have belted him. But I didn't. I just said, "Hey," then watched while he opened his hand and let them drop out, the scrunched-up fags and the packet, onto the floor, like rubbish.

Then he got on to diet; did I eat meat. I shouldn't eat meat, *he* was a vegetarian, that and milk, only this wasn't *good* milk, it had been through too many processes, the best milk was the milk that was closest to the cow. I said, "A runner needs strength, don't he?" He said, "Press down my arm," and rolled up the sleeve and held it out, his right arm, all knobs and cords and veins like the root of a tree, the kind that grows above ground, gnarled and twisted. I looked at it, and I didn't feel like touching it. He said, "Go on, try," and I tried, I put both hands on his arm; it felt hard, like wood, no flesh on it at all, and I started pressing. I was only eighteen but strong, very, very fit, and it should have been easy, I felt almost sorry for him. But I couldn't budge it, however hard I pushed, till in the end I was actually standing up; there was sweat running down my forehead, people were staring but it didn't worry me, or rather it did worry me, I had to do it; I was making a fool of myself, and when I looked down suddenly, into his eyes, they had this look in them, a sort of smile—of triumph really—and more than that, like he was saying, "There you are, I told you so, I knew you could never beat me," which made me press down all the harder, still looking at him, but it was no go, he just blinked once, that was all, and in the end, I give up. I sat down.

I said, "I don't know how you do it," and he said, "Not bad on vegetables, eh? Vegetables prevail over meat!" and then, "Strength is not just the strength of the body; it is the strength of the mind. The strength of the will prevails over the weakness of the body. The will drives the body beyond what the body believes it can do. That is why a great athlete must feed not only his body but his mind. How big was Paavo Nurmi? How big was Sidney Wooderson? He was a solicitor, and in a running vest he *looked* like a solicitor, but when he ran, the mind was greater than the body." And on and on. And on and on and on.

"Why were the Greeks the true, original athletes? Because the Greeks were the inventors of the golden mean. They did not neglect the body for the mind. In our age, we have neglected the body for the machine. What we have to do is to rediscover the body, stop poisoning it with false stimulants, stop filling it with noxious substances, stop treating it only as a means of self-indulgent *plea*sure. A plant needs water, and a body needs exercise. If you deprive a plant of water, it dies. If you do not exercise a body, it corrupts, and the mind corrupts with it. Look at the politicians and the scholars and the businessmen. Look at the people who rule our world and tell us what to do. What a travesty of logic! These are people who *have* no bodies, only heads. And many athletes have no heads, but only bodies. A champion is a man who has trained his body *and* his mind, who has learned to conquer pain and to use pain for his own purposes. A great athlete is at peace with himself and at peace with the world; he has fulfilled himself. He envies nobody. Wars are caused by people who have not fulfilled themselves; I have fought in two, and I know. Look—just here, above the navel; that was Flanders. And here, look, on right shoulder. That was Murmansk. But I bore them no ill will, because I knew I would survive. You can kill the body, but you cannot kill the spirit. There are no limits to what the body can do when the spirit is strong. Twenty years ago, they said a four-minute mile was impossible. I told them then: 'We shall live to see it run in three minutes, forty seconds, and they laughed. But what has happened? The four-minute mile is now a commonplace. Athletes run it every week. Even schoolboys run it. We shall see a three-forty mile and a nine-second 100 meters and a nine-foot high jump and a twenty-foot pole vault. It all lies in the conception. Once these things have been conceived as possible, they are achieved. And that is why athletics are important, why records are important. Because they demonstrate the scope of human possibility; which is unlimited. The inconceivable is conceived, and then it is accomplished.

"Look at me. It was inconceivable that my one arm should resist the pressure of your two, and yet it did. Now it is inconceivable to you that your two arms could defeat my one. But all this is arbitrary. Matter is arbitrary. It is your will against mine, your spirit against mine. Everything depends on the will. I have been in India and seen a fakir stab himself with knives, plunge knives into his body and pull them out again, without a mark. I have seen them walk on fire. If these men desired, they could lift weights which would make the strongest man in an Olympiad look weak. A man like Vlasov of Russia would look puny, although he was three times their size. So this is why I say to you, train. Look after your body. Temper it with pain. And your body will amaze you; you will do things that you thought impossible. That is why running matters. That is why Olympiads matter. Not for gold medals, those little, worthless disks, but for their inner meaning, what they stand for. The Olympic flame is sacred, because it is the flame of human aspiration."

I got excited, listening to him, understanding some of what he said, not understanding lots of it, but still, like I said, being carried along, as much by how he said it as by what he said. I mean, I was eighteen; who had I ever heard who could talk like that, who could spout ideas like that, who could make you believe in what you could do and what you were doing, the way he did?

Up to then I'd just been running, something to do, a race here, a race there, won a few, lost most of them, not knowing what I really wanted—out of that or anything else. But hearing him in that tea shop, I knew what I wanted and I realized it had been there all the time, only, like, it had come and gone. Sometimes I'd felt it when I was actually in a race, when I knew I'd got it in me to win, when I'd feel this sort of current shoot through me, a sort of ambition; other times it was when I was training, usually alone, in Epping Forest or some mornings on the track, early, when I'd been on night shift and I was there alone; you'd be moving so well, so smooth, your body felt so good, that you knew you could beat anyone on earth, bring 'em all on: Elliott, Bannister, the lot. And now I felt it in me again, even without running, even just sitting; this *knowing* that I could be great, that I wanted to be great—and something else: that he could show me how.

Mind you, you might say that was him, that was his stock-in-trade, which I admit; but what I mean is, that was part of it; if he hadn't had one, he wouldn't have had the other.

Out in the street, the Edgware Road, I hardly noticed the crowds. I was in my blue track suit, very proud of it, just got it, with the club crest on the pocket, and Sam was wearing what he always wore off the track, this gray jersey and a pair of blue jeans—never mind what it was, sun or rain, snow or hail.

I remember we walked across Hyde Park, with him still talking, and passing Speaker's Corner, where they was all talking, too, the blackies and the Irish and the nut cases, and him looking around and saying in this loud voice, "Lunatics, the lot of them, pouring out their prejudice and hatred," and it suddenly came to me that this was what he'd kept reminding me of all the time he was talking—the tone of his voice and the way it was one long speech, with you the audience.

All the way across the park, he was talking, I was listening; I think we both just took it for granted he was going to train me. He'd got three or four he was coaching, he said; one was a miler, one was middle distance, and the others sprinters. Sundays they trained on Hampstead Heath; other days it depended on the light and the time people could get off. He said he had this physical education job with the city council—it was long before he opened his gym for businessmen— and he'd done it a year, and when he got tired of it, he'd change. He said, "If I want money, I can always make it. Money is easy to make. Never let yourself be dominated or deluded by the importance of money; it is secondary. I've been a sailor and a soldier and a farmer and a postman and a travel courier. I have cooked in the finest hotels, and I have worked as a garage mechanic. I have written for newspapers, and I have *sold* newspapers. My dear wife is dead, I have no children, and I can exist with perfect comfort in the open air."

Then he asked me what *I* did, and I told him I was working in this cardboard-box factory, knowing more or less what he'd say—partly, I suppose, because it was what I really felt myself—that it was the wrong job for an athlete, unhealthy, that it wouldn't get me nowhere. I must have had half a dozen jobs, anyway, since I'd left school; working in a bakery, then a butcher's shop, apprentice electrician, trainee telephone engineer, and now the factory—nothing that really interested me.

He said, "A job like that erodes the will and stultifies the body. Go out into the air! Be a bus conductor or a park keeper or a swimming pool attendant or even a road sweeper! Do something that involves the use of the body. How can you hope to run when you spend the whole day standing still? How can you hope to master your own body when your body is the slave of a machine?" And I agreed with him; it all made sense; I didn't see nothing funny in it, his taking it for granted this was what I wanted, to be a great runner, whereas up to now it had just been something I did, where in the winter I played a bit of football over the Marshes.

I promised on Sunday I'd meet him on Hampstead Heath to do some training with him. By this time we'd walked right across the park, over to the bridge across the Serpentine, stood there talking, looking at the water, all the willows hanging over it, then back again, to Hyde Park Corner. Once he'd gone, it all felt a bit strange to me; it wasn't my manor, this part of London, but while you were with him you could be anywhere, you didn't think of where you were. When he shook hands, he held on to my hand very tight and looked at me, like an animal trainer or something, right in the eye; he said, "I can make you a great miler. If you want to be a great miler," then left me standing there, all dazed.

I could have flown home, let alone run, and all that night I couldn't sleep; I was running races, winning medals, hearing his voice come at me out of the dark. I don't suppose I slept above an hour.

The oh-so-celebrated Ike Low-Sam Dee partnership nearly came to grief the day it was born, when Dee took the eighteen-year-old Cockney kid out for a grueling, make-or-break training run on Hampstead Heath and found himself faced with a one-man mutiny. "I had to find out what the lad was made of," snaps running's most controversial coach, the man officials love to hate. "It was all right for Sam," cracks Low, the six-foot, Hackney-born boy wonder miler, "He was on a bicycle."

We met up by the pond there; I was a few minutes late, and he was sitting on this bicycle, which was something I hadn't expected: I suppose I'd thought that he'd be running with me. There was no one else, just him and me; I mean, none of the other runners he'd said he was training. I'd never seen the Heath before, and it made quite an impression on me, though by the time that afternoon was finished, I wouldn't have cared if I'd never seen it again. But the sun was shining, and everything was this fresh, bright green— the grass, the trees, even the weeds. And not flat, like a park, but rolling—dips and hillocks and mounds and woods, very round and lush, more like the country. I wondered if he lived around there; he'd been very mysterious about where he lived; I imagined him living in a tent or maybe a caravan.

We strolled across the road, him wheeling the bike, and as we reached the other side, the Heath, he took a stopwatch out of his pocket. He said, "Here is your enemy. Here is the beast you have to conquer." There was a course he wanted me to run, he said, one he'd worked out himself, all along the paths, so he could ride beside me. He told me, "We'll see what sort of stamina you've got; then, when we know about that, we can work out a training schedule for you. The needs of every athlete vary, not just between the distance runner and the middle-distance runner, the miler and the sprinter, but from miler to miler, sprinter to sprinter."

So off we went, him on the bike with the watch in his hand, now and then telling me, "Spring!" then, "Stop!" up and down the paths, dodging the little kids and the prams and the people, over stones and sometimes tree roots, till I wished I'd never worn my spikes, down steep slopes into little valleys, up them again the other side. I'd always hated cross-country, always tried to get out of it when the club was doing a cross-country run, and this was killing, the worst I'd ever known, no chance to slow down or take a breather because *he* was there, sometimes beside me, sometimes behind me, sometimes just ahead of me, turning around and calling me on, talking and talking, telling me to go faster, to take longer strides, to hold my head higher, to use more arm action, to keep my elbows closer to my sides, until I hated him; I tried to block out the sound of his voice, just concentrate on a group of trees I could see, try and make out what kind they were, or a cloud with a funny shape, or try and guess how many strides it'd take me to an oak tree or a pond or maybe someone I could see walking.

But it never worked for long; he'd suddenly raise his voice, shouting, *"Sprint!"* or some other order, or else he'd suddenly ride out ahead of me so I couldn't ignore him if I wanted to, not with him there just ahead, his hairy old face bent forward towards mine. Then, just as I was thinking that all I wanted to do was catch up with him and smash him, he'd spin around and disappear behind me. To make matters worse, it was a warm afternoon and I was in my track suit. I wanted to stop and strip it off, yet at the same time I didn't want to risk no favors, I didn't want *nothing* from him, just finish the bloody run and go home and never set eyes on him again. And then there was another feeling I had at the same time as *that,* that this was how he wanted me to think, he wanted me to hate him. I don't know why, but somehow I knew it from the expression on his face, a sort of mocking look, and when I couldn't see him, from the sound of his voice.

Once he asked me, "Are you hot?" and I said, *"I'm* all right," though the sweat was running down my forehead, stinging my eyes, dribbling into my mouth, all salt, trickling out of my armpits, inside my running vest. He said, "It's better for you than a Turkish bath, this is." Once I asked

him, "How long we been running?" He said, "Thirty-eight
minutes. Are you tired?" I said, "No, not tired," and tried
to kid myself I wasn't, but the longer I ran, the worse it
got, my mouth so dry, my heart pumping away so loud I
reckoned people must be able to hear it for miles around.
Then he said, "Want a drink?" and honestly I loved him;
he had this plastic bottle in his hand; holding it out to me,
he said, "Not too much," it was better than champagne,
and then, "You'd better take your track suit off," and I did,
I stepped out of it, it had practically stuck to me in places,
and with that off and the drink I thought I'll run for miles,
I'll bloody show him, and for a while, maybe for a quarter
of an hour or so, it really was a bit better, I was almost
beginning to enjoy it, which he probably realized, because
soon things started getting harder; there were many more
hills to climb, even a run across the grass. He said, "Down
into that bowl and up the other side. I'll meet you there, I'll
time you," and cycled the long way around the path while I
ran down into this dip, then had to climb the bleeding hill,
like going through some bloody assault course. He was there
at the top with his stopwatch, saying, "Very good, all right,
come on," and cycling off, not looking back, leaving me to
follow like a dog.

So all this feeling good wore off; after a while I was back
where I started, and worse, except for taking off the bloody
track suit; my legs aching, my chest aching, my heart thumping and banging away, the only things to look forward to,
the only things that kept me going, the drinks of water; but
only when he offered them, I'd never ask for them, no matter
how I felt, any more than I'd stop till the old bastard said I
could stop. Except twice to be sick, when he just stood
watching me while it all came heaving out, not saying anything, just standing, waiting for me to go on, while I thought,
*Christ I'll die, I'm going to die, my guts are coming out, I'll
die.*

In the end it got darker and colder; I was swaying about
almost bumping into people, just not seeing them till they
was on top of me, and at last, right at the top of another
bloody hill, or maybe one of the same bloody hills, God
knows, hearing his voice behind me saying, "Okay, that'll
do," and collapsing, bang, right where I was, and bursting
into tears, lying there crying and not being able to stop, not
even caring, just lying there and crying.

He didn't say a word, just stood there by his bicycle, with his back to me, waiting for me to finish, just like when I was being sick. I don't think I've ever hated anyone the way I hated him then—giving me nothing, when it was him who'd got me in this state. People were walking past, looking at me, one or two of them stopping, but I didn't care about that, either. I heard one of them say, behind me, "Is he all right?" and Sam's voice say, "Yes, he's all right," and I thought, *Who the hell are you to say I'm all right, you old cunt; whose body is it, who did all the bloody running?* till at last I stopped crying, and then I felt ashamed; I didn't want to face him, I buried my head in my arms and went on lying there, hoping that he'd go away, but when I looked up, he was still there, still with his back to me, like he was prepared to stand there forever. So I got up, and as I got up, he turned to me; the watch was still in his hand. He said, "You have run for two hours and seventeen minutes. I would estimate that in the first hour you covered ten and a quarter miles, in the second hour, nine and a half miles, and in the final seventeen minutes, less than two miles, making a total of slightly less than twenty-two miles, which is four miles less than the marathon. That, of course, is only an estimate." Not good or bad or well done or how are you. And still up on his bloody bicycle as we went all the way back across the Heath, my feet so sore I could hardly take a step, my calves aching like someone had been going over them with a truncheon, and him saying, "I do not believe in training to exhaustion. The Zatopek training. Zatopek was a great champion, but his achievements have been surpassed. This was not training; this was a test of stamina and will. There were moments when I doubted your will, but I am satisfied that you gave your maximum. Your maximum can be increased, just as your stamina *must* be increased."

I don't even know how I got home, on a bus I think, sleeping most of the way. That night I dreamed that I was flying. He was in it somewhere. He was doing it.

Q. What would you say are the most important considerations in training an athlete?
A. Stamina, technique and will.
Q. In what order?
A. Will, stamina and technique.
Q. How much emphasis do you place in technique?

A. Unlimited.

Q. Coaches like Franz Stampfl believe that technique is relatively unimportant, that great runners often succeed through power, preparation and determination, despite an undistinguished style. Would you disagree?

A. A runner who makes improper use of his body is wasting energy. Style cannot substitute power; power cannot substitute determination. A strong man will run faster if he has been taught rhythmic movement; a graceful man will run faster if he becomes strong. And neither will become a champion unless he strengthens his resolve.

Q. Do you think there are ways of strengthening an athlete's resolve?

A. Yes.

Q. What are they?

A. They are psychological. They depend on the relation between the athlete and his coach. An athlete is generally young and immature. The coach's job is to convince him of his possibilities.

Q. Can you describe the program you would follow with a new pupil?

A. It would vary according to the athlete. First I must test his possibilities, both mental and physical. Then I decide on what area I must concentrate: on his mind, his stamina, or his style. Each athlete must be instructed in the kinetics of the body, on the physiology of propulsion. My runners are not taught to run; they are taught to *float,* so that the maximum effect is achieved with the minimum of effort, like a bird.

Q. Do you advocate the same style, irrespective of distance?

A. The principle of movement, of economy of effort, is always the same. The precise dynamics vary with each event.

Q. You place considerable emphasis on the development of the upper body. Does that mean you subscribe to the belief held in some quarters just after the war that the arms are more important to a runner than his legs?

A. The arms cannot possibly be more important than the legs, any more than the chassis of a motorcar can be more important than the wheels. But the arms and the upper body impart secondary drive to locomotion. That is why I encourage my runners to develop them through weight training.

Q. But you have reservations about weight training?

A. Proportion must be retained between strength, will, and technique. There is a tendency at the moment to believe that everything can be achieved through strength. Brute force may be paramount in the throwing events, though even there, will and technique play their parts. In the running events, it can never take pride of place.

I hated the weight lifting; I'd never bothered with it in the club; smelly old gymnasium and all the big men there, the shot-putters and that, grunting and heaving away like they were having it off. To me, it was like a fetish, everybody had to do it, whether they were throwing the hammer or playing tiddlywinks; it didn't make no sense.

But he insisted on it. He had me along to this gym that belonged to a school in Holloway, one where he was teaching phys. ed. I went one evening, and there was this ruddy great barbell on the deck with great shining disks on it, so big I could hardly bear to look at them, let alone lift them, and he said, "Right, watch me; this is a curl," and put his hands on the bar, bent down and came up again, bang, bringing it up to his chest, arms like twisted rope, red in the face, his eyes practically popping. Then he put it down, one-two, and said, "Now you do it."

There was a few kids standing around and grinning, people that used the gym in the evening, teen-agers like myself, most of them, and I didn't fancy it. I hesitated for a moment. I'd never done curls before, anyway, only squats and presses, and a bit of clean-and-jerk, but in the end I bent down, just about got the bloody thing off the floor, then dropped it. He said, "Right, we'll make it easier for you," and he took off the big disks and put on a couple of smaller ones, twenty-five pounds, and this time I managed it all right, except that right away he said, "Again!" and after that, "Again!" till I felt I was back on the bloody Heath, pounding away with my feet like lumps of raw meat and my legs feeling like they'd drop off. But when I'd done them, he said, "All right, rest," and immediately started clinking about with the weights again, saying, "This time, the press."

He put seventy-five pounds on the bar and made me lift the bloody thing above my head till my arms ached, keeping up the usual running commentary: "All training must be done under calculated pressure. The effort and the intervals must be exactly judged. Training which is not done under pressure is of no real value."

The others in the gym had all of them gathered around by now; they seemed to be a bit amused by him but to respect him. He loved them being there, I could tell that, clowning around, showing the right way and the wrong way to lift the weights, but I didn't enjoy being part of the act, the stooge.

Two of the lads there that night were runners he was training, a quarter-miler called Tony Dash that I knew about, he'd come third in the Southern Counties—he was from somewhere like Clapham—and a boy from Yorkshire, Tom Burgess, that run the longer ones, the mad ones, like the three miles and the six. Tom said he'd come down to London because of Sam; he'd met Sam when he was running for his club, at Chiswick. He was very, very thin, and all he lived for was athletics; everything he did was tied up with it—his job, where he lived, what he ate and drank, whether he got married. I said to Tony once, "I bet he doesn't even crap without thinking will it help me do a better time," and Tony said, "If he thought it'd help, he'd never crap at all."

We went out to a café afterward, the four of us, to have a cup of tea—milk for Sam—and Tom and Sam got down to talking about times, overall times and lap times, what the Americans had done this year and what the Russians had done, what you ought to aim for in the first mile if you wanted to run an Olympic-qualifying time in the three miles, whether it was better to put in a fast second mile and try to kill off the field or to leave yourself something in hand for a spurt at the end, whether in a race you should concentrate on the time, rather than the other runners, till I wondered, *Is this how I'm going to get? Is this all I'm ever going to think about?* because it was like a religion; but once or twice I caught Tony's eye and seemed to see him smile, which made me feel better about it.

Sam was on a lot about Tony smoking, the same stuff he'd given me about the body turning into a chimney. Tony said, "Five a day, Sam, I cut it down to five a day; I've come down from twenty. I can't just cut it off completely, honest; I'd die." Sam said, "You'll die much sooner if you go on filling your lungs with that filth." He ran for Poly Harriers; Tom was with Woodford. Clubs didn't seem to make no difference to Sam; he seemed to take his athletes where he found them.

I heard him say once, "I will not attach myself to any club. My talents are available to the best, whoever they may be. An athletes' club is a contradiction in terms. Athletics is an individual sport, and a club is a collective entity. A club is like a convoy—everyone goes at the speed of the slowest ship—but a race is won by the runner who goes the fastest."

Tom was living over Chigwell then, and we went back some of the way together, on the bus. He said, "Sam's a genius, you realize that. He's years ahead of his time," and he was dead serious; in fact, you hardly ever saw him smile. I said, "He don't half drive you though." He said, "You're lucky to get taken up by him at all. I know people that have come to him and begged him. If there was any justice, he'd be coaching the Great Britain team. But they hate him; they're jealous of him; a lot of coaches are. You'll find that out; you'll see." And in a way I did see, quite soon, as a matter of fact.

The thing was, Sam wanted to see me in a race, and not just any race, a mile. So I went to our own club coach one day, Des Tompkins, and I asked him, I said, "I'd like to run the mile." He looked at me—he was a tall man with a mustache, always very dapper, a bit like a sergeant major, really —and he said, "You? What do you want to run the mile for? You can hardly get round the quarter." I said, "Well, it's an idea I had, that's all. I'd like to try it." He said, "Well, three of the milers are here tonight"—at Paddington, this was— "why don't you join in with them?" I said, "Well, frankly I wanted to run it under competitive conditions, just so I could see how I went." He said, "And frankly, you're not going to run a mile for this club unless you can show me you're better than the boys I've got already," which I suppose was fair enough, though I didn't think so at the time.

So there was nothing else to do but go out and run against them, which I did, though I must say I didn't like the idea. Not that any of them was all that; they'd none of them broke four minutes, the fastest any of them had done was 4.08 or something like that, but it was a new experience. I'd no idea how to pace myself, and I could easily end up looking like a twot.

Anyway, I ran. Des said to them, "This is our new miler; he says he's going to leave the rest of you standing," which made it even more embarrassing; the three of them all gave me an old-fashioned look, then looked at one another. I said,

"Just to see, that's all," and one of them said, "You'll bloody see. It's not like poncing around with quarters." Then Des lined us up and we were off.

I'd reckoned that the best thing to do, the safest thing, was just to stay up with them, then see if at the end I couldn't find a bit of speed to beat them, and in the first lap, of course, it was dead easy, being used to the pace of the quarter; in fact, the difficulty was not to let yourself go shooting out ahead of the rest of the field. The second lap, one of them, Jack Brogan, a lanky bloke with red hair, suddenly spurted out ahead of the rest of us, and I thought, *Do I catch him or do I stay with the others?* but as he got farther ahead, I started worrying, I thought, *I'd better catch him,* and put a spurt on, though it wasn't easy; I was feeling it a bit, this second lap, that feeling in the lungs when they're starting to ache and you think about things like second wind, which is something you never think of in the quarter.

I caught him all right, and once I'd caught him he seemed to let up a little, we jogged along side by side, but as soon as the third lap started, I began to realize that they must have got together, because he dropped back, and another of them, a little short fellow, Roger Coomb, shot past me like a blue-arsed fly, and then I saw it: They were trying to kill me off. So realizing this, I let him go, just jogging with the others, running a much, much slower lap, and Jack turned round to me and said, "What's the matter, are you clapped out already?" I said, "You'll bloody see."

When Roger saw I wasn't following him, he dropped his pace, staying maybe twenty yards ahead, hoping I suppose that I'd come up and challenge him, but I didn't, I was waiting for the last lap, and when we reached it, Des was there at the side, yelling, "Last lap; ding-a-ling-a-ling," for the bell. I said to the fourth one, Charlie Cooper, "Come on, your turn now," and sure enough he went, but of course it was a little late now, they hadn't worn me out like they meant to, and suddenly I found I was starting to enjoy it, the challenge of it all, the working things out, and even the rest of it, the actual running, maybe because that run with Sam had done me more good than I'd thought it had; after that, nothing could be too bad.

So there we were all in a bunch, everyone afraid to go, I suppose—I know I was—I felt I'd got something left, but I couldn't risk breaking, I'd no idea what they'd got. And then

Jack, the red-haired fellow, broke, about two-fifty yards
from home, from just ahead of me in the inside lane, and
there was something about the back of him, his head and
shoulders, something cocky, that got up my nose; I thought,
Right, you bastard, and I went, all or nothing, and he half
looked around when he heard me coming behind him, and I
reckon seeing me made him all the more determined, because he put on even more of a spurt. But I knew I had him,
I was closing in—I wasn't even worried about the others—
and suddenly I was level with him, looking at his face, seeing
it dead white and worried, then past him, and I wanted to
laugh, knowing I'd skate home, that he'd never catch me.
Around the last bend, feeling the cinders kick up against my
leg, then into the straight, just starting to run out of breath,
but keeping it up, keeping ahead, until there it was, the line,
and I was over it, standing there sobbing and puffing away,
Des with his stopwatch in his hand saying, "Not *bad,* 4.11,"
then Jack coming in, then the other two, and Jack collapsing
on the grass and lying there like he'd been shot.

The week after that, Saturday, I ran the mile at Eton
Manor.

*A sports stadium on the fringe of East London, urban and
peripheral, lurking behind a high brick wall; the very grass
appears to be growing on sufferance. A brick-red running
track surrounds the field; on one side, there's a modest
wooden grandstand, on the other, a small collection of
wooden huts, of the kind which appear, ephemerally, on
building sites. There are, perhaps, a dozen spectators scat-
tered around the grandstand in little knots and islands, like
a metaphor of noncommunication. More are dotted about
the field, behind the green railings which separate the track,
the field, from its residual public. On the grass, a number of
athletes in track suits—blue, green, purple, black—are limbering up; spurting forward in sudden, nervous truncated
bursts; standing, feet apart, patting the ground; sitting down,
legs outstretched, their hands reaching elastically to their
toes; or high-kicking like ballerinas. Others sprawl about the
grass, relaxing; still others form groups around older men in
blue blazers—the coaches.*

*There is nothing predicated, here, of triumph, medals,
laurel wreaths, of great stadia full of chanting thousands.
If the athletes have style, the occasion has none, and the*

*athletes themselves have style, for the most part, only in
movement. In repose, strong limbs hidden in their track
suits, there's a suburban gaucheness about them. Yet from
these drab crucibles, champions come, just as boxers come
out of the slums, footballers out of coal mines. The difference
for the athlete is that this and places like this are his milieu,
for most of the year. Some will never go beyond it; others
will do so infrequently, the luckiest more regularly, above all
in the Olympic year, with its special, transmitting alchemy.
Then, briefly, they will turn into lions and roar in the arena.*

*In the middle of the field a tall young man in a pale-blue
track suit is limbering up, gracefully, yet anxious, jogging,
sprinting a few paces, only to stop, like a man suddenly
aware he is going in the wrong direction, jogging again:*
IKE LOW. *His hair is dark and wiry; as a child's, it must have
been curly. Now it gives a first impression of being almost
tiered. He has a fine, straight nose, but the youth of his face
is mitigated by the hollow cheeks of the athlete in training.
His mouth is wide, but narrow; his eyes, gray and rather
small, deep-set and alert, look frequently across the stadium,
where the entrance gate is just concealed from view. Even
in these few, restricted movements, one divines an elegance,
a nervous, thoroughbred power. His tension, indeed, is that
of a racehorse at the starting gate.*

A voice sounds, over the loudspeakers.

VOICE: Competitors for the mile, please. Will competitors
for the mile go to their positions.

IKE LOW *begins.. abstractedly, to peel off his track suit,
revealing broad, slender shoulders, slim, muscular arms, a
chest not large, but firmly developed. The body, though
clearly fit and strong, gives the impression of still-unused
potential; it remains a boy's body, not a man's, and the man
will be bigger than the boy. Suddenly, he appears to see what
he is looking for; his eyes focus on a lean, gray-headed man
who has appeared at the entrance to the track, brisk and
purposeful, walking as if to set the world an example; that
all men his age should be—as fit, as fast, as tautly preserved
as he. The man—*SAM DEE—*is wearing a gray, turtleneck
jersey, blue jeans and canvas shoes. He has a small white
beard, neatly kept—an emblem of defiance, perhaps, or
jaunty eccentricity.*

*Pulling his track suit, now, down sinewy, functional
thighs, hard calves, flecked only lightly with hair,* IKE LOW

raises a hand as if to wave, then drops it again. A tall man in a blazer comes towards him, straight-backed, with a small mustache, a long head, sleekly brushed, a military air; the coach of his athletics club, DES TOMPKINS.

TOMPKINS: Come on, let's have you, Ike. Not looking for anything, are you?

LOW (*a little uneasily*): No, I'm all right.

TOMPKINS: Walder's the one to watch; he always comes in with a strong finish. Don't burn yourself out on the first lap. And try not to get boxed in.

LOW (*abstractedly*): No. No. Okay.

TOMPKINS *follows his gaze and sees* SAM DEE, *who has now stopped, almost level with the starting mark, and is looking about him, for* LOW.

TOMPKINS (*suspiciously*): That's Sam Dee, isn't it?

LOW (*carefully nonchalant*): Yeah, I think it is, as a matter of fact.

TOMPKINS: What's *he* doing here?

LOW (*speculatively*): Come to watch.

Together, LOW *and* TOMPKINS *walk toward the start.*

TOMPKINS: Come to see if he can pinch someone else's runners, more like. You do the work; then he nips in and grabs the publicity. (*With a sudden look at* LOW.) He hasn't been after you, has he?

LOW (*restlessly*): I have been *seeing* him a bit.

TOMPKINS: *That's* why you wanted to run the mile.

LOW: Sort of.

TOMPKINS: I might have known you'd never have thought of it on your own.

LOW: Why wouldn't I, then?

TOMPKINS: Okay, I'll talk to you about him afterward. Only he'd better keep out of my way.

He walks straight past DEE, *who is now leaning over the railings opposite the start, watching him and* LOW, *and goes up to another of his runners, the red-haired* JACK BROGAN, *who is also to compete in the race.* IKE LOW, *with a quick, cautious glance at him approaches* SAM DEE, *who is smiling.*

DEE: Didn't like seeing me, did he?

LOW: Not much, no.

DEE: No, they're all the same, these coaches. Little men. Little men. Obsessed with their own importance. Now I'll tell you how you're going to win this race. The best runner is Walder. He has speed but no stamina. The ideal way to beat him is to kill him off before the last lap, but this you're too inexperienced to do.

As he talks, he continues to smile, with the air of a conniving wizard. LOW *listens to him with total attention; his whole wiry body seems to be hearing, absorbing, almost as if he were under a spell, the young body possessed by, in thrall to, the old.*

LOW: So what do I do?

DEE: The first lap will be slow. Probably about 58.5. The second will be slightly quicker. You will take on Walder not in the last lap but in the third. At the end of that lap, I want you to be ahead of *him*, even if you aren't leading. In the final lap . . .

THE STARTER *speaks, somberly, pistol in hand, like a platonic executioner. He is small and squat, his blue blazer elaborately crested.*

THE STARTER: Get to your marks.

TOMPKINS (*peremptorily*): Get down there, Ike.

DEE (*giving* TOMPKINS *a disdainful glance*): In that last lap, go on the final bend. You'll hear me shouting.

He pats IKE LOW *on the arm, and* LOW, *taking his place in the second lane, beside the inside track, bends down with the others in the ritual starting position, hands to the ground, arms straight and parallel, one knee bent—like men frozen, suddenly, unwittingly, in a posture from race memory.* LOW'S *tongue can be seen to move briefly across his lips, but his face is smooth.*

THE STARTER *points his pistol at the sky.*

THE STARTER: Get set.

BANG: *The pistol finally explodes, the runners rise from their haunches and are off to a thin, dispersed cheer, in which individual cries—*"Come on, John! Let's have you, Ted!"*— are clearly heard. Because there are four laps, four good minutes, to run, the start has none of the drama, the irretrievability of the sprints; nor is it as casual as the ten thousand meters or the marathon, where the runners merely stand at the start, one foot in front of the other, in a ragged phalanx. The pace of the runners now is brisk rather than urgent, the interest, in these early laps, a connoisseur's: tactical, stylistic. Dotted about the track, the coaches watch anxiously, calling sharp words of advice.*

TOMPKINS (*as the group still compactly together, passes for the first time*): That's right, Ike, stay with them!

DEE (*as* IKE LOW *goes by him*) : Now remember, remember!

TOMPKINS: Remember what? *I'm* his coach!

DEE (*impervious*): Remember Ike!

TOMPKINS *looks at him with rage, his chest heaves, the blood springs cholerically to his cheeks, but in the end, he says nothing.* SAM DEE, *meanwhile, is intently looking at his stopwatch, held in the palm of his hand like a charm or talisman.* TOMPKINS, *jerking away with a movement of exasperation, takes out his own stopwatch and regards it, as though in silent competition. As the milers come around for the third lap, both men look up. The red-haired* JACK BROGAN *is leading now, moving not gracefully but crisply, his knees rising a little too high, his elbows pointing slightly too far out, the expression on his face one of remote inner communion. Behind him, compact and contained, running in an almost palpable aura of optimism, smug expectancy, lies* WALDER, *a square-built man in a black-and-yellow vest, with the broad calf muscles of a sprinter rather than a miler. He takes short, swift, bouncing strides, which seem to reflect not merely his physique but his disposition.* IKE LOW *is running fifth; his action is rhythmic, feline, and economical. By contrast with the first two runners, it seems wholly unself-conscious. He simply and naturally runs; he has no concept of himself as a man running.*

TOMPKINS (*as* JACK BROGAN *passes*) : Stay there, Jack!

DEE (*as* IKE LOW *passes*): Now, Ike!

At once, virtually from one stride to the next, IKE LOW *accelerates. The long, white almost tubular legs, which have been so effortlessly churning, suddenly gain speed and urgency, like a voodoo drummer abruptly raising the beat. From around the field, there goes up a faint sigh of surprise. This new and hectic pace carries him quickly past the fourth runner, then the third, until he is level with* JACK BROGAN *and, at length, past him, as well. For an instant, a stride or two, his speed appears to relent, then* SAM DEE'S *voice is heard again.*

DEE: Keep going, Ike!

At this IKE LOW'S *legs resume their faster rhythm, and he draws irresistibly away from the other runners, like a man drawing on an endless length of elastic. Now the field, a shaken kaleidoscope, regroups, defining a hierarchy.* WALDER *in his black and yellow, sets out in pursuit of* IKE LOW, *the elastic contracting, while he, in turn, is chased by* JACK

BROGAN. *The other five runners straggle out in ones and twos behind them.*

TOMPKINS (*in loud soliloquy*): He's daft. He'll kill himself.

DEE (*shouting*): Stay *ahead*, Ike!

TOMPKINS (*with a darting look at* DEE): Bloody insanity.

As the runners come around for the fourth and final lap, an official in a soft gray hat and a blue blazer pulls the rope of the bell, which responds with its cacophonous, ritual jangle, like a ship lost in the fog. IKE LOW *is still ahead, but* WALDER *is now only some fifteen yards behind him.* IKE's *pace is the same, but he is clearly maintaining it on borrowed energy; the lolling of his head, the radically changed expression of his face, denote as much. His brow is contracted into sharp furrows of concern; his eyes have a look of anxiety premature for his years, as if on this third lap he has made bewildering discoveries.*

DEE: Keep in front, Ike!

TOMPKINS (*scornfully*): Him! He's got nothing left.

DEE: *Go!*

Now WALDER *is only ten yards behind* IKE LOW, *now five; now, as they go around the third bend, he is almost level. It seems a trial of will as much as stamina,* IKE LOW *willing his body to maintain its pace,* WALDER *willing him to fail. There are these few seconds in which the race is to be decided, in which* IKE LOW *will falter, fall behind, or* WALDER's *challenge will evaporate. And in the event, it is not so much that* IKE LOW *moves ahead as that* WALDER *gradually falls back, the gap increasing from a hand's width to a stride, from a stride to two strides, till at the straight* IKE LOW *is two yards clear, moving inexorably away as* SAM DEE, *even* TOMPKINS, *shout him home; increasing it to three yards, five yards, and at the tape, which he breaks with a look of saintly anguish, suffering tempered by the joyful certainty of reward, it must be almost ten. At once there's a convergence of people and voices around him and upon him;* TOMPKINS *rushes up to him; a solicitous* OFFICIAL *throws a blanket around his shoulders;* SAM DEE *leaps the fence and comes dashing into the middle of the group.*

VOICES: 4.01! . . . Can't possibly. . . . First mile he's run. . . . I made it 4.01 . . ." First competitive mile. . . . Four and eight-tenths. . . .

SAM DEE *and* TOMPKINS *confront each other over* IKE LOW *like two dogs over a bone,* TOMPKINS *the dog which lays an owner's claim,* DEE *the marauder who disputes it. Neither concedes; each decides, after a few silent moments, on a fragile truce.*

TOMPKINS (*with emotion*): Ike, you've run a 4.01 mile.

DEE: I'm proud of you, Ike. Proudest of all that you're still on your feet. (*He looks scornfully at* JACK BROGAN, *who, comforted by sympathizers, has now reached a sitting position.*) A true champion never runs himself into exhaustion.

IKE LOW's *head droops to his chest; weariness and a sense of sudden anticlimax combine to wrap him in momentary isolation. When* WALDER *pushes through the crowd to congratulate him and shake his hand, he limply allows it to be taken. His lips move in some polite, reflexive formula, but his eyes remain focused on the ground.*

TOMPKINS (*proprietarily*): Okay, Ike, let's get you into the dressing room.

An arm around IKE LOW's *shoulders, he steers him out of the crowd, towards a gate in the railings.*

DEE (*addressing those around him, as he turns to accompany them*): And this is only the beginning! Within a month, he will break four minutes! Within six, he will be running for Great Britain! When I first saw him training, I convinced him he was naturally adapted to run the mile!

Indifferent to a virulent look from TOMPKINS, *his aura of silent hostility,* DEE *hurries forward to take* IKE LOW's *free arm.*

DEE (*to* IKE LOW): Remember! We are just at the beginning!

II

The week after that first mile, I got sacked from the factory. I don't remember what it was, exactly: an argument with the foreman, something about taking too much time off. Anyway, I was glad to be out of it. For a month I went on the dole, which was lovely; nothing to do but go down to the old Labor Exchange, draw your money, and pretend to be looking for a job. There wasn't a lot going at that time, what with the credit squeeze and that, and for people like me, unskilled, it wasn't easy to find things.

Not that I exactly went out of my way, because all I wanted to do now was run; I was training every day, sometimes up at the track, sometimes over the Heath, with Sam and the others, and actually racing about one a week, sometimes twice.

Sam was well pleased; he'd got it all worked out; he said, "You're preparing to represent your country's prestige, so why shouldn't your country pay for you? They do little enough for their athletes." Though that wasn't the way my old man saw it. Dole—well, to him, that was something disgraceful, something you ought to be ashamed of, reminding him of what it was like before the war. He worked as a storeman now, in a factory out at Walthamstow, but back in the prewar days he'd gone eighteen months once, unemployed. He was pleased I'd done so well in that mile, of course, but what he said was, "Where does it get you? It ain't like football or boxing; you can't make a living out of it," and Mum agreed with him, which she usually did.

In the end I brought Sam home to see them; he wanted to come; in fact, it was his idea. He started talking the moment he got in the door and never stopped the whole of the time he was there; they'd never met nothing like him; they listened to him with their mouths open.

He said, "Your son, Mr. and Mrs. Low, has the ability to

become one of the most celebrated figures in the world. He is one of the chosen few with God-given talent, for which there is no substitute. Talent can be developed, but nothing can take its place. A man who has been given this talent has the responsibility to make use of it."

The old man said, "Yeah, but what about his living? It's unsettling for him. He ought to put his living first." And so it went on.

SAM: In the Communist countries, a great athlete is not *obliged* to earn a living. His importance to society is recognized.

DAD: Yeah, but this ain't a Communist country.

SAM: No, and that is why athletes must struggle for everything. That is one of the freedoms guaranteed in a democracy: freedom to struggle.

MUM: Why, you wouldn't rather live in one of *them*, would you?

SAM: As a human being, no. As an athletics coach, yes.

DAD: Everything behind the Iron Curtain, though, it's all just used for propaganda, ain't it?

SAM: Sport is always propaganda. Great sportsmen will always reflect credit on the countries from which they come. When you think of Great Britain, who do you think of?

MUM: Winston Churchill?

SAM: But not only Winston Churchill; of Roger Bannister, of Fred Perry, of Stanley Matthews. Who is the Prime Minister of Australia? You don't know. But everyone has heard of Ken Rosewall and Herb Elliott. Finland is a small, obscure country. But when Paavo Nurmi was running, Finland became famous.

DAD: Yeah, but you can't live on medals.

At this, SAM DEE, *who is dressed, as always, in his gray turtleneck jersey and his weatherworn blue jeans, begins an antic dance about the little room, with its cheap and garish comforts, its leather-cushioned chairs and sofa, its china knickknacks behind glass, his movements reflected in the pink, scalloped mirror which hangs above the mantelpiece, over the electric fire of artificial logs.*

SAM: You and *I* can't live on medals, we know that medals are nothing, but a *nation* lives on medals! A nation lives on *heroes!* It lives on the example a hero sets to its youth, whether he's an athlete or a general, and an athlete is greater than a general because a great athlete represents life, whereas a general represents death! A victorious general evokes hatred as well as love, but a great athlete is an inspiration to the world.

MR. LOW, *who is a lean, grave man, largely bald, smoking a pipe and wearing a dark-green cardigan, watches* SAM *with quiet amazement, half-impressed.* MRS. LOW, *a good-looking woman of surprisingly young appearance, with clear features and an accepting smile, is wholly impressed. She is smiling, her lips slightly parted.* IKE LOW *himself sits, legs stretched out, in the attitude of an indulged youngest child, watching and listening intently, though his face lends no clue to what he thinks.*

SAM: Yet we reward the people who bring death and we ignore the people who bring us life. A medal is an insult to an athlete! His achievement is sufficient in itself. But (*to* DAD) you are right, sir! An athlete has to eat; an athlete is particularly involved with what he eats. An athlete must have a roof over his head, even if it be only the roof of a tent. So why is it that in our Western world, we force him into humiliating trickery, in order to obtain the very essentials of life?

MRS. LOW, *smiling, shakes her head and clucks her tongue; whether in admiration or in sympathetic disapproval is not clear.*

SAM (*to* DAD): Sir, there are ways, even in our world, that these necessities, and more than necessities, can be provided. I know them. I have access to them. To me, they are unimportant. I have enough. I will always have enough. But I have no compunction in obtaining them for my athletes, in making use of the society which is using *them.*

What he meant, of course, was fiddling: expenses. I'd heard it mentioned often enough by the other lads in the club and one or two that were training with Sam: what this one had got and what the other had got, but mostly what people they'd heard about had got—like this bloke up in the north, this sprinter, that was meant to have bought a house and furnished it, just on his expenses.

In fact, about a week or so after I'd run this four-oh-one mile, this bloke rang me up from somewhere in the Midlands, would I like to run in some meeting he was putting on, and when I said well, maybe, it was sort of rather a long way, he said very quickly, "We pay generous expenses." I said, "Oh," and then, when I didn't say nothing else, he said, "The fare and hotel and any incidentals; shall we say fifteen pounds?" which, as the fare was only London-Birmingham and you could do the whole thing easy in a day, meant you'd come out maybe ten quid ahead—not bad. As a matter of fact, I didn't go to that one, but later in the season, after I ran for the first time at the White City, I'd get offered things like that and better, mostly from the north, practically every week. When I told Sam about them, he'd say, "I haven't heard you. Fifteen quid?" and then later, maybe running over the Heath, "Ask for twenty." Or he'd come to me and say, "You're running at Hitching next week. If they give you an envelope, don't tell *me* about it."

Now and again, too, he'd ask me was I all right for money and slip me a couple of quid, or he'd turn up with a new pair of running shoes or maybe shorts. He even got me a barbell set. One morning a bloke staggered up the stairs and delivered it; several of the other lads over the Heath told me they'd got them from him, too; he had some sort of deal with the people that made them. When I thanked him, he just winked and said, "When you break four minutes, I'll give you Jack Straws Castle," which was the pub at the top of the Heath.

I won't say I actually enjoyed the training, I can't say I'd ever enjoyed *any* training, but it was nowhere near as bad as that first time, with him on the bicycle. He ran with us himself now, he was amazing for his age, bouncing along so easy he made you ashamed of yourself; he didn't think nothing of doing ten miles in an evening. He was a great believer in hills, he called it resistance training; he'd lead us down these dips and up the other side, one after another, and sometimes when we reached the bottom, he'd shout, "Sprint!"—he wouldn't sprint himself—or up certain hills, he'd time us; you had to be able to do it in so many seconds.

Other times he'd take me to the track, to Paddington or Parliament Hill, and there it was mostly sprint work, change of pace; you'd be going around, and suddenly he'd yell at you to accelerate, and you'd go flat out for fifty yards, a hundred yards, maybe more, until he shouted, "Relax." He was very much against what he called one-pace runners, "zombies." He'd say, "These are the parasites of running, the jackals, who prevail on other people's weakness rather than their own strength. They can sometimes set records, but they will never win important races, because the spirit is not in them. I would rather *compete* and lose bravely than plod my way to a flabby victory."

Then there was all this movement stuff, position of the arms and legs; he'd have you at that for hours, stopping you and showing you where your arms were held wrong or your stride wasn't right or there was something wrong with your shoulders. He said, "Training is the chrysalis from which the glorious butterfly emerges. One is impossible without the other."

After that first mile I didn't do so good for a time, which depressed me. When you're very young like that, you get overconfident; I think I expected to go out there the next time and run a four-minute mile straight off, whereas what happened was I started running a string of 4.05's, 4.06's. It's the same with most things, I suppose: You do something *because* you don't know what it's really all about; then when you start finding out, taking things apart, suddenly it gets difficult. One or two up at the club was taking the mickey, saying they reckoned the stopwatches must have been bent that day, and I knew there was a bit of feeling at first among the other milers, me coming in and showing them up like. The first time I turned up for training with them after it happened, Jack Brogan wouldn't hardly speak to me.

Most of these races I won; a couple I didn't.

Des Tompkins was on to me about Sam; I'd been expecting it. He said, "I suppose Sam Dee's taking all the credit for that mile of yours. I suppose he's told you you owe it to him."

"Well," I said, I was being a bit cautious, "in a way I do, don't I? I mean, it was him that got me running it."

He hadn't got no answer to that, because it was true, so it stopped him a moment; then he said, "You'd better make up your mind who's coaching you, me or him. Don't think you know it all just because you've run one good mile. You've got a lot to learn, and you aren't going to learn it from him, I can tell you. And what the hell's the point of my telling you one thing when you go off to him and he tells you another?"

As far as I was concerned, there wasn't no question who was coaching me, but I could more or less see his point, and

I didn't want to leave the club—it was useful for facilities and meetings and things and getting recognition—so I didn't answer. He said, "Sam Dee isn't a coach, he's just a sideshow. What runners has he ever produced?"

I said, "There's Tom Burgess, isn't there?" and he said, "Sam never discovered him; he'd run for Yorkshire before Sam even met him." I said, "Well, he's improved him," which made Des practically do his nut. He said, "Im*proved* him? You look at the bloody record books and see how he's improved him. You look at how he ran in Melbourne last year, in the ten-thousand. Where did he finish? Twenty-eighth!"

I said, "He pulled a muscle, though, didn't he?" He said, "Yeah, it's amazing how all Sam's runners turn out to have pulled muscles, after they've lost." I said, "I'll have to think about all this, then, won't I?" but he still kept on. He said, "What's his background in athletics, anyway? What's he ever done? You ask any coach in London, any coach in this country, they'll you the same thing; he's a phony."

I didn't say nothing to this, either, because I'd already heard about Sam and the other coaches, how they'd got it in for him, and anyway, there was something else I'd realized about Sam: Either you were for him or against him, there wasn't no in-between, and as far as I was concerned, myself, I was for him.

After that month on the dole, he turned to me one day when we was running, and he said, "Got a job yet?" I said, "No," and he said, "I'll get you a job."

A couple of days later he took me to see this man, this Stanley Ling, in his flat over near Marble Arch. It was the biggest flat I'd ever been in, I'd never seen nothing like it, ours would have fitted three times just into this drawing room. There were great, thick, furry carpets and white leather walls and a bloody great chandelier and a cocktail bar and an enormous big television set; the whole place must have cost a bomb. And the funny thing was, he just seemed an ordinary sort of Cockney chap, shortish, with wide shoulders and the kind of face I'd seen on people around our part of the world that had been boxers: broad, a lot of black hair growing down low, creamed back, and these little dark eyes that looked at you like two little stones.

I'd heard about him vaguely before, about his being interested in athletics and other sports, that he was a million-

aire that had made it all out of scrap metal or war surplus or
something. He looked at me; then he looked at Sam, and he
said, "Is he good? Is he going to be good?" Sam said, "Stan,
he is already good, he is going to be *great*. In his first competitive mile, he ran 4.01." He said, "I know that, I know
that, but he hasn't done it since." Sam said, "Believe me,
before this season ends, he will have broken four minutes."

Then Ling got up. Like I said, he was very short, and he
was wearing a sort of camel hair jacket, like half a dressing
gown—the other thing I noticed was his crocodile shoes,
which I wouldn't have minded myself—and he sort of *wad-
dled* toward the bar; you couldn't put it any other way. He
said, "What about that last one, that bloody lay-about?
Never did better than 4.08. *He* was going to be a world
beater, wasn't he?" Sam said, "That was because my work
was undermined. That was because he was corrupted by
people who are envious of me; he listened to them instead of
listening to me, and everything I did for him came to nothing. I told him, 'If you want to follow your club coach, not
me, if you want to immerse yourself in mediocrity, then
carry on, but remember there is no turning back.' Stan, you
are drinking too much," and he went over and patted his gut.
He said, "Your physical condition has *man*ifestly deteri-
orated."

Ling didn't seem to mind; he poured himself a whiskey
halfway up the glass, and he said, "I take it the young man
doesn't drink." Then he said, "I did those exercises of yours
for two bloody weeks, and I'd rather be unhealthy." Sam
said, "If you'd continued with them, you'd be feeling better
than you have ever felt in your whole life. Why should you
treat your body worse than you would treat your car?" and
Ling knocked back the drink, he took it neat, and said,
"You're wasting your time with me, Sam. If I'm going to go,
I'd sooner go my own way."

Then this bird come into the room, a real little dolly, she
couldn't have been half his age, wearing a silk blouse and
trousers all in the same colors, mostly pale green, with a lot
of blond hair done up on top of her head and little, sharp,
pointing breasts. Sam said, "How *are* you, beautiful? Whenever I see you, it makes me feel young again," and she said,
"Oh, but you *are* young; I mean, young in spirit. I only wish
Stanley was as healthy as you are."

Sam said, "There you are, Stan; doesn't that give you an

incentive?" but Ling just asked her did she want a drink, then said, "This is Ike Low, dear, another of Sam's discoveries. He runs the mile," and she said, "Oh, isn't that fabulous?" giving me this look, and shook hands with me. Her hands were small and very warm; I got this feeling that she liked me, and that Ling knew it, that he was watching me, and when I looked around, so he was. I met those eyes, no expression, weighing me up. He wasn't a bloke to cross.

He said to Sam, "So he wants a job?" and Sam said, "If you could find him one, Stan, you'd be doing everyone a service." He looked at me again, this look, and he asked. "How much do you want?" Well, what do you say to that? I just sort of stood there feeling stupid, hoping Sam would step in, which he did. He said, "Whatever you can afford, Stan. He doesn't need much. He's living at home. If you can manage the same as you were paying Wally."

Ling said, "Fifteen quid a week? All right," then to me, "Can you drive?" which fortunately I could. I'd had one or two clapped-out cars I'd bought off blokes I knew, never for more than ten quid, though since the last one had packed up on me, I hadn't had none. He said, "Okay. You can be a sales representative for my ball-bearing factory at Tottenham. Sam'll tell you where it is. Go in and see the sales manager on Monday." This time, when he looked at me, he seemed to be almost smiling, but you couldn't be sure.

Just then a bloody great china clock they had on the mantelpiece, all the colors of the rainbow, like it was made out of barley sugar, suddenly began chiming, and that sent Sam away, he sprang to his feet with finger pointed, and he was off:

"Time is the enemy. Time is what we are fighting in our lives, as we fight it in our running. We can never achieve a total victory, but every time we achieve a partial one, every time we extend the boundaries of man's capacity, we affirm our human dignity. In the air, we have flown faster than sound. On the ground, we have broken the barrier of the four-minute mile. In the operating theater and the laboratory, we have learned ways to prolong the life of the human body far beyond what was ever dreamed. The day will come when each human being will be able to choose for himself exactly how long he wants to live, just as the day will come when we travel not merely beyond the speed of sound, but beyond the speed of light. Every record that is broken on the running track, on water, in the air, on the salt flats, is a gesture of human independence. The day will come when we will smash every clock in the world, because we shall have conquered time, and clocks will no longer be necessary."

The job was a giggle, really. When I went there, to the factory, the sales manager looked at me and said, "Oh, you're another of them, are you?"

I had this nice little Cortina to run around in, and all I had to do was go in and see a few distributors, all over London. You could have done the whole lot in a day, probably you could have done it just with a few phone calls, but I was expected to do at least three days, which meant three mornings, and the rest of the day to myself. Or rather, the rest of the day to go training with Sam, either the running or the weight lifting or all this movement stuff, getting what he called the perfect action.

At home they were beginning to think I was a bit daft, not eating meat no more and having all these nuts and vegetables that Sam had put me on, a lot of them raw. The other thing was that getting home at night, I'd be so tired I wouldn't want to go out again, whereas before I'd always been off somewhere with the other lads, to the bowling alley or the pub or one of the cafés, or, if it was a Friday or a Saturday, maybe to a dance. Not now, though, not with the way he was driving me. Training with the club was a doddle by comparison; Des Tompkins seemed to have more or less decided to let things go on as they were, probably because I was winning races. Mum got a bit worried about it; she asked me once, "Is it all worth it, Ike? Don't you think you're overdoing it?" I said, "No, I don't think so," though to tell the truth there were times when I wasn't sure. Not till I ran my first four-minute mile; then I was sure.

And now the third lap of this invitation mile at the White City, and Ike Low, this eighteen-year-old miler, running only his second race here, still keeping up wonderfully well with a very strong field. The time of that lap, the time of that last lap, we'll have it for you in a moment, the time of the second lap was 58.2, no records in sight, but still a pretty fast pace. There you see Ike Low now, a tall boy, beautifully built, only eighteen years old, a sales representative from

Hackney, running very smoothly, staying in fifth place. What do you think of his action, Wallace?

A *very* smooth, easy action, Derek, very rhythmic; long strides, strong, economical, *piston*like movement of the arms. Still seems to be running well within himself. A *very* exciting prospect.

So it's Goetz of the United States in front, Goetz from San Jose, who has already run three sub-four-minute miles this season, Goetz the favorite for this race, followed by Leroche of France, then our own McAllister, always a fine competitor, followed by Ihuru of Uganda, this tiny little man, bounding along, full of energy, a police corporal, father of eleven children, and Ike Low from Hackney.

So slow, this track; you're fighting it every stride. Great now, going around this bend, around in front of the crowd, them cheering for you, giving you just that little bit. . . . Old Sam there, I heard him as I passed, "Stay there. Stay with those four." I feel good. The way he always said. Like I was flying, like something else took over. Like I could go right out in front of the lot of them, now. Waiting for that old bell, clang-a-lang-a-lang; *then I'll go. That's when he's told me I can go. Past them all. Past that little old blackie. Look at him bouncing along. And that big Yank. I've never felt so good; all being done for me. By him, he's done it, but it's me. He's worried now, the little blackie, I can feel it, feel it coming off him; look at the way his shoulder's moving; he wants to look around, but he can't; I'll close the gap, then let him get away again. And the big Yank out in front, not giving a fuck for anyone, so bloody sure he can just walk away with it; we'll see. Wonder will I get a cheer coming past this end. . . . Great, that was, really gives you something. Now Sam and the bell and Des Tompkins there shouting a lot of bloody nonsense and go when we're halfway round.*

Clang-a-lang-a-lang.

Up in your chest, that's where you feel it.

And at the bell, Goetz is moving away, this very big, powerful American, fourth in the Olympic final, look at him hotting up the pace. I don't think anyone can live with him here, do you, Wallace?

Very difficult. The lap time, by the way, was 58.1.

And Goetz is ten yards ahead of Leroche now; McAllister is following behind; I think Ihuru is going to overtake them both.

Now, Ike, now!
A lean old man running around the outer perimeter of the track, capering like a witch doctor.
Now, Ike!

And my goodness, Low is coming up! Ike Low! What a burst of speed! You can see him there; past McAllister, past Leroche, level with Ihuru, now he's passed him, too, and he's gaining on Goetz. He's cut the gap to fifteen yards. Running beautifully. Ten yards. As they move down the back leg to the straight, there can't be more than five yards in it.

Give up, you bastard, give up! My legs, my bloody chest! I can't. . . .

Now, now, NOW!

And suddenly Low is level, shoulder to shoulder with Goetz, Low in the inside lane.

Keep that fucking elbow down; I'll kill you!

The British boy is level. Twenty-five yards to go; I think he must be just ahead. He *is* ahead! A foot, a yard. Low in the lead, breaking the tape now, there can't be more than a couple of paces in it, a wonderful win for the eighteen-year-old British boy. Ike Low has won this mile for Britain.

Christ, I'm going to die.

Ike, that was great. . . . 3.59.2, Ike.

I've done it! I've broke four bloody minutes!

All right, now just take it easy. Stand away from him, please. Stand away.
Congratu*lations,* Ike.
Thanks, yeah, thanks.
Ike, I could kiss you.

Thanks, Sam.

Good running, kid. You surprised me.

Yeah, thanks.

What's this twot with the bloody microphone, then?

Out in the center of the track now with Ike Low, the winner of this fantastic race. Ike, that was absolutely fabulous.

Thanks.

Why doesn't he fuck off?

Tell me, Ike, were you running to a plan?

Well, in a way, yes.

What was it?

Stay more or less up there with the leaders till the middle of the third lap, then go.

Whose plan was it?

My coach.

That would be the Spartacus club coach, Des Tompkins; a very, very fine coach.

Well, no, as a matter of fact. Sort of a personal coach, actually.

A *personal* coach! You have your own personal coach, Ike?

What I mean is, he's not the club coach, see.

Ike, did you believe you could win this race *and* beat the four-minute mile?

I hoped I could.

You *hoped* you could?

Yeah.

How do you feel, now?

Well . . . very tired, to be quite honest.

Tired, but I imagine, very, *very* happy.

Yeah.

We won't keep you then, Ike. A wonderful race, a wonderful victory. Congratulations, and thank you very much.

Thanks.

Now all these others waiting: one or two of them I've seen. The bloke that won the medal. The other one from Track Monthly. *Thank God Sam's there.*

Well done.

Congratulations.

Bloody marvelous.

Terrific, Ike.

Thanks.

You'd never broken four minutes before, had you, Ike?

No.

What was your fastest time till today?

He ran 4.01 at Eton Manor last July.

Did you plan the race like that, Ike?

Sort of, yeah.

What exactly *was* your plan?

Well, to keep up with them, like, and see if I could do it at the finish.

That big bloke, jutting his face in yours like a bleeding copper.

Where do you live, Ike?

How old are you, Ike?

What's your job?

Who coaches you?

I coach him.

I thought he was with Spartacus.

I *am* with Spartacus.

But *you* coach him, Sam?

How long have you coached him?

Just this season. Since I discovered him.

Was that your plan today?

Of course it was.

Did you expect it?

Does he run with you up on the Heath?

Got any hobbies, Ike?

How did it feel to win?

How does it feel to have broken four minutes?

Now, steady boys.

And in the Sunday papers next morning, there it all was. I was famous.

WHITE CITY CROWD LIKES IKE
TEEN-AGER BEATS YANK AND FOUR-MINUTE MILE

If you want to talk to sprightly, fifty-four-year-old Sam Dee, Britain's off-the-beaten-track coach, you have to run. So that was what I did on Happy Hampstead Heath: pulled off my jacket, took off my tie, and ran beside this oh-so-different sporting Svengali whose eighteen-year-old prodigy, Ike Low, crushed the might of the world's mile in Saturday's White City classic.

On my right loped the Cockney kid himself, on Sam's left ran ten-thousand-meter titan Tom Burgess and half a dozen others, but Sam kept pace with them all.

"I bet even you were surprised on Saturday," I told the wiry, weather-beaten former merchant seaman.

"Rubbish!" he yelled. "The only thing that surprised me was that Goetz made such a close race of it. I'd reckoned Ike would win by at least five seconds."

Jumping over a fallen tree trunk, Low cracked, "I didn't care how much it was, as long as I finished in front."

Britain's best hope for the mile since Bannister hands Dee all the credit. "Sam's fabulous!" he enthused. "He looks after everything; your running, your training, even what you eat. Before I met him, I was just an ordinary quarter-miler, going nowhere. But Sam took one look at me and said, 'You'll run the mile.' Fantastic."

"You have conquered the barrier of the four-minute mile, but you have still to contend with the barrier of pain. Until you have experienced pain and learned to use it, until you have fought with it and conquered it, you can never be a champion. Nurmi, Zatopek, Kucs—these men all learned to live with pain and overcome it. Pain and time. These are your opponents, and they are inseparable, because in defeating pain, you are defeating time, and in defeating time, you are defeating pain. Moreover, they have this in common, that no victory against them can be complete. In fact, no ultimate victory can be *won,* because the body ages and the body dies; the body can only attempt this victory in youth. All the attention you have had—the television and the chatter in the newspapers—is the crackling of thorns under a pot. I deal with such people because they are necessary to promote my work, although they will always distort what I do and what I tell them. I need them as a mouthpiece to fight back against the bureaucrats, against the enemies of true human progress. But they can do you no good. They will flatter and weaken you while you are strong, and undermine you if they think you are weak. To them, you are always replaceable, just as you have taken the place of whoever they were publicizing before. I can detect signs

in you since that race of self-satisfaction, a tendency to relaxation. Remember you have not even *begun* to express
your potential. I told you that before this season ended, you
would run a four-minute mile. You worked well, and you
have run it. Now I tell you that even greater achievements
are within your powers, if only you continue to work.
devotedly."

This thing, this pain thing, in a way I saw what he meant,
but in another way, I didn't understand it. Why run at all if
it was going to hurt you? Sport, to me, was something you
enjoyed, and if you didn't enjoy it, you packed it in. On the
other hand, I could see he was right, that this sort of attitude
wasn't going to get you nowhere, not with everybody else
so dead serious and more or less dedicating their lives to it.
Either you did it properly, or you might as well let it alone.

And mind you, it wasn't like there was no enjoyment in it
at all, that it was *all* slog. The training was hard, of course,
and all the things you had to give up, but the races, they
could really be great, if things were going well; so exciting
that everything else in the world seemed dead; that moment when it was time to go and you felt this power thrum-
ming away in you like a great, big engine and you knew you
were going to do it, beat the lot of them. In a way it was
better than actually doing it, like a meal or making love to a
bird; I mean, it usually looks better beforehand. Though
winning was great, too, breaking that old tape, the little,
light touch against your chest, and the first feeling you
always had, didn't matter how tired you were, was always
this flutter in the guts, like to say, I've done it.

The other way I could see Sam was right was obviously if
you want something, you ain't going to get it for nothing,
not unless you inherit it, and you can't inherit running, and
there was a hell of a lot to want in athletics—breaking records, running for Britain, traveling abroad, and maybe one
day, please God, an Olympic medal. Because records, they
were here today and gone tomorrow, but an Olympic gold
medal they could never take away from you.

And another thing, whatever Sam said, though I supposed
he was right, it *was* nice, the publicity, at least to begin with:
the way suddenly everybody wanted to know you at home,
it was funny how some of them changed, and being looked

at in pubs and tubes and places, and having your picture in the papers and all. At eighteen, it wouldn't be natural if you weren't impressed by it.

At home they were delighted; even the old man had to admit it couldn't be bad, getting all this praise, and with a job to do as well, that come directly out of running.

Stan Ling was there at the White City the day I beat four minutes; he was really bowled over. The week after, he had a bit of a party around at his flat for Sam and me, to celebrate, though we neither of us drunk anything. His wife was there again, all over me, wasn't it wonderful and she'd been there and she'd seen it, but I could feel him looking at me, just like the other time, and Sam, too, if it come to that, so I didn't try chatting her up, which I think she wanted.

Sam talked to me quite a bit about birds; he said that now I was becoming a successful runner, I was going to meet a lot of them, on and off the track, and the ones on were often more dangerous than the ones off, because in a way they intruded into your real life, where with the others, you could take them or leave them. He didn't have no time for women athletes by and large, only for one or two; he thought most of them were just playing at it, they was only in for a giggle, because they liked the traveling and having all the men around. He said, "Combined track meetings are a fiasco. And when the Iron Curtain countries add up men's and women's points together and calculate a match on that, it is worse than a fiasco, it is downright dishonesty. Women are lovely and wonderful in their proper roles, but their proper role is not on an athletics track, where they only ridicule their feminine image and distract the men. Women have a vital place in every man's life, but it must be the proper place: as an inspiration, not as a temptation. This is particularly true for the athlete, who is subject to much more stringent physical discipline than the average man."

I asked him did he mean a runner shouldn't have nothing to do with girls then, which seemed a bit overdone to me, but he said no, he didn't expect athletes to live like monks, that was bad for them, too; it was a question of priorities. He said, "Sex is a beautiful thing when it is used *by* the body for the good of the body, but where the body is used by sex, is subordinated to sex, it becomes no more than an instrument, and then it is corrupted. The penis is a *part* of the body, it is not the whole body, and the parts must never become greater than the whole."

I thought about it very seriously, like I thought about everything he told me, though it didn't really affect me much, not then, what with my coming back so tired every night and not wanting to go out again, and not really having a regular girlfriend at the time, just odd birds I'd take out now and then.

Tom Burgess took it very serious, too. When I mentioned what Sam had been on about, he said, "He's right. You've got to make up your mind what you want to use your body *for*." He was engaged himself, his fiancée taught phys. ed. in a school over at Tooting, quite a good-looking girl, big, with ginger hair. He said, "I made this perfectly clear to Mavis, and she understands it." I said, "What? You mean when you do and when you don't?" He said, "I made it clear from the beginning. As long as I'm an athlete, then running comes first. She accepted that." And I sort of had this picture of them, her pleading with him, and him with his deadpan look of his, pushing her away and opening up a little book, looking through it, then saying either yes or no; probably no. I didn't ever want to be like that; to me you either felt like it or you didn't—I mean, provided it was a bird you were having it off with anyway—but that was Tom, he did everything by numbers.

We was both in the team that went to Leipzig that August to run against East Germany, my first international, and when I got the invitation, I was dancing all over the house, I can tell you, waving it around, and when I saw Sam that day, up at the Heath, I shouted, "They've picked me, they've picked me! I'm running for Britain!" and he shook my hand and said, "That's marvelous. Now you've got to *win* for Britain," and he put me through the hardest afternoon I'd had for weeks.

He had this thing that you could exhaust yourself in training, but you should never be exhausted after a race, that collapsing afterward was a sign of weakness, even if you won. He said, "In training, you are deliberately pushing yourself beyond your maximum, so that your maximum can be extended. You are deliberately challenging pain. But in a race, the first object is victory, and this may sometimes be achieved *without* reaching or exceeding your maximum. Your first enemy is the other competitor, and if you cannot defeat him without exhausting yourself, then you have not really beaten him at all. There is no disgrace in being beaten yourself *provided* you have given your maximum, *provided* you have tried to drive yourself through the pain barrier. Even so, if training has been sufficient, you should not be exhausted, even in defeat, because in your training you will have pushed yourself far beyond what is needed in the distance you race. A well-trained miler should not reach exhaustion under at least five miles; a well-trained three-miler should not approach it till ten."

So anyway I went and got fitted for my Great Britain blazer with the Union Jack on the pocket, and when I'd got it on, I never wanted to take it off; I remember walking miles through the streets wearing it; when you're eighteen, things like that tend to go to your head a bit. If it hadn't been for the creasing, I'd probably have slept in it, and all.

Having Tom in the team was great, because it meant I didn't feel quite so strange, suddenly meeting all these new people, going abroad for the first time in my life, and flying in an airplane, which was the first time, too. We met at this hotel in Lancaster Gate, just near the park; we had to be there on the Thursday afternoon. I'd never stayed in a hotel either, and I must have walked past it, up and down the street, a good half a dozen times before I could make myself go in, and even then I was shaking. At the desk I was telling them who I was when this big, booming fellow, wearing the British blazer, come up to me and said, "Ike Low? I'm Jack Brady," which was the coach, and crunched my hand like he was squeezing an orange.

He said, "Congratulations and welcome to the team," but in a funny sort of way, like he'd said it so many times before that he'd forgotten what it meant, it was just automatic. He said, "That was a good race you ran at the White City. If you can do as well for me in Leipzig, I'll be satisfied." I thought, So will I, and all, but I didn't say nothing. He said, "You're training with Sam Dee, aren't you, like Tom Burgess?" and when I said, "Yes," he said, "Well, remember, when you're running for Britain, *I'm* your coach, you're running for *me;* you remember that, and everything'll be all right," which was a good beginning.

Then he took me into this big lounge they had there where everyone was sitting about, the whole team practically, men and girls, all in blue blazers, looking sort of restless, and he introduced me around. Some of them I'd met before: Tom, of course, and Peter McAllister, that I'd run against at the White City and was going to be the first string now in Leipzig. I liked him, he was easygoing, smiled a lot; he shook my hand and said, "Maybe I'll stay a bit closer to you this time!" One or two of the girls were all right, too, and there was a big one, Jane Cobham, a discus thrower, that give me a smile.

Then after we'd been more or less around the room, Brady seemed to take a bit of a deep breath and said, "And now, I suppose you'd better come and meet the officials." He took me over to a corner of the room to where there was these four or five men with bald heads sitting around a table, all of them wearing blazers, talking together very, very serious like they was the only people in the room. Brady stood over them, and he said, "This is our new 1500 meters man, gentlemen," which of course was what I'd be running over there, and one of them looked up at me like the cat had brought me in, he said, "Low?" I said, "Yes; yes, sir," and I wondered did he want me to salute him. But he shook hands, quite polite, though he didn't get up, none of them did, and he said, "Well, good luck, young man!" and the others said, "Yes, good luck," and Brady told me who they all were. The one that spoke to me first, he was the vice-president, Arnold, and next to him, a long face, very sad, a bit like a bloodhound, that was the chairman, Ron Vane, who I'd seen before on television, and Molloy, the team manager, and Atkinson, who was deputy chairman, or some such. As we moved away, Ron Vane said, "Don't forget you're running for your country, young man." Then they all turned back to whatever it was they were discussing as if we'd never been there.

Brady said, "That's the officials," and I looked quickly at his face to see was he putting the boot in, but you couldn't tell nothing. To me, that table seemed like a little private island where they lived and didn't want nobody else. From the way they looked, the sound of their voices, they seemed to me like they was complaining, and when I got among the athletes, *they* was complaining.

> When I think of all I've done.
> All the things that Ron has done.
> All the things he's done for sport,

In a voluntary role.
All the hours that he's put in.
All the contacts that he's made
And the sacrifices, too.
Thirty years without a break.
Never took a penny out.
Someone's got to run the show,
While these youngsters come and go.
Make the fixtures, plan the trips.
Pick the coach and choose the teams.
Last five years, the athletes do,
While old Ron's done thirty-three.

Now they want two quid a day.
Don't appreciate a thing.
What the hell's it coming to?
Ron's essential to the sport.
If they don't watch out, he'll go.
That'd serve 'em bloody right.
Should be happy with a quid.
When I think of what he's done.
All the years that he's put in;
Well, you'd think they'd show respect.
Youngsters these days, all the same.
When you think of all the rows,
I'm amazed he carries on.
Like to kick their bloody arses.
All the same, the bloody young.

Did you hear what Ron Vane said?
Diabolical, it was.
That we couldn't have two quid.
Should be happy with a pound.
That a pound was quite enough,
When we know he's made a bomb.
And the way he spoke to Jack.
Said, "Remember, you're the coach,
And it's *us* who pick the team."
When they're all so out of touch.
All so old and out-of-date.
All so mean and double-faced.
When we win, you'd think it hurt.
Then they worry what we'll want.
All so keen to keep their jobs.

And the little perks and trips.
All just riding on our backs.
Never give the sports a thing.

I shared a bedroom in the hotel with Tom. We talked a lot
about what it was going to be like out there, the big crowd,
the stadium and all, and how Sam had told us to run, but
I felt very nervous, knowing Sam wasn't coming, that he
wouldn't be there; it was like suddenly not having your
father. I hardly slept at all, going over and over his instructions; he'd written them down, and by now I knew them by
heart.

The trouble was, not only was it my first trip, but it was
my first 1500 meters, which of course is shorter than a mile.
We'd done a bit of practice on the track at Paddington, Sam
shortening the course and Danny Spence, one of the other
lads, going around with me, but it wasn't the same, and I
admit I felt frightened.

That evening they came around with a petition to sign,
about the expenses, saying we ought to have two pounds a
day. Well, as far as I was concerned, I was that pleased to
be going I would have *paid* two pounds a day, and another
thing was, I mean, after all, this was my first international,
and I was afraid if I signed, maybe they'd never pick me
again. So I said, "Do I have to sign? I mean, I don't really
know nothing about it," but the bloke that was bringing it
around, a quarter-miler called Harry Price, said, "If we don't
get unanimity, there's no point in presenting it all," and Tom
said, "You don't have to worry. If everybody signs, they
can't touch anybody."

Then Harry Price said, "Have you any idea what someone
like Ron Vane's making out of athletics? From broadcasting
and television and journalism? At least two and a half
thousand a year. *Plus* the trips he doesn't have to make, that
fit in with his business. *Plus* whatever he makes out of his
business itself." So I signed, because there didn't seem no
way out of it, and next morning, when I was down there
having breakfast with Tom, Ron Vane walked past our table
and he give me this old-fashioned look, sort of "I'm surprised at you," which was what he actually said when he
got me alone, later, "I'm surprised at you."

He said, "You want to watch out you don't get into bad
habits; there's a few ringleaders in this team, and all they

want to do is stir up trouble. No conception of what's done
for them. All the work. Take everything and give nothing.
Why spoil everything on your first selection? They talked
you into it, didn't they? You ought to hear the other side.
Have you any idea what we lose every year, the three A's?
Do you know what it costs to send a team abroad? Do you
realize what a struggle it is to raise enough money to send
you to the Olympic Games? Other countries, the Communist
countries, they're government-subsidized. What the govern-
ment gives us is a drop in the bucket. Look at myself and
the other officials. All honorary. All sweated labor. I'm not
joking—we are. If I told you the hours I put in. Interfering
with my business life—*and* my home life. The number of
times my wife's begged me to give up. I've offered my
resignation on three occasions. That surprised you, didn't
in? Three times. Turned down every time. You know why?
They know they'd never find anyone else prepared to do it.
I don't expect appreciation. What I *do* expect is cooperation.
Don't get led astray. You're a good runner, I've seen you;
you've got a very good future. Concentrate on your running.
Leave the rest to us."

You can imagine how this left me feeling. Tom had seen
us together; he said, "He's been on at you, hasn't he? Just
like he did with me, when *I* came into the team. Hinting that
you won't be picked again if you oppose him. Don't believe
it. If your times are good enough and you win your races,
he can't stop you, he daren't, and Jack will fight for you."

In fact, Jack was quite friendly that morning, when we
was all in the coach on the way out to the airport. We had
a jet plane all to ourselves, just the team, and as I was about
to go up the steps, they took a photograph of me with a girl,
Mary Baldwin, one of the sprinters, who was new as well.

In the plane, everyone was chatting and laughing and taking off their blazers; it reminded me of some of the trips we
used to have as kids, in the bus down to Southend. I sat in a
window seat with Tom beside me, and I wondered what it
would be like, the going up; there was something knotted
inside me, not that I was afraid we'd crash; it was something
else, I don't know what, just this going up.

So I sat there looking out of the window, looking at that
great big silver wing and the jet engines, only half hearing
Tom, who was saying something. Then the stewardess come
around, a blond one, and my seat belt wasn't fastened; I'd

never even thought about it, and I didn't know how to do it. Tom did it for me; then I looked out the window again. We seemed to go round and round the airport for God knows how long; I wondered when the hell we were ever going to take off; then suddenly it stopped, and the engines come on full blast with this enormous roar, frightening; you could see the air blowing back out of the engines; then it went forward again, only much, much faster, and one, two, three, we were up, nothing in it; one moment down on the concrete, the next looking down on all these squares of brown and green, and suddenly this funny thought come into my head, *Blimey, why bother to run?*

Tom said, "Are you all right?" I said, "Yeah, I'm all right," sitting back in my seat, and he said, "Some people never get over flying."

I suppose I was one of them, because I never really did. I could never take it for granted; to me it always seemed an amazing thing that a great big heavy machine like an airplane could whisk itself off the ground like that; a miracle, really. Not that it was ever quite the same as the first time, even coming back from Leipzig, it wasn't as strong, and anyway by then I was so choked I wasn't noticing much. But in a way it did stay with me, like Tom said.

People moved around a lot on the plane, changing places, sitting next to one another, and when Tom and the bloke next to him went off, Jack Brady, the coach, come and sat down beside me. He said, "Now I'll tell you the race I want you to run, and we must plan it very carefully. Kraus has run the fastest 1500 meters in Europe this year, and Manfred's a great competitor; see you keep away from his elbows on the bends. They're always five yards faster in front of their own crowds, too; nearly everybody is." Then he went on and told me how I was to run each lap, how they'd try and box me in here and kill me off there, how it was no good thinking I could run the same race I did at the White City, when nobody knew about me. He said, "They all know about you now, strong finish, and they'll do their best to see you're not in a position to use it."

But the more he talked, the more it was obvious to me that it was McAllister he expected to win the race, that my job was to take on the Germans and make the running for *him*. Everything he said pointed *to* this, and all the tactics that he told me were different from Sam's, who'd been looking at the race from my point of view, so by the time he was finished, I didn't know if I was coming or going. He kept on saying, "You understand? You're following me?" and I kept saying, "Yes," and nodding, just to make him happy, but when he went off and left me, I got into a panic. I wondered, *What the hell do I do, run* his *race or Sam's race?* If I ran *his* race, I knew I'd got no chance, but if I ran Sam's race, I could see I'd probably be in dead trouble.

When Jack Brady had gone and Tom come back, I told him all about it, and he was quiet for a bit, which was his way—you'd start to wonder had he heard what you said; then suddenly he'd speak, like now—he said, "It's up to you, isn't it?" I said, "What do you mean?" He said, "Who's your coach, your real coach, Sam or Jack?" I said, "It's Sam." He said, "Well, there's your answer then." Only, of course, it wasn't that simple; I mean, it might have been all right for *him,* an experienced athlete, but not for me, who was just beginning.

One or two reporters that was on the plane came over and talked to me, too. I'd already been told you can trust this one, watch out for the other, but in fact, I don't think none of them got much out of me, because I was still very shy. I noticed, though, that they asked very different kinds of questions, like the blokes with the posh papers, the *Times* and that, wanted to know about lap times and how you trained and tactics and all, whereas the ones with the popular papers, they wasn't interested in that; it was all how did you think you was going to go, what had Sam said before I left, had he give me any secret instructions, did I have a girl-friend, and that.

As for the town itself, I hated it; you couldn't have picked nowhere worse to go abroad the first time; thought, *Blimey, if it's all like this, I'll stay in England.* It was ugly, for one thing, great, big ugly buildings—there'd been a lot of bombing in the war, and this was what they'd put up—but more than anything it was the atmosphere—there was no life in the place; it was quiet; it was more like the country. Everybody seemed dead scared; they sort of shuffled about whispering to each other; then suddenly you'd be walking through a square, and a voice would start up right beside you out of nowhere, very loud, bellowing away—one of the loudspeakers they'd got, attached to these columns. I don't know what they were saying, because I didn't speak no German, but apparently it was some kind of propaganda. I thought, *Poor people, having this coming at them all the time,* and even when they took us round the sports institute with all the wonderful facilities, everything done for the athletes, I still felt the same, even when some of the others was saying, "If only *we* had this sort of thing." I thought, *If this is what you've got to pay for it, I'd sooner go on running around the Heath.*

They put us in quite a nice hotel, though. I shared with Tom, and that first evening I was lying on my bed reading Sam's instructions for the five hundredth time—Tom was out somewhere—when there was a knock at the door and this girl come in, Jane Cobham, the big one, the discus thrower. She said, "Do you know anything about taps?" she was laughing. I said, "No, not much, I never did no plumbing. Why?" She said, "We can't get our hot-water tap to work. Every time we turn it on, the whole thing shakes and shudders as if it was going to blow up."

Well, I didn't think about it at the time; I said, "All right, I'll come and have a look at it," and went out after her; she had the room next door. When we got in, there was only her and me; she said, "Pam's gone out to see the sights. I told her she could have 'em; I know these Iron Curtain cities," and she give this giggle. Then she went to the washbasin, which had old, brass taps; she turned the hot one on, and sure enough it made a hell of a din, like there were people hiding in the pipes with hammers. She asked me, "What do you think?" I said. "I don't know. If I was you, I'd have them up to look at it."

I was standing quite close to her by now, and when I looked round, she was smiling at me, this smile, she took a step towards me, and next thing I knew, we was kissing each other, she was saying, "You're so nice, you're so nice," and feeling for my trousers, and I mean, what do you do? I remember this word floated into my mind, just *"Sam!"* But only for a moment. Then she'd pulled me over to the bed—she was a very big girl—then reached out and locked the door, and after that I've never known anyone get undressed as quick as she did. And I enjoyed it, too; she did a lot of things I'd never come across; she kept saying, "Do you like that? Do you like that?" where most of the birds I'd had sort of let you do it as a favor.

Afterward, when I'd come and we were lying there, she

run her hand all down my body, down my chest and over my legs, and she said, "You're smashing, aren't you? I know you're going to be a marvelous runner, I can feel it." Then she started kissing me all over, bit by bit, till she was sucking me, which again I'd never had and come as a bit of a shock at first. But then I liked it, and it was only after, back in my room, laying on my own bed, that I started worrying, what had I done, how would it affect me, terrified what Sam would say if Tom found out and told him.

And of course, he did find out; someone or other must have told him, someone who saw us going into her room and not coming out. He said next morning, after breakfast, "You had Jane Cobham, didn't you?" I said, "What do you mean? Who told you?" He said, "I just know. I should have warned you. I didn't know she had the room next door. She's always looking for new blood." I said, "You won't tell Sam, will you?" He said, "No, but you're a bloody fool. If you're going to do that sort of thing, do it *after* a race. At least then it can help you to relax. Before a race, you *need* tension; you relieve it in the race. Besides the physical thing." Which meant I'd got that on my mind as well.

I went training that morning in the stadium—nothing very much, just limbering up, really, sort of getting acclimatized. It was very big, the stadium, just outside the town, all wooden seats. It was supposed to take ninety thousand, and they said they expected about sixty.

Peter McAllister and I sort of chatted about how we was going to run, and this was something new as well, because in the past, except in 440 relays, I'd always run for myself; even in the club team, I'd always run to win like. But this was different, this was for your country, this was for points, and although I hadn't got nothing against Peter, it stuck in my throat, this business of him being first string. In fact, it give me an incentive to beat him again, because if I did that, maybe I'd first string, and the next time I could run my own race, not someone else's.

Sam's plan had been more or less like before, at the White City, stay up in the field then go in the last lap; only like he'd said, it wasn't so easy when there was only four in the field; you couldn't hide yourself. Whereas Brady wanted me to take the two Germans on *early* in the race, to do a fast first lap, which he thought would shake them, because I was new to them, staying out in front for the second, and for

Peter to move up late in the third and really start going at the bell. To me this seemed ridiculous, because I knew I had a faster finish than Peter, I'd proved it at the White City, and anyhow, what happened to *me* after the third lap? I'd asked him, Brady, and he'd said, "On the third lap, you can ease up a bit when Peter comes through; on the fourth, give him the best support you can," which to me meant he didn't care what I did.

Jane got down there later on; she was in the middle of the track, and she smiled at me as I come around; I sort of half smiled back. I noticed, while I ran, that she was spinning the discus up in the air and catching it, then doing these little, short sprints, kind of, "Look at me." I felt a bit embarrassed by her, I didn't know whether I wanted to have her again or not; I didn't know if I even wanted to speak to her. In a way, yes, I'd enjoyed it, but in another way, seeing her dancing about with her big white thighs and worrying about the race and would it affect me, I wished I'd never laid eyes on her.

Jack Brady got hold of us both, Peter and me, and told us again all what he wanted us to do, the same old nonsense; then while the two of us was sitting there, this bloke come up, Alan Bell, the sprinter, and sat down beside us; Peter introduced us. I knew who he was, of course; he won the bronze in Melbourne for the 200, and I'd noticed him on the trip, but never spoke to him. To tell the truth, there was one or two like him in the team that made me feel a bit uncomfortable, people from Oxford and Cambridge with their accents and their fancy way of talking. I felt then they were outside my range, they talked a different language, and Alan was from Cambridge, though I think at that time he'd just left, he was going to be a lawyer, or something. The funny thing was, I found out later that his old man worked in a factory in Birmingham, he'd won scholarships, though you'd never have guessed it. They said he never went near his family, not now.

He was quite small but wiry, fair-haired, with a load of freckles, and these little, quick blue eyes that always seemed to have a smile in them, like whatever he heard or saw was funny. He said, "Has the great man delivered his pronounciamento?" Peter said, "Yes"; he seemed a bit uneasy with him, too; he was one of them that liked Brady, in fact, quite a few of them were really fanatical about him—he couldn't do no wrong. Alan said to me, "You train with Sam Dee, don't you?" I said, "Yeah," and then he said, "How does it feel to change dictators?" I said, "I don't know what you mean," and Peter said, *"Och,* don't take any notice of him. They shouldn't have given him the bronze medal; they should have given him the wooden spoon for stirring." But Alan just smiled; he said, "Well, benevolent despots, then," which didn't mean nothing to me. He seemed interested in Sam, though; he asked me a lot of questions about the training; he said that he'd gone up there once, to the Heath, a few years ago, Sam had asked him, but he didn't think there was nothing in it for him, not for a sprinter. He said, "Anyway, it's not the training, is it? It's the charisma." Peter said, "The what?" and Alan said, "The magic influence, the witch doctor stuff. Sam's an old witch. Three hundred years ago they would have burned him. I suppose it's just a question of whether one's susceptible to magic or not. Or leaders."

Peter said, "I don't think athletes want leaders. Most of them are individualists," but Alan wouldn't have it; he said, "No, they're not. They're selfish. They think incessantly about themselves, and when anything goes wrong, they need someone to lean on. Like children." Peter said, "Speak for yourself," and Alan said, "I am speaking for myself."

I *was* speaking for myself, just as now, in a sense, I'm writing for all of us—for what all the rest of us probably think and would probably say, if they were only articulate. Verbally. Because, of course, they *are* articulate in a physical sense; they express themselves with their bodies, running and jumping and throwing, often quite beautifully, and the rest is marginalia, like a physicist running for a bus. Sometimes you get the two; in Bannister, possibly in Chataway, perhaps in me. I don't know. The whole man. That's a joke! Yet in a sense, one's irrelevant to the other. It doesn't *matter* if a high jumper can write poetry or a poet can high-jump. If he can, he's really a freak, and one will probably interfere with the other. Which makes me ask myself, why am I going on? I'll never do better than that bronze medal; in fact, that was better than I was entitled to do. Sprinters don't last two Olympiads. So why? The notoriety? The applause? It *is* a drug. Not easy to go back to being nobody in a solicitor's office, a rich nobody one day, if you're lucky.

But if everything's going to be anticlimax? Driving and driving one's body beyond what it wants to do. Putting up with these whiny, jealous, petty bourgeois officials. And the pompous, messianic coaches, all believing that they've got the Word. And the other athletes, with their squabbles and their narrowness and their endless, endless monologues about lap times and minutes and seconds and pulled muscles. God, it's a price to pay. For what?

This new miler, Low, seems to me the classic athlete. I mean the ideals, the quintessential athlete, built to do nothing else on earth. The perfect shape. A perfect, natural rhythm. And no self-questioning; too young to ask himself questions, too young to do anything but run. Sam Dee does his thinking for him. Sam Dee gives him his sense of purpose. Running's his religion. It's a sin and a shame people like that can't spend their whole lives running. After all, it keeps them happy, they do no harm, they bring pleasure to people who watch them or support them. *Another glorious gold for Britain!* God! What a pity people aren't like insects; how sad they should outlive their function. They should be like butterflies: beautiful, flying about for their short span, then expiring; no anticlimax. A runner should live till his legs give out, a singer while she still has a voice, a film star till she's lost her looks. It would be so much kinder.

I shouldn't have teased him like that. He didn't understand a word I said. But I can't bear blind innocence; that's the serpent in me.

I must give up. This season, if I can.

This was something new to me, this crowd—the size, the noise they made, and knowing it was none of it for you—not like the old White City, where anyway there wasn't a quarter as many. Another thing about a foreign crowd is it makes foreign *sounds*—which can upset you, if you aren't used to it. This sort of *"Hoy-hoy-hoy! Hoy-hoy-hoy!"* they had in Germany. Jogging around in the middle of the track, watching the other races, it depressed me, it got on my nerves. This great, white sea of them, all in their shirt sleeves with the sun shining off them, and the noise, this *"Hoy-hoy-hoy."*

The nearer my race got, the worse it was; I'd never felt nothing like this before, not even that first time at the White City. And there was no one to go to now, no Sam, who'd understand how I felt, who had this way of just sort of saying something to you, to give you confidence. A lot of them wished me luck, Tom and Peter and Alan, and Jane, and Jack Brady went through the plan with me again, how I was to run, which made things worse, and Ron Vane come up and said, "Good luck, and don't forget you're running for your country," as if I *could* bloody forget, and I felt completely on my own, I was in a sort of daze; the crowd chanting and the races going on and the announcements coming over the loudspeakers in German, it was like a sort of dream.

I went in the dressing rooms and had a massage, I thought it might make me feel better, and it did in a way, except there was this atmosphere there, everyone keyed up and muttering to themselves, and Jack Brady coming in and going out and giving orders like a sergeant major, so instead of relaxing you, you felt more tense than what you did, outside.

Then at last it was our turn, the 1500 meters, and I can tell you I was shaking; I got down at the start, and it was like I'd never run before in my life. I thought, *Maybe it'll wear off once I'm running,* this feeling everything was separate, nothing was coordinated, each leg on its own, both arms on their own. It was probably *because* I was so anxious to go that I made this false start, heard the pistol go bang-bang, and realized it was for me, feeling like the biggest twot on earth, coming back into position, the crowd going, "*Oh . . . oh,*" and the starter saying something to me, it could have been in German, it might have been in bloody Arabic, for all I was hearing then.

I'd drawn lane three, Peter was in lane one, and the second time, we did get off, it was all right; I was going to make bloody sure that if there was another false start, it wouldn't be me. But nothing else was all right, because I ran terrible. As if things weren't bad enough, the way I was feeling, this big bastard in lane two spiked me coming round the first bend—not badly, but enough to hurt, enough to upset me, which was probably what he wanted. All I could think of for the rest of that lap was, *I'll get him, I'll get him.* I jostled him around the next bend, and the crowd started whistling me which was frightening, really, this piercing noise sort of beating down on you, shrieking in your eardrums.

So by the end of the first lap, whatever plan I'd come out with, whether it was Sam's or Brady's—and to tell the truth I couldn't have told you, not even at the start—had just gone.

I suppose if anything, it was Brady's, because I just ran; it was desperation, really, just tried to keep up with the Germans, running much faster than I ever meant to, and halfway through the third lap I blew up. I got this terrible feeling, this wanting to stop, this thinking, *Oh, fuck it,* and hating the whole thing, everybody: the Krauts, the crowd, Brady, running, everything. Wanting just to step off the track and put two fingers up at everybody; even slowing up a moment and very nearly doing it—then slogging on, seeing these three backsides disappearing, Peter and the German two, and forcing myself like I did in training, through the pain barrier or whatever the bloody hell it was, except it was more than just the pain—it was just not wanting to go on, wanting to pack the whole thing in.

Low's had it; look at him.
He had Jane Cobham.
What, last night?
Like an initiation, that.
They ought to use her on the opposition.
Ran that first lap far too fast.
Just hasn't the experience yet.
He has now.

If only Sam was there, shouting. Sam at the bell. Or running around inside the track. Telling me what to do.

Like all Sam Dee's bloody athletes; can't run unless the boss is there.
Don't be hard!
They're not athletes; they're marionettes.
Twenty yards behind Peter at the finish. I was crying, I admit it. I wished I could disappear.

WONDER MILER FLOPS IN LEIPZIG
In a frank, no-punches-pulled, after-the-race interview, Ike Low told me, "I don't know what went wrong. The strength just seemed to go out of my legs. Maybe I missed coach Sam Dee."

Never fucking spoke to him.

Looking back, Ike still calls it "the blackest day of my running life." He confesses, "I felt I never wanted to run again. It seemed to me I'd let everybody down: my coaches, my country, my fellow British athletes. And after a performance like that, I could never imagine being picked for Britain again."

I remember *her* coming up to me and saying, "Bad luck, Ike," and I just turned away without a word because I blamed her—and myself for going with her. I knew what Tom would say; I knew what all the others would think. I hated myself just then, I'd have liked a bloody great hand to come down into that stinking stadium, pick me up, and carry me away.

He was indeed dropped from the British teams which met Russia at the White City and Czechoslovakia in Prague, but a string of sub-four-minute miles forced the teen-aged Low back into the international reckoning and led to his brilliant White City victory against Poland. Modest miler Low takes little of the credit for himself. Instead, he gives it to that stormy petrel of British athletics, Sam Dee, whose absence many felt accounted for Low's Leipzig debacle. "It was Sam who put me right again," says Low. "He'd watched the whole thing on television, and he knew exactly what had gone wrong, just as if he'd actually been there."

"It was not your fault. I do not blame you in any respect. The pity of it was that your first international had to be abroad, where you were at the mercy of the pygmies. The pygmies with their poisoned arrows and their poisonous jealousies. Men who did not *want* you to win, because they did not want *me* to win. Men who were happy to say, 'Sam Dee coached him, and he's failed.' The instructions you received were ridiculous. Every runner has the right to try to win his race. If he does not feel capable of doing so, he has no business to take part in it. Selectors have no business to choose him. You could have won that race. If I'd been there, you *would* have won it. You should have closed your ears to everything they told you, everything conflicting with what *I* had told you. In time, you will be able to do this. You will have the maturity, and you will have the confidence. For the moment, you are still too young. I blame myself for letting you go without me. We should have found some diplomatic reason to decline, some muscle injury. But I felt it unfair to stand in your way; I know how hard it would have been for you to turn down your selection. You would have believed, erroneously, that a second chance might never come. Next time you run abroad, I shall be there, wherever it takes place, even if I have to walk all the way, even if I have to swim rivers."

He did it, too; it was amazing the way he turned up: Paris, Milan, even Warsaw, wearing the same old jersey and blue jeans, with a ruddy great knapsack on his back, sometimes on his bicycle, sometimes after hitchhiking. I don't believe he ever took a train. God knows how he did it—the frontiers and all, the distances, not speaking more than a few words in any language. But it was marvelous to watch him, how he could get on just with signs and smiling at them; you'd see him in the middle of a group of people, talking away, all of them beaming, and I'm sure they hadn't an idea what he was on about.

Sometimes he wouldn't get there till the day of the race, sometimes he'd arrive so late I'd have give up hope, I'd be feeling really depressed, but he'd always turn up in the end. Like in Budapest, in another of those bloody great stadiums, they'd actually called us for the 1500 meters when I see this figure, this gray-haired old boy, struggling with a copper, wriggling away from him, and jumping over the rails onto the track, when I realize that it's Sam. He'd got up to me, he was telling me, "I walked the last ten miles," when two of them caught up with him, two coppers, and there was a right old commotion, officials and interpreters and me trying to explain who he was, till in the end it sorted itself out.

The British officials didn't like all this; they resented him; in fact, they as good as told me that if Sam was going to follow me about all over Europe, then I wouldn't get picked no more. He had a right old row with Brady in Paris and another one with Ron Vane at the White City. Brady told him, "You keep away from my athletes," and old Sam said, "They are not *your* athletes, and they are not *my* athletes. They belong to no one but themselves." Brady said, "While they're running for Great Britain, they are coached by *me*," and Sam said, "I am not attempting to coach the boy. Who in their senses would try to coach an athlete half an hour before a race? I am simply encouraging him."

At times like these, he was like some holy hermit out of a desert cave, the kinds that spent all day fighting with their baser nature in a barrel of water. Dancing and capering about, bringing the Word from the wilderness. What an exhibitionist he was! I was immune to him, but I could see how so many people fell; he had his terrific vitality, this fanatical belief. It must have been hard to resist him if you were as young as Ike and hadn't any of your own.

No wonder the officials hated him. He embarrassed them, with all their stuffy, bourgeois ways, and yet he got through to the athletes, straightforward and they couldn't. In Jack Brady's case, of course, it was a straightforward business of zones of influence; you could hardly blame his resenting the way Sam would skip in to steal his thunder, especially when so many of the athletes had made Jack a sort of licensed martyr. Besides, their approaches were utterly different. Jack was a good, blunt, solid, orthodox coach with a chip on his shoulder, and Sam was a traveling sideshow. Jack did it by sweat and Sam did it, I suppose, with intuition. Jack could talk all night about physiology and force *times* mass, isometrics and isotonics, cardio respiratory fitness, and the rest, like someone who'd learned it all at night school, where Sam's feet never touched the ground; he talked an incredible goulash of originality and nonsense, most of it wild and some of it brilliant, but always exciting to listen to; at least for the first few times around. I don't know which was the better coach; you might as well try and compare fire and water. They both got results with some athletes—or they seemed to. Projecting yourself is part of being a coach, after all.

The rest of that year was fantastic, I could hardly believe it. All over Europe we went, to all those places I'd only heard about, and not only that, but I was going there and winning; I'd put this Leipzig thing behind me. By the end of the season I was first string for Britain, and I reckoned that with Sam there, I could beat anybody in the world. In fact, between Leipzig and my last race, in October, I only lost twice more, once to Vargas, when quite honestly I wasn't really fit, I had trouble with this hamstring, and once in Sweden to the Australian Rod McCall, which wasn't a very serious race. The good thing about these Scandinavian tours was you always made a bit of money on them and . . .

well, they was nice tours socially as well, let's say. By now
I'd more or less understood how things were over expenses
and that. The officials knew about these things, but they
didn't too much mind their going on so long as you didn't
rub their noses in it. Which suited me, because although the
job I had wasn't much work, you couldn't get rich on it
either.

Running was more than ever my life; I seemed to be living from race to race, and as for the training, well, at least
it wasn't as hard as what it had been in the beginning, and
like Sam said, you couldn't have one without the other.

I *needed* these races, though; they gave me a feeling I
couldn't get nowhere else—that power coming up inside you,
jogging along with the rest and smiling to yourself inside,
thinking, *Just you wait, you wait till I go,* and the moment
when you did go, the *flying* moment when you were off on
your own, the wind in your face, and *knowing* this was it,
they couldn't live with you. And just now and again, the
awful feeling when you found they could, when you heard
their feet coming up behind you and you had to force yourself through that bloody pain barrier, beyond what you knew
you could do.

I did a 3.57.8 that August at White City against the Poles,
and that was because I heard him coming, this Volanski, and
when I broke the tape, it was one time I'd like to have fell in
a heap; only out of the corner of my eye I saw Sam, and I
didn't dare.

It was all split seconds now, race times and lap times; if
you weren't worrying about your own, you were worrying
about somebody else's, what someone had done in Sweden
or Russia or even California. You'd think, *If I can do, say
57.5 third lap on a slow track when I'm not pushed, what
ought I to be setting myself on the fourth if I'm really flat
out?* They were in my head all the time, these figures: when
I was running, when I was training, driving in the car, or
lying in bed at night when they raced around in your head
till you thought you'd go crackers. Sam was amazing, though
—the way he could tell you before any race almost exactly
how it was going to go, what each lap would be run in, so
that you knew what you were going to need. Often he'd be
there to shout at me as I was coming around, say, "58.2,"
or whatever it was, to put me right.

There was nothing he didn't think of, even the old bumping and boring. After I got back from Leipzig, he had me out on the track showing me how to anticipate when someone was going to try to spike me or elbow me, how to elbow them back, just at the right point, at the hip, to put *them* off-balance, and what to do if they deliberately boxed you in. It was very useful, too; you'd be amazed at what goes on in some of these big races. He said, "These things should be beneath the notice of a real athlete, but unfortunately it is necessary for him to be able to defend himself. That is what I am teaching you: self-defense."

When winter came, it was a terrible feeling, like all the air suddenly going out of you: no more races, nothing to build up to every week, no more trips abroad, and even the training got harder, over the Heath, partly because you weren't working toward anything, but mostly because of the miserable bloody weather, the rain pelting in your face or dripping on you off the trees, and the ground all squelchy and heavy. Sam didn't mind; the only difference it made to him was he didn't run bare-chested no more. He was still smiling away, though; he said it reminded him of when he was in the navy. There were a few indoor meetings, of course, but they aren't the same, the boards, the banking and all. You have to develop a completely different technique on these corners, and although it was better than nothing, you couldn't really compare it.

Since the summer we'd got quite a few more running with us, partly I suppose because of the publicity Sam had with me winning those races, though Sam was very careful who he took—and he never charged anyone a penny. He said, "My satisfaction is to see athletes grow, not to exploit them to financial advantage." And this was the one thing they couldn't get away from, any of the ones who used to knock him; whatever they criticized, they couldn't say he wasn't sincere. It was like Tom Burgess once said, "They all get something out of it except Sam. The coaches get their jobs with the association. The officials get their perks and their prestige and their free trips. But Sam gets nothing. He's completely clean. He's the only one who genuinely lives for athletics."

As for me, I hadn't got no doubt about it. He'd made me. I owed him everything.

And now, from Sportscast's Young Footballer of the Year

to our Young Athlete of the Year. A choice with which I'm
sure everyone in tonight's star-studded studio audience and
all our millions of viewers will agree. Because *this* year's
Sportscast Young Athlete of the Year, ladies and gentlemen,
is . . . IKE LOW!

*Wonder if they'd applaud like this if that twot wasn't
standing at the front of the stage there, waving his arms at
them?*

Ike Low, who emerged in 1957, this post-Olympic year,
as a wonderful British prospect in the mile.

*How long do I have to keep jogging up and down in the
spotlight then?*

Ike, *many* congratulations.
Thanks.
How does it *feel*, Ike, to be nominated Sportscast's Young
Athlete of the Year?
Fabulous.
Well, you certainly deserve it, Ike. And just to remind
you *why* we've chosen nineteen-year-old Ike Low—I be-
lieve you were actually nineteen this week, Ike?
That's right.
Well, *many* happy returns!
Thanks.
Why we have chosen Ike Low as our Young Athlete of
1957, we're going to bring back to you three of his out-
standing victories, starting with that wonderful White City
mile last August.
I could watch that a hundred times.

Now another magnificent race by the nineteen-year-old
Londoner, again at White City, this time for Britain against
Poland. We join the runners halfway through the final lap,
Volanski of Poland still in the lead.

*It's like living it again, the same feelings. Me going ahead
—and now he's after me. Christ, doesn't it look as if he'd
catch me? But he hasn't; look at it! I've come away. I've
done it!*

Finally Paris, and an incredible finish against France.

Much, much easier. This is where I leave you behind now, mate. Wish they was all like that.

And the Sportscast Young Athlete of the **Year** Trophy, awarded to the athlete judged most promising by a panel of international experts, will be presented to Ike Low by Sir Raleigh Cunningham, vice-president of the British Olympic Committee.

Jolly good show.

Thank you, sir.

It gives me particular pleasure to present this trophy to a young athlete who I hope will worthily be carrying our colors not only in the Empire Games next year, but also in Rome, on the occasion of the next O*lym*pic Games. It's to you, the *new* generation, that we must always look for the preservation of the Olympic ideal, the awareness that in triumph, *as* in disappointment, the important thing is not winning but taking part.

"The important thing is not winning *or* taking part. There is no merit in an easy victory. There is no virtue in having taken part if you have given less than your best. The Olympic ideal is false. If it were not false, there would be no prizes. There would not even be any races, because to win a race is in itself a prize. It was not the Greeks who formulated this so-called ideal; it was a rich French nobleman whose whims are now indulged at the expense of the athletes, at the expense of the young. How strong is the Olympic ideal? Is it observed in Russia, where the best athletes are given sinecures and devote their lives to sport? Is it observed in the United States, where athletes are given college scholarships, even though they may be scarcely literate? The Olympic Games are a magnificent event, the very pinnacle of sport and physical endeavor, but the so-called ideals behind them are a hypocrisy."

Yet in a way, everything you did was the Olympics; every race you ran, even every training session, you'd got that in view, that on the horizon, the old gold medal; that was, like, your sun. All the other races, they were stepping-stones, and even the records, like I've said before, they took second place. I mean it was marvelous at the time, breaking them, but you knew inside you that they weren't what you was really after.

I could never know enough about Olympiads; anyone who'd been in one, I'd ask him about them. Tom Burgess said there wasn't nothing like it; he said the atmosphere was just fantastic; in the Olympic Village, it was like you could feel the electricity in the air, everyone getting worked up for their event, nothing else in their minds, just winning, just this medal. Then, he said, in the last few days, when the tension lifted, everything changed; it was like a great big party, everyone behaving like kids. He said, "No one who hasn't competed in an Olympiad can know what it's like. It's a world on its own. You can forget all this stuff over here, the White City and that. Even competing in places like Los Angeles and Moscow, in big meetings, it isn't the same. You don't know how alone you can feel at an Olympiad. In an international, you're only up against three people. In the Olympic Games, you're fighting the world."

I talked to Alan quite a lot about it, too; after all, he'd won a medal. Of course, he took the mickey, like he always did; he said, "Ah, the Olympic Games, the crown of every athlete's career, that festival of gilded youth." When he'd been through all that, I asked him how he'd felt before his races; he said, "Scared to death, like everybody else. Scared in the heats, frightened in the semifinals, and terrified out of my wits in the final." I said, "Even when you was running?" and he said, "Oh, once the pistol goes, your automatic pilot takes over. Besides, the sprints are over so quickly that you haven't time to think." I said, "And what about when it's over? Was you delighted?" He said, "I was furious, because I knew I should have won. If only I could have got off to a better start, I was certain I would. That's the thing about the Olympics; there's only the gold. Anything else is a failure."

Then there was this thing about peaks, when you reached them and when you didn't, and the more I heard about it all, the more it worried me. Everyone talked about it, how this one had reached his peak exactly at the right time and the other, that was a much better runner, had mistimed it and lost. The trouble was, they all had a different answer. For example, Alan reckoned that he *had* reached his peak at Melbourne; he'd been running up to the beginning of August, and then he'd just laid off; he'd even gone abroad for a fortnight to Spain and sunbathed; he said, "I never put on weight anyway." Then he'd come back and trained but not run any races; he'd told them he wouldn't be available even for the internationals, and they hadn't liked it, but his times had been so good there was nothing they could do. He said Ron Vane had told him, "You've got a duty to your country," and he'd said, "I know. That's why I'm not running." He said it wasn't a question of physical fitness, it was a question of mental fitness. He said, "When you reach a certain level, what *physical* advantage does one runner have over another? Anyway, nobody even knows what makes one person faster than another, despite all this physiological mumbo-jumbo that the coaches have picked up from the sports medicine doctors. It's certainly not determined by size; it may not even be determined by strength. In any case, what *is* strength? And don't give me all that tripe about force *times* velocity, because that's simply restating it in other terms. If you ask me, ninety percent of the whole thing's psychological."

Whereas Tom's opinion was that there wasn't no such thing as a peak; he said, "You obviously try to prepare yourself mentally for certain races, but unless you train hard all through the year, your body won't have the power to do what your mind wants it to. I don't believe all this stuff the Americans talk about leaving it on the track. Naturally, when you've got a big race coming up, you're not going to dissipate your energy over a lot of little races; naturally, you have a break from training just now and again, but that's as far as it goes."

When I asked Sam, he said, "You are still too young and inexperienced to worry about peaks. What you need is the maximum experience in races and the maximum quantity of good training behind you, so that you may draw on both. Besides, there is no such thing as a peak. A peak is for mountaineers, not athletes. It exists only in the imagination. What do people mean when they talk about a peak? They mean the day on which a runner runs his best, but when *is* that day? How can it be guaranteed? It may come in an Olympiad. It may come in a race of no importance. That is the mystery and the fascination of athletics. Obviously an athlete can overtax himself with too many races in too short a time and may need a rest, just as he may occasionally require a rest from training. But no two athletes are alike. There are some who can only give their best on great occasions, others who need to be kept tuned to the highest pitch, or they will lose their tone. Sprinters must be distinguished from milers, milers from distance runners, and all of them from competitors in field events. If training is properly planned and intelligently varied, an athlete will not grow tired of training. If he goes stale, it means one of two things; either his training has been wrongly conceived, or he has run too many races. But to work deliberately toward a peak may mean that when the time comes, you are not equipped to reach it."

III

How long have you been in track, Ike?
How long have you been running the mile, Ike?
Is this your first visit to the States, Ike?
Is this your first indoor meet, Ike?
What's the name of your coach, Ike?
Is that right they wouldn't let him travel with you, Ike?
Is that right he paid his own way out here, Ike?
How do you like Madison Square Garden, Ike?
What do you think of New York, Ike?

Fabulous. I think New York's fabulous.

British boy miler Ike Low, whose aitches fall like leaves in a gale and who may just be the miler Britain has been looking for since Bannister, ran around Central Park yesterday morning and pronounced New York "fabulous." It's a word he uses a lot.

Mind you, the nineteen-year-old Cockney kid has problems here, main one being that his personal coach, one Sam Dee, at whose name stately British track officials change color and reach for their starting pistols, was banned from traveling with the four-man British team. Since Low's relation to Dee is apparently slightly closer than that of Barnum to Bailey, Laurel to Hardy or, come to that, David to Jonathan, you'll see that things around the British team right now could be a whole lot more tranquil.

Puffed British athletics boss Ron Vane, "This is an official party, and Dee has no official connection with our association."

Heigh-ho. Seems like we've been here before.

P.S. Latest news is that Dee is expected momentarily. "If I know Sam," cracked one British scribe, "he's walked across the Atlantic."

You've talked a lot on the show about pain, Sam. What *are* you, a masochist?

A masochist enjoys pain. I do not enjoy pain.

Then maybe you're a sadist?

A sadist enjoys inflicting pain. I do not enjoy inflicting pain. I believe in *using* pain. I believe in *conquering* pain.

You mean like a Christian Scientist?

A Christian Scientist denies the existence of pain. I acknowledge its existence; I also comprehend its purpose.

Ike, do *you* enjoy pain?

Not enjoy it, no.

But you reckon you can use it?

I reckon it can *be* used, like Sam says.

Tell us how you'd use pain tomorrow night, in Madison Square Garden.

Well, it depends how the race goes, don't it?

You mean, if it's a tough race, you may need it; if it's an easy race, you won't?

Sort of, yeah.

What you're saying is, if it hurts, you reckon you'll run better.

That is a *trave*sty of what I teach. The athlete grows with each new conquest of pain, both as a runner and as a human being. He cannot *court* pain in a race, as he can in training, but if he is required to run through the pain barrier and he succeeds, then his performance will inevitably improve.

Will he be required tomorrow, Sam?

I have no idea.

Can you define this pain barrier for us?

You cannot *see* it, if that's what you are asking. It is not like barbed wire. It does not resemble the water jump in the steeplechase.

So what does it resemble?

The pain barrier represents the physical limits beyond which an athlete thinks he cannot push himself.

But he can?

Yes, if he is prepared to accept the pain involved.

So really the barrier isn't physical; it's psychological.

It is both physical *and* psychological.

I loved everything about that trip except the race. And

the arguing, of course, but I was getting used to that. Any time you went away, you got the arguing. Us and the officials. It might be spending money, it might be the accommodation—them taking all the best rooms—it might be over Jack Brady (who hadn't come with us), or it might be like it was this time—over Sam. There'd been a bit of trouble about Jack, too, before we left; the old petition stuff, only this time they decided there wasn't time to get enough signatures. Harry Price, who was one of the team, was on about it being disgusting that people like Ron Vane and Ted Arnold, the vice-president, should just come along for the ride, and leave the coach at home.

Of course, it all got back to Ron Vane, and of course, he was very, very upset about it. In fact, the night before we flew to New York, and we was all staying in Lancaster Gate, when Jack came around to wish us luck, Ron wouldn't even talk to him. Later on, when Jack had gone, he give us all this long talk about why it was so important for him to go to New York, all the things that had to be arranged for us, the conferences he had to attend there, the people he had to see. He said, "I assure you I am losing both time *and* money by this trip. I would far rather stay at home and attend to my business affairs." We didn't say nothing.

On the plane, I knew he'd be after me, I felt it, and in the end when Harry moved out of the seat next to me and he did come and sit down, I pretended I was asleep. He said, "Ike?" but I didn't answer, so he just sat and sat there, till in the end he said, "Well, you may be asleep and you may not, but I'll take a chance. I want to give you some advice, Ike. Don't let yourself be dominated. There's always a tendency for a young athlete to allow his coach to run his life for him. He always regrets it in the end. Now, you've got great potential, but you're still only at the beginning. I've seen it happen before. I've seen careers destroyed. I've been in athletics forty years, and I'll tell you this: It's much easier to be a coach than an administrator. Much easier. An administrator's there to be shot at. An administrator has to take the broad view. He sometimes has to make unpopular decisions; an unscrupulous coach can play on that. A coach has none of the same responsibilities. Let me ask you something. What would happen if every athlete in a team took his own coach abroad? It would be

chaos, wouldn't it? So just try to see the other point of
view, Ike. That's all."

> When I think of all I've done,
> *When we think of all he's made,*
> What I've given to the sport,
> *What he's bloody taken out,*
> I'd do better to retire.
> *Why the hell doesn't he retire?*

It was Stan Ling who'd paid Sam's fare. They come over
together, Stan and Sam and Stan's wife and a couple of
friends of Stan's. Early in the morning, me and the other
three would all go running in Central Park, and Sam would
join us; he'd pop up suddenly like he'd come out of the
ground. It was lovely that time of day, very cold but quiet,
with nobody about, and wherever you looked, these great
big skyscrapers, jumping into the air like rockets. It was
nothing like Hampstead Heath, the park—a lot of grass, but
no trees to speak of; instead, these little rolling hills, gray
rock sticking out all over the place, and squirrels, ever so
many of them, so tame that they practically ran across
your feet.

We went training in Madison Square Garden the afternoon after we arrived, and when Sam turned up, there was
a row. Ron Vane came rushing up to him and said, *"You've
no right to be here! You're not attached to the party!"*
Sam said, "I'm attached to my athlete," and I thought old
Ron was going to burst; that whole bloodhound face of his
went red; he was yelling, "All you want is the publicity! I
know the stories you've been spreading here! If you don't get
out, I'll tell them to have you thrown out!" Sam was very
calm; he said, "Well, I'm sorry you should take that attitude,
Mr. Vane, because all I came out here to do was help. I want
to help Ike, and I want to help the team." Ron said, "You
came out here to make trouble!" and so on and so on while
Sam just stood there watching him, with his eyebrows sort
of raised and his hands on his hips, like he was saying, "Let
me know when you're finished," and, when he *had* finished,
said, "Will you permit me one thing? Will you permit me
to ask the athlete whether *he* wants me to stay and help?"
Ron said, "You know perfectly well what he'll say! The
boy's too young to know what's good for him! I'm telling
you to go; now go!" So Sam looked at me, still with this same

expression, and I said, "Quite honestly, Mr. Vane, if Sam has to go, I don't think I'll feel much like running." So he turned on *me* then; he shouted, "Are you trying to blackmail me?" Sam said, "Of course he's not. He didn't say he wouldn't run; he just said he wouldn't feel like running. You may be able to control what an athlete does with his body up to a point, Mr. Vane; even you cannot control his feelings."

So Ron turned his back then and went thumping off to talk to Ted Arnold, the vice-president, who'd been lurking around in the background, like he usually did; they both disappeared with their heads close together, muttering away, Ron turning around every now and then to give us a glare. I was shaking, I can tell you, but Sam said not to worry about it; there wasn't nothing he could do. I said, "He can stop picking me; that's what he can do," and Sam said, "If he stopped picking all the athletes that he and the other officials have quarreled with, he wouldn't have a team. I've told you before, if your times are okay, if you win your races, there's nothing they can do; that's the way to fight them." Which soothed me a little, but it still wasn't very nice, your first time in a city like New York, everything so strange, your first time on an indoor track, and then, on top of it all, this.

And the indoor track, I don't mind telling you, was very worrying, this business of twelve laps to the mile for a start, then the boards themselves, and the steep banking on one side. I don't know what I would have done if Sam hadn't been there, showing me how to adjust my stride and all and warning me what to expect, coming around the bends. Not that I was ready for it when it happened.

There was going to be five others in the race. Goetz was one of them, which encouraged me in a way, three more Yanks, Vitali, Baker, and Spence, and an Australian, Gill. They was all of them sub-four-minute milers, but the main thing was that all of them had done a lot of running indoors, which was big in the States, but still nothing much in England. Three of them had run better times than I ever had, but Sam said not to worry; it had mostly been in California, where everyone knew the conditions were such a help, and to get the equivalent of a White City time, you could add on a couple of seconds. He was always good before a race, like that.

This Madison Square Garden depressed me, though, with

no one in it—all so dark and cold and quiet, and thousands and thousands of empty seats looking down at you, stretching right up to the roof. I imagined them being filled—and that was worse. Previously whenever I'd heard Madison Square Garden, it had always been boxing; I tried to imagine Joe Louis in the ring there, winning titles and that, but it didn't work; there was just no life in the place; it still depressed me.

Not half as much as what I was after the race, though; I hadn't run so bad for I don't know how long. It was all so strange, the spotlights shining down and dazzling you, the way they introduced you, like a load of boxers, then trying to get used to the track. And as if all this wasn't enough, getting a right old going-over on that first bend, wallop, bang, elbows from everywhere, one in your ribs, another in your stomach, then bang again from the other side. By the end of that race I realized something: In indoor miles, it was belt or be belted; you had to get in first, though by the time this had sunk in, the field was spread out, and it was too late.

It was a nightmare, the whole thing, in a way worse than Leipzig, because there, even when the crowd was whistling you, they were a long way off, whereas here, they was right on top of you, and you could understand the language, "Come on, Limey! What's the matter with you, Limey?" and the rest of it. The only thing that was better than in Leipzig was Sam, I think if he hadn't been there, I'd have give up. He'd got right down there at the edge of the track opposite the start, his normal place, and most of the time, when I couldn't see him, I could hear him shouting, telling me to come on and I could do it, but no lap times, though, because how could you, with twelve laps, and lap times helped you; they gave you an idea how you was running.

On the twelfth lap I was last, just behind Gill, the Aussie; I heard Sam yelling, "Sprint, *sprint!*" and hearing it, I did sprint, God knows how, God knows where I got the energy; it was automatic, I suppose, from always doing what he said on the Heath, being used to pushing myself when I was nackered, and I went past Gill, I went past Baker; there was this roar from the crowd; I thought, *I'll show you now, you bastards.* I passed another of them on the last bend, and I ran in third; I thought I'd die. I was staggering about when Sam caught me; he said, "All right, all right, at least you finished well." I'd done a lousy time, 4.04, I was disgusted with my-self, but like he said, I'd shown something at the end, which I suppose was better than starting out well, then packing up.

Ron Vane didn't come near me; in fact, he didn't say a word to me till we was on the plane on the way home, and then it was only something about he hoped maybe I'd learned something, and I felt like saying yes, I've learned what a twot *you* are, and I've learned how they carve you up around the bleeding bends, but I was young, and I didn't say nothing.

The other lads that was with us, though, come up and said hard luck and all, and even Ted Arnold, who used to be a runner himself, quite a good one, about a hundred years ago, come up and said, "Well, they certainly gave you a going-over," like he thought it was funny. Then there was all the reporters asking you questions, but the British was nothing to the Yanks, they practically bombarded you; in fact, I was very glad Sam was there, because he was able to take some of the questions off me.

Later that night a whole lot of us went over to this Green-wich Village place, there was Stan Ling and his wife, and Al Vitali, who was a New York boy and knew his way around the place, and Robin Cuthbert, another of the team, a big shot-putter, and Sam, of course, and we ended up in a jazz club where this black was playing the most fabulous stuff on the piano. It was dark in there, and some of the birds were great; they went in for this long black hair a lot, a lot of eye makeup and very white complexions, and if you looked at them, they looked right back at you.

When this colored bloke wasn't playing the piano, they'd got a little group playing up on a stage, and people danced, this very serious kind of stuff where you're really dancing on your own, I don't know what they called it; it was before the twist. Anyway, these birds would sort of stand there, wriggling their hips, no expression on their faces, till in the end Sam said to Mary, Stan Ling's wife, "Come on, let's show them," and when they went on the floor, he did this take off of the way they was dancing, still in his blue jeans and jersey, wriggling about like they did, holding his head like them, with just the same sort of blank look, until we was falling about, and even some of them had to laugh. In fact, after a time there was only Sam dancing and all the rest just standing laughing and applauding; when the music stopped, he did a handspring in the middle of the dance floor.

Later on I found myself dancing with Mary, the normal dancing; she'd been drinking quite a bit, I think, and she was all over me; she was pressing herself so close I was getting a stand, and I knew he was there at the table, watching us. She said, "Why don't you come and see us more often?" I said, "Yes, I must. I will," trying to back off, but she was holding me so tight I couldn't without practically shoving her away. She said, "Promise?" and I said, "Yeah, of course, I'd love to," which was true in a way, because she was a cracking little dolly, but I was scared to death what might happen after.

By this time, Sam was holding court at the table, America this and England that, it was amazing. He could do it anywhere.

IV

If people asked me to characterize the athletics world in one word, I suppose it would be "hatred." That's only with hindsight, of course; I don't suppose I'd have thought so at the time I was actually competing. Yet I think it's true. The permanent war between the officials and the athletes, with the coaches in the middle like lightning conductors—or *agents provocateurs*. I remember once hearing Ron Vane say, in one of his pompous speeches, "The athletics world is one big family," and I thought, *Yes, that's exactly what it is, one great, unhappy family, with the parents forever squabbling with the children.* Because the athletes *do* behave like children, spoiled, quarrelsome children, just as the officials behave like Victorian parents. There's no change; I don't suppose there ever will be. Both groups are frozen in their own attitudes.

I'm not saying that the athletes are always childish and the officials always adult. Quite the reverse. After all, children can sometimes be right and adults wrong, just as parents can be childish and children precocious, but the roles don't change. The awful thing, looking back, is how one was forced to assume them. You started out with the best possible intentions, with the best possible case, and ended up being as petty and vindictive as they were, the officials, constantly being pulled down to their level. The fact was, I suppose, that it was implicit in the whole relationship; once you'd committed yourself, your part was written for you. Even when the athletes formed the International Club in the fifties, things didn't really improve. I mean, they improved to the extent that the athletes had a pressure group and could get more of their own way, but the whole setup was still authoritarian, not democratic; there was still this polarity between the young and the old, the old men everywhere keeping the young off the committees. In fact, the old French chestnut, *si la jeunesse savait, si la vieillesse pouvait!* The problem being that whereas age had to acknowledge it couldn't, youth thought it knew. Hence I suppose, the jealousies, the awful inevitability of the athlete-official relationship, paternalism degenerating into paranoia.

I found this in my own case, congratulations turning into sulky acknowledgment, till you really felt they *wanted* you to fail, though it was much easier to see from outside, in the case of someone like Ike Low, where you really found it at its purest. In one sense, of course, he was a special case, an especially hard case from their point of view, because he brought Sam Dee along with him from the first, so they couldn't even begin by taking credit, they were faced right away by their *bête noire,* an intransigent coach, one they weren't even paying, so they couldn't even persecute.

Yet in a sense, it seemed to me that Sam was Mephistopheles, while they were only a bunch of peevish old men. What tended to complicate things was that you could warm to Sam, but you couldn't possibly like *them;* the most you could feel for them was an occasional pity. Sam gave much more than they did, but he wanted much more—he wanted his athletes body and soul, whereas all they wanted was a certain deference; they wanted people to be grateful to them, to appreciate all the committees they sat on, all the phone calls they made, all the paper work they did. They wanted to be wanted; they wanted to be accepted at their own valuation. And they'd always win, by the very nature of things, because you can go on doing paper work forever, but you can only run and jump and throw for a few years. The funny thing was that with a little more intelligence they could have handled us so easily, because athletes are the most selfish, egocentric people on earth; it took the most extraordinary, protracted crassness to force them into banding together. *Si la vieillesse savait . . .* But they didn't; they never learned a thing.

I still remember Ron Vane's face at Cardiff, when Ike won the Empire Games mile. I was sitting just near him, and I watched him all through the race, you would have thought he'd bet thousands on it, leaning forward, his expression changing all the while, delighted when Ike was falling behind, more and more worried when he came through on that last lap, then, at the end, absolutely shocked, incredulous, as if he somehow thought God had let him down.

That was the first real row we ever had, Sam and me, down at Cardiff, and even at the time, I suppose I knew he was right. But there's something *about* an Empire Games, it's not like an Olympiad; much friendlier, none of the same pressure; in fact, if you know what I mean, friendlier in every way.

Sam was in the athletes' village practically all day, when he wasn't in the stadium—though I think they'd have stopped him if they could—but at night he had to sleep at some hotel in Cardiff. He had three of his runners in the English team: me, Tom Burgess, and a quarter-miler called Gerry Sands, a little fellow from the northeast, I couldn't hardly understand a word he said. Then there was a half-miler, Freddy Morris, that Sam was very sore about, because he'd trained with us three months while he was doing some course in London—he hadn't run for Britain then—and afterward gone back to Manchester. Then later, when he was in the British team and won a few races, and someone asked him on the telly wasn't he another one of Sam Dee's runners, he'd said no, he wasn't, and the man who'd done most for him, that he'd really learned from, was Jack Brady. Sam was on about it for days, and he still was whenever Freddy's name come up: how Freddy had betrayed him just to get in with Brady, how he hadn't been nothing when he come to London, how he'd never asked anything from him, but the least he expected was a bit of loyalty, and this was the reward he got; he said, "I should have made him sign a statement."

In fact, I was afraid of what would happen when they met in the village, which they were bound to—Freddy was afraid and all—but when they did come face to face in the restaurant, Sam just said to him, "I wish you luck. I wish you success. I do not need acknowledgment. Your success is my acknowledgment."

Alan was there at the time. He said to me afterward he wasn't surprised; he said, "It's a religious matter. Coaches are like prophets. Before the sun goes, thou wilt deny me thrice. If anything, it simply confirms Sam's view of himself." I saw what he meant, more or less. Still, I knew how Sam felt; I mean, there was no need for Freddy to say what he did, even if he thought it.

Peter McAllister was running for Scotland in the games, so that meant the English second string was Don Maitland, from Sussex, a blond boy, sort of stocky, very cheerful; he was quite a good runner, but he believed in enjoying himself as well, and I admit that he did have an effect on me. He was always chatting up the birds in the restaurant and up at the club there; when we'd get our food in the restaurant, he'd always look around the room to see was there a couple of good-looking birds on their own, and if there was, he'd lead the way there. There was a fabulous selection, too, you couldn't go wrong, really, not just athletes from our own team—most of which weren't all that, in any case—but from all over the Empire; and not just them but the swimmers and gymnasts and everything, too; Australians, Canadians, New Zealanders—and some of the colored birds weren't bad either.

When Sam was around in the restaurant, I had to be a bit careful, but when he wasn't, I let myself go more. I wanted to win that mile all right, it was very important to me, and I knew the field was very, very strong, but I'd been going without it so long that it was like being put in front of a bloody great meal when you're starving; you know you shouldn't, but you can't help it. What I told myself was I wouldn't *do* anything till after the final. As long as I went on with the training—and there wasn't much chance of avoiding that, not with Sam there—it wouldn't make all that difference, just a little dancing and that.

But what happened was we got in with these Canadian girls, these swimmers, and started having parties and things in their quarters. Of course, I didn't drink nothing, never more than just a glass of beer, though old Don put it away, but there was a little girl there I really fancied, blond curls and a lovely little figure, and she like me as well.

One night, while three or four of us was up at their place, I asked her would she come for a walk, knowing there'd be nobody in ours. She said yes, we went back together, and— well, that was the first time it happened. I remember practically freezing every time I heard someone going past the door, and her saying to me, "If you can run as well as you can make love, you must be pretty good."

Next day at lunch in the restaurant I was sitting there with Sam when she come by; she said, "Hi, Ike, how are you?" and the damage was done; I mean, I couldn't very well ignore her or tell her to bugger off, and though Sam was all right to her and paid her a lot of compliments, like he did when they were pretty, I think he could tell from how she looked at me and how *I* was that there was something going on. And I had a new kind of feeling—new with Sam, that is, because I'd had it with my old man over smoking and staying out late and that when I was younger—I was definitely feeling annoyed with him for making me uncomfortable. Yet afterwards, when we was alone together, training, I felt ashamed and I knew that he was right; I felt I'd let him down.

So there were these two things, pulling at me, all through the games, or, if you like, these two people, him and her; at different times I was choked with both of them, and it got so as I was avoiding the restaurant when I thought they'd both be there, slipping in very quick when I was sure one or the other wasn't because sitting there with both of them was too much for me, him wanting this, her wanting the other.

In the end he turned to me one day at the training track—we'd just finished—and he said, "Tell me the truth, Ike. You're sleeping with her, aren't you?" I said, "Not exactly sleeping with her, no." He said, "Don't try to wriggle out of it. I can tell. I can always tell. Even if I'd never seen the two of you together, the way you look at each other, I could tell from your running. Look at you now, the way you're breathing. You're a fool, Ike. I can't stop you. I can only advise you. But it's one thing or the other. You can go with girls, or you can win races. And if you prefer girls to winning races, fine. That's *your* decision. But you're wasting your time and you're wasting mine."

I didn't answer, I was too upset. After a time, us standing there, he put his hand on my shoulder; he said, "A girl like that has nothing to lose. Her life is not devoted to swimming, the way yours is to running. To her, swimming is only a means to an end. But the decision is yours. I leave the decision to you." Which put me in a terrible position, because I knew what my decision was, or what it should be; it would have been easy if I didn't see her every day, but I did, and the other thing was that every time I saw her, I felt the same about her. At first I made excuses, which wasn't difficult for a couple of days because I had this semifinal coming up; I run badly, but I qualified. I come in second behind Murphy, the New Zealander, with a bad time, 4.02, and the trouble is that even when you know you can run much better, second is second; the bloke that wins it has a sort of advantage over you. Sam said to me afterwards, "There you are," and I got angry again. I thought, *What do you mean, there you are; how do you know it wasn't your fault, going on at me, mucking things up with me and her?*

In a sort of roundabout way, I tried to talk to Alan Bell about it, I asked him what he thought about athletes having it off. He said, "It's like everything else; nobody really knows; there's just a lot of received ideas, a body of unverified prejudice. Why? Are *you* having it off?" and he looked at me in this way of his, smiling, like he had you under a microscope. I said, "No, no, I was just sort of interested, that's all." He asked, "What does Sam think?" and I said, "He's against it," and Alan said, "He would be. Sam isn't very keen on rivals," which struck me as a funny thing to say. He said, "I don't think there's ever been any research into it. There are two schools of thought—aren't there?—one that *any* sort of screwing exhausts you and the other that it can relax you. All those stories of the fellow who gets straight out of bed to win an Olympic medal. Obviously if you spend all night screwing before a race, it's going to take something out of you, but I don't think one can go much further than that. Personally I keep away from it before any important race, but for emotional reasons rather than physical ones; involvement tends to distract one. I think that may be at the bottom of it, actually. Singleness of purpose. Asceticism. The athlete who's dedicated his body to his sport. The mortification of the flesh. Oh, yes, Sam would certainly be all for it." Which left me like it always did when I'd talked to Alan: more mixed up than what I'd been when I started.

In the end it worked itself out, because Jackie, that was her name, got pissed off because she thought I was avoiding her—which I suppose I was—so she started avoiding *me*. Which upset me, I don't mind telling you, but what with the final coming up and all the training, I was able to put it out of my mind. In fact, I don't think I even spoke to her again until after the final, when she suddenly come running up to congratulate me; she give me a kiss, and she congratulated me. That was something I could never get used to with birds: the way they forgive you.

Congratulations, Ike! Is that how you planned the race? No, I didn't; no.

Who'd *plan* a bloody race like that? That finishing kick of Burke's, the way he went away from me around that second bend, just *leaving* me. So fucking hopeless. Then hearing Sam, God knows from where, "Come on, he's kidding!" when I hadn't got nothing left and I had to find something, and driving, driving myself like my body was a horse; get on, you bastard; the pain in my chest, hardly even knowing where I was 'till suddenly—bang!—the last bend and him a yard in front of me; then side by side, hearing him puffing and gasping, hating him; and then alone, ahead of him, just the tape in front of me, and breaking it, winning; I mustn't collapse, I mustn't collapse. Winning.

No, I didn't plan it. He surprised me; yes.

V

Rome has snubbed us, I suppose; yet perhaps she's right to see us as she obviously does: barbarians camped outside the gates, clean-limbed and empty-headed, no different from all the other infinite invasions except that we were going to throw our javelins into the ground.

A lot of athletes in the Olympic Village feel hurt by it; an athlete's ego can be awfully fragile. He's convinced the world revolves around him; he has to be egocentric to be successful, but indifference hurts him terribly, perhaps because it confirms what he inwardly feels about himself: that what he's doing, despite all the public acclaim, may not be important at all; it may even be completely marginal. I don't know whether I'd have thought like this in Melbourne, where I was bursting to win and knew I could. Objectivity's inclined to be a luxury, but here I can afford it, because I'm only a tourist. I haven't a hope of winning; I know it, so does everybody else, but my times were good enough so I'm here, enjoying it, guiltily. Noninvolvement tends to breed guilt; I imagine war correspondents must feel it badly. After all, men are getting killed.

Still, no wonder Rome despises us. I've never seen such beauty, natural and historical; I've never come across such a massive domination by the past. Whatever one does seems to be taking place under a great umbrella, so that things like running and swimming and cycling seem doubly peripheral, and I wonder why they ever decided to hold an Olympiad in Rome, though of course one knows.

It's just like them to have it in August, under that hot, heavy sun that makes everything look so dazzlingly beautiful —the white marble of the stadium set against those dark-green hills of nodding trees, so peacefully irrelevant, so implicitly disdainful—but at the same time turns the Olympic

Village into a concrete desert. A cyclist has died; a sacrifice, I thought. A human sacrifice. Wasn't it what they'd been wanting when they made it Rome in August, those terrible old men? Wasn't this their revenge for incapacity? *Si la vieillesse pouvait* . . .

Standing in that glorious stadium during the opening ceremony, all of us, every nation, in ranks and uniform, like a military tattoo, while the old man spouted rubbish at us— youth of the world, pure amateurism, the Olympic ideal, and the rest of all the nonsense—thinking that if we were like troops, he was like a general, sending us into battle before he went back comfortably to base.

Yet one can't be completely detached; there's this thing in the air, the Olympic thing, that even Rome can't kill. This electricity, this high-strung expectation, tension; you can reach out in the Olympic Village and touch it.

The heat apart, the village isn't really unpleasant, provided one can escape now and then. They'd built it across the Tiber from the Olympic Stadium, little concentrations of two-story brick buildings, the men's section divided from the women's as usual. Rome itself is a stupendous corrective, practically deserted in the heat, the light so glorious on all those orange walls and climbing leaves, on those extraordinary roofs, with the tiles crawling across them humpbacked, like red tortoises. I find I need the corrective, the relief: from the patter and the chatter and the monomania, from our nice, dingy running girls; from the giggling swimmers, from the heavy men, the throwers and lifters, with their ugly, bulging limbs, ambling like dinosaurs.

Besides, I'm sharing my room—how I detested sharing rooms—with Ike Low and Tom Burgess, another of Sam Dee's runners, which means we have a lot of Sam, hectoring and philosophizing, a little more than I can stand, and all the intensity of Ike and Tom. Tom, who's intense anyway, and Ike, because he wants so much to win. You might ask why not? What else is there to do but win, despite all the windy double-talk about taking part? Hadn't I been keen enough to win myself four years ago.

Yet the thing about Ike is it seems to me that this is *all* he wants or all he's been conditioned to want; he can't see an inch beyond it, this medal, it doesn't symbolize anything, it doesn't lead to anything, and when he's won it—*if* he wins it—he might as well drop dead, like a posthumous VC.

One afternoon, siesta time, when both of us were resting on our beds, I found myself asking him, "Ike, do you enjoy running?" He'd been talking endlessly about lap times, about relating the mile to the 1500 meters, about how the other runners in his race would run, about *their* lap times, and it jolted him. He said, "What do you mean? Of course I do. Don't you?"

I said, "While it's happening? While you're actually competing?" and these words popped into my head, from God knows what repository: "He rejoiceth as a giant to run a race." What giant? What race? Why a *race?* Why not just to run? And why rejoice? Because he was a giant? Because he knew he'd win? Because it was a race against ordinary men? Would he have rejoiced if the others had been giants, if he hadn't been as sure?

Of course, it worried Ike; it was like taking the mechanism out of a clock or asking a bird how it flew. Except that flying was a primary function, while running races wasn't. But Olympiads were no time for philosophy; they were for competition, singleness of purpose, monomania, and I was sorry that I'd asked him; it was unkind and unfair; it had made him think when he'd no business to be thinking. He said, "It depends on the race, don't it? Some of the time you do, some of the time you don't. The good times are when it clicks, when you feel this is it, this power in you. You enjoy it then. But running through the pain barrier; you can't enjoy that, can you? It stands to reason; you can't enjoy pain." I said, "Some people do," which again wasn't fair; then I heard myself say, "Anyway, *what* pain barrier?" though it was Sam I should have asked, not him, poor fellow, parroting what he'd been told. The words always annoyed me, though—the bogusness of them.

He said, "Well *you* know what I mean. When it hurts so much you think you can't do it, there's this barrier there, and you've just got to drive yourself, force your way through it. That's coming through the pain barrier." I said, "In other words, it must be an imaginary barrier." "Oh, yes," he said. "I mean, it's all in the mind."

Then he asked me did *I* enjoy it, which was reasonable enough. I said, "Now, yes. Now the pressure's off. The actual running, yes. Before—I don't know. Yes, at the be-

ginning. Less and less as it got more tense. I liked it when
I'd won." He said, "Oh, yeah. We all like winning."

Here in the Olympic Village, where one meets the
world and his (athletic) wife, where the heat in the
Roman air is rivaled by the almost tangible tension, I
asked Sam Dee a blunt question: "Do you think Ike
Low can do it?"

For more than a hour, this extraordinary coach and I
had been discussing strength and style, tactics and
stamina, the merits of interval training and sheer, hard
running, the importance of technique and the crucial-
ness of character. We were joined now by bronzed
American boxers, now by intrigued Australian swimmers, while the whole stupendous pageant of this Olympiad drifted: Dutch girl swimmers in orange bathing
wraps, a mysterious cyclist in a solar topee, massive
Russian discus girls in sleeveless white dresses, earnest
walkers undulating along on a training spin. And I
wondered how many other journalists felt as I did, that
it was a privilege simply to be here, to partake, even at
secondhand, at this unique festival, where the world's
youth met in peaceful contest.

Dee looked at me steadily for a moment; then he said,
"Ike knows he can win. I know he can win. There are
only two other competitors in this race who know they
can win, who truly believe in themselves. The others
only regard it as a possibility. They have no chance."

I knew what he meant, this remarkable moulder of
champions, who can rouse love and hatred with equal
facility, whose eccentric ways have led to so many bitter battles with officialdom. For the pressures of an
Olympiad are such that nothing short of total confidence is enough; anything less will crack under the immense strain. And Low has total confidence. Twenty-
two years old, a lean amalgam of grace and power, you
have only to watch him perform the simplest actions—
eating a meal in the Olympic restaurant, writing a letter to his East London home—to know that he is perfectly composed, as ready in mind as he is fit in body.

"Yes," he said, when I put the same question to him
across the restaurant table, "I think I can do it." Then,
after a pause, "I know I can do it."

Of such stuff are potential Olympic champions made.

"In an Olympiad, you are not running only for yourself; you are running for the millions of people who believe in you, the children who would one day like to *be* like you, and the adults who wish they had been. You are running for the old and the young, the sick and the well, the good and the bad. The athlete is not only important in himself, he is important in what he stands for, and he has never been as important as he is today—in a time of motorcars and mechanical jobs, a time in which the body is forgotten and neglected. When they watch you on the television screens, they are watching *themselves:* Your victory is *their* victory; your defeat is *their* defeat. You are an example to youth and a reproach to those who have abused their bodies, who have allowed the flesh to corrupt. So an Olympiad should be a *challenge* to the old and an *inspiration* to the young."

Some people asked you, "How do you like Rome? What do you think of Rome?" and I couldn't answer them; I didn't *know* Rome. Rome, for me, was the village and the stadium, and when they asked me, "Don't you think the Olympic Stadium's beautiful?" I couldn't answer that one either. Beautiful? You didn't think about it like that. Maybe it *was* beautiful if there'd been nothing going on and no one there— no noise, no races to run in, if you hadn't just come here with one thing in mind.

It was like the sun; I mean, in a way, if you was there on holiday, the sun must have been wonderful, this warmth every day, blazing down at you, but if you was a runner, not used to it, then it was terrible. I got sick of the bloody sun. I'd wake up every morning and hope to Christ it was raining.

As for the stadium, well, it was just too much for me. After I'd been in it three or four times, I stayed away from it unless I was actually running, I'd go to the training track or I'd stop in the village, which could be boring at times, it could wear at your nerves, but at least there wasn't all the row, the tension, eighty or ninety thousand people packed in every day, the Italians cheering the Italian runners, the Germans cheering the Germans. In fact, the Germans made more of a din than anyone. They seemed to be organized; you could pick them out if you looked, all at one end on the terraces. Every now and then they'd give a sort of chorus, it sounded like

> Hoy-hoy-hoy!
> Hoy-hoy-hoy!
> Rah Rah!
> Rah-rah-rah!

again and again, till it began to drive you crazy.

The scoreboard, too; this big, black scoreboard. It was electronic; electric lights lit up on it, spelling out names and giving times, one little bulb after another, but very, very quick. But watching it, it wasn't other people's names I saw go up on it but *my* name, wondering where would it be, would it be first, what time would there be against it? Then, other moments, while all these different names appeared, name after name, Japanese and Russian and Italian, not being able to imagine mine at all, thinking it could never go up; maybe I wasn't even here.

Yet this was funny, because most of the time, specially away from the stadium, I knew I could do it, I knew I could beat any of them; in fact, I *had* beaten most of them, and only three had ever beaten me, two of which I'd beaten later on. The ones you worried about, though, were the ones you'd never run against, and there was two of those—two important ones—the American, Jim Driver, that had beaten the world record in their Olympic trials, which they pick the team on, and then this Hungarian, Budai.

Obviously holding the world record made him favorite, Driver, though like Sam said, it was an advantage in a way not to be favorite, there was less pressure on you, and the thing was, it could just be a flash in the pan, this record. Besides, another thing Sam used to say, records were one thing and races were another, and I'd had a lot more experience of *them* than what he had. Still, he'd got that over me, the record. That was something I'd never had, a world record.

We'd never spoke, me and him, but we knew each other by sight from the training track in the Foro Italico, and now and again, when we passed each other in the village, we'd sort of look at one another, sort of weighing each other up, more like two boxers, really. He wasn't very much to look at—a little, thin fellow, sandy hair and rimless glasses—but you could feel this determination about him—even just in the way he looked at you—and I suppose he felt the same about me.

It's difficult, really, knowing how you should behave with your opponents, especially in anything that matters as much as an Olympic Games. You don't want to treat them like a load of enemies, but in a way, I mean, they *are* enemies, at least until the race is all over. They'd give anything to win, and you'd give anything to win, so really, unless the bloke's from your own country, you just kind of smile and say, "Hi!" and, "How are you?" and leave it at that. Or if he's from a different country like Budai, one that speaks a foreign language, then there's no problem, because you couldn't even talk if you wanted to. Sam says quite a lot about what he calls channeled aggression, which means sort of *having* this competitive feeling, this always wanting to win, but not letting it go out of hand.

From what I'd heard about Driver, he was a bit like me; he got off to a very busy start, and he had this fantastic finishing kick as well. In fact it wasn't a year since he'd moved up from the 880 to the mile. Budai was a bit different: He liked to get out in front at the beginning and stay there; apparently he had fantastic stamina but all one pace; he hadn't got the acceleration, which meant he had to try and kill you off early.

There was others as well, of course: Goetz again, and Manfred, this big East German that had sorted me out in Leipzig that time, and the Aussie, Jeff Burke, that had nearly beaten me at Cardiff; we'd run against each other once again, in Los Angeles, and we'd done the same time, though they'd give it to him. But I wasn't running well that day—it was in the middle of the winter anyway—and I knew I could beat him here. Though, of course, in an Olympiad another thing was you could never be sure who'd come through, maybe somebody you'd never heard about; it had happened before, and it could happen again, but usually not in the mile.

The trouble was it wasn't just one race, it was three: your heats, your semifinals, and your final, which meant you had to build yourself up three times, up and down, up and down, because after a race you always went down—and all in less than a week. Another thing was how to run each race, how far did you push yourself in the first two? It wasn't so much that you'd give anything away, because most of us, like I said, we knew each other, we'd run against each other before, but if a bloke beat you, say, in the semi-final, he'd have this over you in his own mind, even if not in yours, so maybe in

a way it was better to win every race and build this advantage. But then in *doing* that, especially in this heat, you
might take too much out of yourself.

Of course, I went into all of this with Sam. His opinion
was that you had to wait for the draw, to see who you'd got
against you. If it was Driver or Budai, someone new, maybe
it would be better not to show them too much. He said,
"We'll see. Don't worry. *I* am here to do the worrying for
you. *You* are here to do the running." But how could you
help worrying? What else was there to think about? Especially with all these reporters jumping on you the whole time,
these interviews, question after question—did you think you
could win, what did you think of this one, what did you think
of the other—some English, some American, some that
could hardly speak English at all, some with notebooks,
some with microphones, getting on to you while you was
eating, even coming into your room. One or two, the ones
you really knew, were okay, more like friends, but some of
them drove you nuts.

Confident, Ike?

Who's your coach, Ike?

You will please tell me what you think of the chances of
the German runners?

Is this your first Olympic Games?

What do you do at home, Ike?

You prefer a fast race or a slow race?

Could you describe your methods of training?

Did you know Driver ran 3.37.8 in Zurich on the way here?

You heard Burdai did 3.38.6 in training yesterday?

What do you think of interval training?

Does the heat bother you?

What is your opinion of training with weights?

Are you married, Ike?

How do you like the track?

Got a girlfriend, Ike?

Do you think that there will be a new Olympic record?

Is that right you don't eat meat?

What is your best time for the 1500 meters?

Would you rather run this or the mile?

Who's going to get to the final, Ike?

In the White City you were running a 56.3 first lap, but
in Stockholm only 57.2; how do you explain?

How many times have you broken four minutes?

How old are you?
How tall are you?
What is the length of your stride?
Do you like Rome?
What do you weigh?
Who do you fear?

On top of that there was the usual business of Sam and the officials. The coaching thing wasn't quite so bad. Jack Brady had more or less accepted Sam was looking after me; he didn't give me no detailed instructions before a race, just little general things, and even those in an offhand sort of way, like he only did it because he had to. He and Sam never spoke; he didn't often speak to *me*.

But with Ron Vane and the others, it was different; they were still gunning for Sam, and about the third day we was there, we had this big row about his not being allowed into the Olympic Village. He hadn't got no official pass, which was something they could get very nasty about, even if you was an athlete, so Sam had been coming in *with* athletes; only this time, when he did it, they stopped him. So then there was a hell of a carry-on; they even had the police in on it, till in the end they phoned through to the British headquarters, but instead of them helping, Ron Vane come down to the gate and said yes, it was him that had given the instructions. He said, "You've nothing to do with us; you've got no official status." Sam said to him, "What do you mean? I've got two of my runners in your team," but Ron wouldn't have it, he just said, "And if I see you in the village, I'll report you," then walked off.

But you couldn't keep Sam down. He was back in the village that afternoon; he'd got a pass from the Canadian television, I think it was, as a commentator, and there wasn't nothing Ron could do about it. In fact, I was there later on when Sam walked up to Ron, he said, "Good morning, Mr. Vane, I wonder if you'd oblige me with an interview for television?" and I nearly pissed myself. But Ron didn't see the joke; he never could. He looked at Sam, then turned his back and walked away.

We made a bad start, the British team, which didn't help, because although athletics is so individual, all but the relays, it's funny how it can affect you. If a team starts well, then everyone feels good, but if it starts bad, you begin to think,

I'll do badly, too. To make it worse, Tom was one of
s that come unstuck. I don't think right deep down
cted to do all that well in the ten-thousand, but he
ly bumped around the first bend, and he come in
th.

After that, all he wanted to talk about was what went
wrong, the way they sorted him out around that bend, then
boxed him in later on—it's a rough old race, the ten-thousand; there's so many in it, for a start—and how he'd change
his tactics if he could run it again. I could understand how
he felt, but it didn't do *me* no good, hearing him, yet at the
same time you couldn't very well tell him to belt up.

Sam cheered him up as much as he could, telling him he'd
been unlucky and that he hadn't run bad, if he'd done that
time in Melbourne he'd have come in fifth; but it wasn't
much use. By the time I had to run in my heat I was wondering would I qualify, though, in fact, the draw wasn't a
bad one, really. Manfred was in it, and old Don Maitland,
and Gill, from Australia. It was in the morning, so the
stadium wasn't all that full, which I liked, but I still didn't
feel too good before the start, wondering how I'd run. Still,
I jogged a bit on this red track they'd got, and I liked it—it
was nice and light; there was some speed in it. Then, when
the gun went off, I forgot the rest, I was just running, what
I'd come there to do, and nothing else mattered.

I was drawn in lane two; Manfred was in the outside lane,
thank God, the big dirty bastard, and I think I was so pleased
to be running at all after all the waiting that I was like a dog
let off the bloody lead in that first lap, I went like the
clappers, and when I come round, I must have been ten yards
clear of everybody else, and I knew I could win. In fact, I
heard Sam's voice shouting, "Steady, Ike!" and I coasted a
bit in the second and third laps, till at the bell there was two
of them up there with me, Manfred and some African bloke
I didn't know. So I let Manfred out in front, partly because
I'd always rather have him where I can see him, and partly
because I knew I could catch him, which I did. About two-
fifty yards out, when I was running with Gill and this darkie,
I opened up, and when Manfred heard me coming, he really
turned it on. It was a great feeling, him giving it everything
and me knowing that I wasn't really pushing myself, nothing
like flat out, but still coming up with him and going past him,

beating him by about a yard. It wasn't a bad time either: 3.39.2.

The best moment came when I saw my name go up on that scoreboard, the little yellow lights twinkling away till they said LOW; there it was, my name; if it could go up there once, it could go up there again—on top.

When I saw Ike win his heat, I thought he'd win the final; I still believe he would, if he hadn't been so unlucky. He ran a beautiful, arrogant race, slightly nervous at the start, pawing round like a horse, but once he was away, glorious to watch.

There was a moment, when they were on the far side of the track, when I suddenly saw it as a painting—the step back, the tourist's advantage—under the hard, strong light: the marble and the trees, white against deep green, the runners, frozen in their colored vests; near enough to see the power and grace, far enough to miss the sweat and pain and effort. I was sitting on the bottom step of the terrace, Sam on my right, Tom Burgess on my left, Sam shouting, "Look at him, look at him!" with this infernal pride in his face—I made him, I made him!—the most intransigent smile I'd ever seen. I thought, *Pygmalion,* except that nobody had made Ike, nobody needed to; he was simply *there,* waiting to be quarried.

And he ran as if he knew he could win when he liked, not that the field was really stronger or his time exceptional; it was the manner of it all, the power that *wasn't* being used. Each time he came by us—we overlooked the start—Sam would yell at him, and although he didn't turn, you could tell by a slight lifting of the head, a sudden stiffening of the body, that he'd heard. But it annoyed me; I felt he didn't need Sam—not there, not then—and that this was an attempt to make him think he did. One that worked, because when he'd broken the tape, and Sam was yelling, "Well done, Ike! Well run, boy!" he looked around until he saw him, and he smiled at him, like a boy at his father.

As for Tom, he and I were by then in the same boat: We'd both failed; we were both peripheral. The difference was that I'd done better than I thought I would, and he'd done worse. I'd got to the semifinals and been beaten out by one place. It stung for an hour or so—it's curious how a conditioned reflex goes on twitching—then I'd accepted it.

Tom hadn't; he was still terribly depressed, and **I felt** awfully sorry for him and angry with Sam, maybe unfairly. Perhaps Tom would have been the same in any case, with **or** without him; he already had this one-track disposition. You could easily see that pale, ascetic face of his in a cowl. Not Ike, though. Ike had been manipulated.

It was this, and the extension of this, the same sort of thing reflected everywhere—irrespective, as they say, of race, creed or color—that mitigated one's enjoyment of it all, even as a tourist. It was like being at some stupendous circus, where the more you admired the performing animals, the more you worried about how they'd been trained to do their tricks. The less one knew, the more one could appreciate it, the more one could sentimentalize it as a pageant of youth, see it simply in terms of flesh, bodies in movement, through air, through water, swimming and jumping and running and wrestling and tumbling, and all against this overwhelming background, which at once set it off and corrected it.

Poor Ike. I heard him shouting in the night after that race, that semifinal: "I'm falling!" God knows what he dreamed.

It was heartbreak day again for British hopes as wonder miler Ike Low, powering into the lead in the back straight of his 1500 meters semifinal, pulled up suddenly, then hobbled off the track, victim of a torn thigh muscle.

I call this Britain's bitterest blow on this red Roman track, which has so far brought us nothing but athletic anticlimax. In my view, and that of Europe and America's top coaches, Cockney miler Low was well on his way to striking gold for Britain.

"It just went," Ike told me, afterward. "One moment I was going like a bomb; the next, I was in agony."

Ike's coach, stormy sporting petrel Sam Dee, angrily denied charges that he had been training twenty-two-year-old Low too hard. "There's not a word of truth in it," snapped the bearded, fifty-seven-year-old miling mastermind. "Ike was fighting fit. He didn't train any harder than he normally does."

Amazing how Sam's runners always pull muscles in Olympiads, isn't it?

Ike Low? Would you like to come over to the restaurant there and give an interview to Canadian television?

Not now, mate. I can hardly bloody walk.

Well, you know how it is in television, Ike. Today it's one story; tomorrow it's another.

Yeah, well, not now.

I mean, of course, the boy was overworked. If he'd only listened to us, if he'd only been left alone.

From the very beginning, Ron.

Driving the boy, never letting him rest. *We* knew what was best for him, but he wouldn't listen. *We* had his interest at heart, but he wouldn't believe it.

Perhaps he'll have learned from this, Ron.

I hope so; I hope so.

Stopping like a man who's been shot, like a bird hit in full flight, so you could feel the pain go through your own leg, the red-hot jab of it down the back of the thigh, the dreadful feeling of impotence—how well one knew it. And moving so beautifully until it happened, with such economy and strength. You had to be another runner to feel the full pain of it, physical and mental. And I felt something else besides: that this should have been his moment, and his moment had passed, his chance had gone, just as mine had gone, in Melbourne.

And I was feeling so strong, so good. Letting Burke make the pace with Budai, staying in there behind them, then in the back straight, finding I'd got so much left that I knew I could take them, though it didn't matter—this was the ridiculous thing—I'd have qualified in any case. So that for weeks I couldn't get it out of my head: If I hadn't accelerated, would it have gone, would it have been different? If I'd come in, say, third, would it have been all right? Or would it have gone in any case, like a lot of people said; would it have gone in the final? You could never know; you could never be sure. Even the doctors, they all give you a different answer.

This terrible feeling, this *plunging*. Nothing in between. One moment you're going like a bomb; the next you can't even move—this pain, this spasm down your thigh, and worse than the pain, the knowing that you've failed, you're finished. Them all coming past you, one after the other, even the ones you could walk away from, like those nightmares where you can't move, till there's nothing to do but step off the track, onto the grass, into the middle, into nowhere.

That moment I honestly wished I was dead; there was nothing left to live for. Two or three officials come running up to me, jabbering away in Italian, which I didn't understand, and one of them threw a blanket across my shoulders, all prickly in the heat; I threw it off again. Then Ron Vane turned up from somewhere, saying, "What's the matter, Ike, did you pull?" and I couldn't speak, I was too choked; I only nodded. He asked me did I want a stretcher, but I shook my head. It hurt enough, but that was all I needed, being carried across the stadium on a bloody stretcher, in front of all them people. So they sort of carried me across, Ron and one of the officials, I had an arm round both their shoulders, and I was able to see the race just finishing; it looked like Burke first, then Budai, and when that tape broke, I closed my eyes, because I knew I was crying. In fact, next day there was my picture, in all the bloody papers, Ron and this official carrying me, and me with my face screwed up, crying.

Some of the others in the race were quite decent about it; Burke come across and said, "Tough luck, sport," and Budai, he couldn't say nothing, but he got hold of my hand and sort of shook it. Then Sam was there, thank God, and I found myself saying, "Sorry, Sam, sorry, Sam." It was all that come into my head. And Sam kept saying, "This is *only* a setback; this is *only* the beginning," more like he was talking to himself than he was talking to me, and I think, looking back, that he was nearly crying, too.

Then Jack Brady come across; he said, "Hamstring pull?" just like that, like a doctor; he said, "Get him back to the village; then let's put him to bed." Sam took my arm instead of the official, and we went down the tunnel, then waited there outside the stadium while Jack got hold of a car. He didn't speak to Sam, and nor did Ron. In fact, Sam and Ron stood either side of me, both speaking to me, but behaving like each other didn't exist. From the way they was behaving, Ron and Jack, you would have thought it was all Sam's fault, that he'd come running out onto the track and done it to me himself.

When the car come up with Jack in it and an Italian driver, Ron said to Sam, "I think we can manage now, thank you," but Sam didn't take no notice; he said, "Easy, Ike," helping me into the back seat; then he got in beside me. Nobody said a word on the drive, but Sam got hold of my arm above the elbow, and every now and then he'd squeeze it.

As for me, I thought, *I'd like to cut that fucking leg off,* which was how I felt for days. It was like it wasn't part of me, that leg; it didn't belong to me; it hadn't got nothing to do with me. Because *I* felt just the same inside me; that was the terrible thing; I had the same confidence, I felt the same power in me, just like I did out there on the track when I begun to turn it on. It was like having a great big engine inside a clapped-out old car, except that you could always buy another chassis, while I was stuck with what they'd give me.

Then, when it started to get better, it was funny, there was *only* that muscle; you couldn't think of nothing else; it all narrowed down to that—the pain of it, from just below the buttock right down nearly to the back of the knee, the weakness in it as it started to improve, the ache in it when you tried to stretch it, which Sam made me keep on doing.

He took me to some clinic there in Rome for treatment: the diathermy heat with this coil wrapped around your leg like a black snake, all warm, and the ultrasonics, you lying on your back while they rubbed the oil on your leg, then this rod going up and down, up and down, very hot and nice unless they forgot to move it, when it burned like hell. It was all to get the muscle fibers expanding and contracting. Sam would give me long lectures about what had happened, the internal bleeding; he'd run his finger down the muscle, and he'd say, "It's tracking well; light training in a fortnight," but for me, I couldn't see ahead a fortnight; all I wanted was to get out of Rome, away from this Olympiad, out of the fucking village, where everything reminded me.

I pleaded with Ron Vane and Des Victor, the team manager, "Can't you send me home?" But they said no, the charter flights had been booked, and that was that. Ron said, "I know you're disappointed, Ike. We all are. But treat it as a holiday. A free holiday." Some fucking holiday.

Sam had a lot to say about it:

"This is a setback, but no more than a setback. It depends on you. A great champion learns from his misfortunes. A great champion uses them to grow, just as in the process of evolution a man walks upright or a bird grows wings. You have failed honorably. You have proved to yourself and to the world that you are a great runner, and not only a great runner, but one who can produce his best on the greatest possible occasion. In four years time you will be a greater runner still, stronger in mind and body, fuller in experience.

"I think you would have won these games. No one can be sure, but I think you would have won, just as you, in yourself, believe you would have won. I say this not to tantalize you but to give you faith in your own potentialities. Between now and the next Olympiad, there are many fruitful possibilities. Remember: You have not been defeated, only temporarily betrayed. Your victory in Tokyo will be a *greater* victory than in Rome, because you will have conquered your adversity."

Which was fine while he was talking and for a little while afterward, but then I'd get depressed again. I've often wondered since, would it all have happened if I'd won, or if I'd gone straight home, the way I wanted to—the whole thing of Jill and me? Would it have happened if I hadn't been in the mood I was, down on the floor, pissed off with everything?

I didn't even want to get out of bed; at least in bed I was away from things; I only had to see Alan and Tom, when they was there, and the ones that come in for visits; sometimes when they did, I'd pretend to be asleep.

When I did come out, it was terrible; terrible not even to be able to walk properly, let alone run, so that I hated that bloody leg all the more. It would have been bad enough at any time, just out in the street, hobbling along while everyone went past you, but here, where you weren't among ordinary people but athletes, fit people, the fittest people in the world, all using their bodies, you felt a kind of double cripple.

I knew Jill before, of course; she'd been in the team on and off about a year, and she'd come abroad with us a couple of times; I'd thought to myself, you know, *very* nice, pretty face, lovely little figure, and thought she seemed different from the other girls. They sort of tended to be very much the same, sticking together and giggling a lot and never bothering about their appearance very much. Even the ones that come across, ones like Jane Cobham, who I'd had it off with that time in Leipzig, weren't really like ordinary birds. When they did go to bed with you, it was all a bit of a joke, run of the mill, like having a drink or going to the pictures. But Jill didn't giggle at all, thank God; in fact, there was something serious about her, the expression in her eyes—she had these very nice brown eyes—the way she looked at you. And when she did laugh, it was always *about* something, and it was wonderful the way her face changed, how she looked at you when she was laughing, like you were the only two people in the world, you and her. I'd talked to her now and again, but I'd never tried to chat her up, partly because of this thing about her, that she wasn't on, the way some of the others were, and partly because, being the Olympic year, I was behaving myself, especially on the tours, before the races. I'd promised myself that if I won that gold medal—*if* I bloody won it—I'd have the time of my life, I'd make up for it all, but until it was over, nothing. Well, nearly nothing.

She was from Manchester, Jill; it always surprised me a bit when I heard her speak, at first: her dark, little, pretty face, and this northern accent coming out of it. I'd always had this idea, being a Londoner, I suppose, that northerners were sort of comedians, and I couldn't really fit the two together, her and her voice. Anyhow, the way I felt after that injury, the last thing I was interested in was getting off with any birds; in fact, to tell the truth, I don't think I'd have even had the confidence.

One afternoon, though, I come into our Olympic restaurant. I come in late, because I didn't want to see people; I didn't want to talk to nobody. I brought my tray across to one of the tables, sat down, and then I heard this voice, *her* voice, say, "How's your leg?" She was sitting just across from me, just a few places down. I'd never noticed her; that was the sort of state I was in. To tell the truth, I wasn't that excited now that I had; I didn't really want to talk to no one. My attitude was, what does it matter how my leg is? I've dropped out, I've been eliminated, it's another four years before I can try again, so what difference does it make one way or the other? Still, I got to admit that she looked very nice in this pink blouse they'd issued to the girls, nice bare brown arms, slim but, you know, nicely turned, sort of strong without being heavy. She was a sprinter, 100 meters, and as a matter of fact, she hadn't done bad, getting into the final, finishing one or maybe two from last.

I said to her, "It's better than what it was," which I suppose wasn't all that friendly, but like I said, it was something I didn't fancy talking about. She said, "I was there. I could

have cried. You were running so well," and for some reason, that got me; it brought it all back, and the tears come
into my eyes, I bent down over my plate and started eating,
not wanting her to see me. When I still didn't speak, she said,
"I'm sorry to upset you; I know how you feel about it," and
that made it worse; in fact, I wanted to get up and just run
out of the restaurant, except that I still couldn't run and it
would look ridiculous, me leaving my dinner there and hobbling out.

So we both just sat there in this stupid sort of way, me trying not to cry, her trying not to upset me, till suddenly I
found myself hoping that she wouldn't go, getting frightened
that she would, and I looked up then, I made myself, and I
said the first thing that come into my head, "Going to the
stadium this afternoon then?" Which was the most ridiculous
thing, because it was the final of the 1500 meters, the one
thing I'd have gone a thousand miles not to see, which I suppose was why she looked at me the way she did and didn't
answer for a bit; then she said, "Yes, I am," and I said, "Let's
go together."

We sat in the athletes' part, which was in the middle, quite
low down, opposite the grandstand. I didn't remember till
we'd sat down, and when I did, it was too late; there was
nothing to do but stay and go through with it. Quite a few of
our team was there; a lot of people said hello, but I could
feel them looking at me, wondering how would I take it,
probably, or perhaps in some cases wondering at my being
there with Jill. An Australian come up, a hurdler that I'd
met at Cardiff, and he said, "Who do you fancy, Ike?" I
thought, *How bloody thick can people be?* I said, "I don't
know. Very, very open," but in fact, it hurt me to think
about it, knowing that I ought to be out there, that I could
have beaten every one of them.

Then the loudspeaker announced it, and the names started
flickering up on the scoreboard—all those names, not mine,
just like I'd imagined when I saw it first. Budai was in it, and
Driver and Burke and Manfred. They were all jogging
about, stretching, limbering up, first in the middle of the
track, then by the start, peeling off their track suits, and
suddenly it was just too much for me, I dropped my head, I
couldn't look, and that was the moment that she took my
hand; it was wonderful, really, suddenly feeling these fingers
pressing on mine.

When I looked up, it was to look at her, not the track; she had this beautiful expression in her eyes, like she really knew what I was feeling and was sorry for me, and I looked back at her and that was it; it didn't need no words; we were in love.

It was like being drugged or something; I could look out there now, at the runners and the race and all, and I didn't feel nothing; it didn't sting no more; it was just a lot of blokes getting out of their track suits, standing around in colored vests till this gun went off, then running, like in some dream. Several times during the race I turned around to look at Jill, and once she was already looking at me when I turned to her, and she smiled. This great smile.

In the end, it was Burke that won; he went away from them halfway through the last lap, and Driver just blew up; he couldn't live with him; in fact, by the end he was lucky to come in second; there must have been a good fifteen yards between them. But even then, at the finish, even then with all the excitement, even though I was properly focused on it now, this drug thing was still working so it didn't upset me. Not even later when they give the medals, when I see Burke standing up there where I should have been, though I can think of it today, and it makes me choke.

That night we went into Rome for dinner, Jill and me, to a restaurant down near the river, where we sat and ate outside. To tell the truth, I didn't notice a lot else about it, because this was something new to me, this feeling; I'd never had it like this, so strong that you couldn't think of nothing else, that you hardly knew where you were.

I remember the river, though, the Tiber, standing with Jill by the parapet, there, below the trees, looking at the water, not speaking at all, holding hands and looking, then kissing her. When I got back, they told me Sam had been up there, looking for me. To tell the truth, I'd honestly forgotten all about him.

Arrivederci, Ike! You take away a cruel memory of Rome, but leave us with a sympathetic one, the memory of a young and ardent athlete, full of vigor of youth, who came to win, but lost without being beaten; the memory of an athlete typically English, tall and slim, with the profile of one of those aviation heroes of twenty years ago, a classic type, an Olympic type, pursuing victory, but always within the limits of fair play.

Alas, like so many heroes you have been betrayed, betrayed not by any human being but by a traitor closer and more intimate, one which every athlete must beware of: his own body. They call it a pulled muscle, that disaster which struck you as you ran so nobly round the red track of the Olympic Stadium, full of confidence in your powers, in those legs, so long and muscular, which were about to let you down.

And when the muscle went, one saw in your face a double agony, the agony of failure and the agony of betrayal, the agony of a man abandoned by his closest friend. That race was one which you were going to win, just as you must feel you would have won the final. But you did not win the final. You did not even run in it. You had to look on, in bitterness, while the officials hung the medals around the necks of those you could have beaten.

You return home in the torment of anticlimax, like a plant that is not allowed to grow, but to us you leave the image of your sportsmanship, your virile grace, your loyal combativity. Which is why we say: "*Arrivederci, Ike; a Tokio!*"

> If he'd listened to us then,
> Never listen, never learn,
> Taken heed of our advice,
> Done the things we said he should,
> Realized *we're* the ones who know,
> He'd have won the bloody gold.
> Well, it serves him bloody right.
> Hope he's learned his lesson, now.

VI

HAMPSTEAD HEATH. *An autumn afternoon. The scene has a mellow, domesticated beauty. Among the copses, yellowing leaves spin slowly in a gentle wind. The light is soft; the mild air holds a promise of rain. An unemphatic sun plays over grass which has moistened and modulated to a winter green.*

Over a slope, out of one of those dells, brief undulations, which cover the Heath like parentheses, two runners appear: a MAN *and a* WOMAN. *Both run with an air of purpose, dedication, as if toward some specific goal. Both wear white singlets and flimsy white running shorts. The* MAN *is taller, six inches taller than the* WOMAN—*handsome, with wavy brown hair, a face young but tempered by hard physical experience, like that of a soldier or perhaps a young religious. His body has a lean, pared muscularity. His complexion, like hers, is almost olive. She has dark, short curly hair; her limbs are slight, yet supply developed. As the two of them clear the crest, she turns her head to look at the* MAN, *her expression one of admiring fidelity. He does not look back at her.*

The next moment they are joined, over the hill, by three more runners, all wiry and thin: an ELDERLY MAN, *with a short gray beard and the vigorous movements of some mechanical doll, and two* YOUNGER MEN, *one pallid, tall and tense, the other blond, shorter, running with a crisp self-sufficiency. These three now overtake and surround the first two, the* TALL MAN *going to the* MAN's *left, the* BLOND RUNNER *to the* WOMAN's *right, the* ELDERLY MAN *moving in between the* MAN *and the* WOMAN. *They run in silence for a while; then the* ELDERLY MAN, SAM DEE, *speaks.*

SAM: Right, now we'll get in a little sprint work. Whoever's name I call sprints until I tell them to jog again. *Jill!*

JILL DAILEY, *the* WOMAN, *accelerates over the grass. Her stride is short and brisk, her knees come up high in a pumping action.* SAM (*calling*): Arms higher, knees lower; arms higher, knees lower! All right: *jog!*

JILL *relaxes into her former, steady pace.*

SAM: *Ike!*

Now the MAN, IKE LOW, *sets off at a sprint, raising his pace without manifest effort in a few strides, his movements powerful and controlled, so smooth and economical as to seem automatic. He runs beyond* JILL *and is some fifty yards ahead of her when* SAM *calls to him again.*

SAM: Jog!

IKE *jogs.*

SAM (*whimsically*): Sam!

He himself now sprints, swift but not smooth, giving an impression, as his gray head inclines, bobbing, to his left side, that his body is being consciously driven. When he reaches JILL, *he stops, trotting beside her, then, after a few paces, turns his head to shout again.*

SAM: Tom and Alan! Come on! See who's first to Ike!

The tall man, TOM BURGESS, *and the shorter blond man,* ALAN BELL, *set off in competition, swift and serious.* TOM *has the longer stride,* ALAN *the sprinter's dynamism. After thirty yards, he's five ahead of* TOM, *who shows, however, no sign of giving up. His head lolls; his mouth sets in a thin grimace; he gives the impression of a man approaching the end of a marathon. After two hundred yards, when they are now past* IKE, *the gap is wider still, some fifteen yards, but by the time* SAM *cries, "Jog!" it has begun to decrease.* ALAN *jogs, but* TOM *runs sourly on till he has reached* ALAN. *They are then caught up by* IKE.

TOM (*to* ALAN): I'd like to see you over five miles.

ALAN (*cheerfully*): I couldn't run five miles.

TOM: And I can't bloody sprint.

IKE: Don't let it get you down, Tom!

TOM (*bitterly*): *I* don't let it get me down.

IKE (*turning to look back at* SAM *and* JILL): I got my eyes on you, Sam!

SAM (*immediately*): *Ike!*

IKE *obediently sprints away alone, while the others laugh.*

SAM (*to* JILL): *We* know how to get rid of him, eh?

When IKE *is a good two hundred yards away,* SAM *calls again.*

SAM: Okay, jog!

IKE *jogs.*

TOM (*glancing back*): Never knew you were a dirty old man, Sam.

SAM (*putting an arm around* JILL's *shoulder*): Jill knows
   that I regard her as a daughter.
ALAN (*looking back in turn*): A dirty old father then!
SAM: We shall ignore that.
   The run continues, the runners, like so many molecules,
now coming together in clusters, now drifting apart. Describ-
ing a large semicircle, they arrive, at length, at a fringe of
the Heath which borders a quiet suburban row of large,
detached, two-story houses. There, by the Heath, two cars
are parked; one, IKE's, *a Ford Cortina sedan, the other,*
ALAN's, *a blue two-seater sports car. Unlocking them,* ALAN
and IKE *produce and hand out track suits to* JILL *and* TOM,
a gray, high-necked jersey and blue jeans to SAM.
IKE: Thought you was looking old today, Sam; eh, Jill?
JILL (*squeezing* SAM's *arm*): I thought he looked smash-
   ing.
SAM (*kissing her cheek*): That's my little darling.
IKE: *Your* little darling!
SAM (*hugging* JILL): If all women athletes were like her, I
   would take women's athletics seriously.
JILL: You *should* take them seriously!
SAM: I take *you* seriously, darling, because you are feminine
   and beautiful.
JILL: You see! Not because I can run!
SAM: I *know* you can run. But to me, your femininity will al-
   ways come first, your running second.
IKE (*putting his arm around* JILL's *waist*): Quite right, Sam!
   Tell her she wants to stay at home and do the cooking!
JILL (*breaking away from them both*): You've got a cheek,
   the pair of you!
SAM: Darling, you are our inspiration! You are our Atlanta!
   If it was within my power, I would award you every gold
   medal in advance, just for being what you are!
JILL: I'm interested in running, not in winning beauty con-
   tests!
SAM: If there were beauty contests among runners, you
   would win them all!
JILL: I give you up! You just don't believe women athletes
   can be dedicated.
SAM (*hugging her, again*): Of course I believe they can be
   dedicated. Why, if every male athlete was as dedicated
   as you, if *Alan* had been as dedicated as you—
ALAN: Here we go, again.

SAM: He would not have won only a bronze medal—

JILL: *Only* a bronze medal!

SAM: He would have been the most *successful* sprinter of his day.

IKE (*in a mock-American accent*): World's fastest human.

ALAN: Serves me right for not listening to you.

SAM: Well, you had your chance. You came and trained with me. I was prepared to take you.

ALAN: Too late now, Sam.

SAM (*declamatory*): There is a tide in the affairs of men.

IKE: Yeah, but the tide's gone out, eh, Alan?

ALAN: Irrevocably. Never mind, Sam; I'll still drive you home.

SAM: In that rocket of yours? I don't know if I want to.

ALAN: Fine. I'll take Jill then.

SAM (*embracing* JILL): My little doll? I wouldn't trust her to you for a minute.

IKE: When Alan slowed down, he bought the car.

ALAN: Perceptive of you.

ALAN *opens the driver's door of the sports car and climbs in,* SAM, *with a grimace to the others, getting in at the other side.* IKE *and* JILL *climb into the front seat of the Cortina,* TOM *into the back.*

SAM: Ah, but there's nothing to compare with *human speed.*

The cars drive away.

She's a *grave* girl; that's the word to describe her. Not dull, not humorless, not heavy—*grave.* What the French call *sérieuse.* And Ike isn't really serious; he's only serious about running. *His* running. He isn't very interested in what happens to anybody else's, to athletics as a whole, the way they're being run. He won't join committees; you have to badger him to sign petitions, so that at times people get angry with him; I do myself.

I suppose, in a sense, we're like Marxists; there's no neutral position. If you aren't for us, you're for them, by default. There has to be commitment—and Ike's commitment is to running. And to Sam, of course—which partly explains his attitude, when most of the opposition seems to crystallize around Jack Brady. And now, to Jill.

One wonders at times how far one's own motive would stand examination; is all this committee work just a means of postponing the cutting of the umbilical cord? Was this how Ron Vane and all the rest started—as rebels, meta-morphosing with the years into authoritarians? I don't really believe it—I don't want to believe it. There's that plaintive quality in Ron, that longing to be misunderstood, which surely doomed him to administration, made actual partici-pation just an overture, a hiatus. He must have been born middle-aged. As for Ike, when we blame him for his selfish-ness, how far are we blaming what we sense in ourselves and envying it in its natural, undiluted state? Besides, who *really* does more for athletics; the devoted committee man or the runner who just goes out and runs and excites the world simply by running? You have to be careful. If you plump for the committee man, you're only half a stride away from Ron Vane.

But how lucky Ike is in Jill; that she should take him, his possibilities, as seriously as he does, as Sam has taught him to. How doubly lucky; for he's lucky to have her at all. Any-body would have been. I'd fancied her myself, but the grav-ity defeated me; she wasn't one for quick fucks on tour, esca-pades. When she turned you down, it was with a sort of re-proachfulness—"A-lan!"—all the more tantalizing because she was obviously a sensual girl.

It had been fascinating in the Olympic Village, to see Ike in love—Jill was made to be in love—to see him with that re-mote, besotted look in his eye, and to know that for once he wasn't thinking about records, lap times—that was a differ-ent sort of look—but actually of someone else. I'd wondered how Sam would accept it; but initially, at least, he has. This seems to be the honeymoon period in almost every but the technical sense: one for all and all for Ike. Because Jill is perfectly prepared to be a sort of handmaiden, quite happy to put his running first and hers nowhere. You get the feeling that if she goes on running at all, it's to help Ike, to train with him, to be in the team with him on foreign trips. I suppose she's a girl who *wanted* to sacrifice herself to something, some ideal, preferably embodied by some man.

I was standing with her once, watching him in a race, and she was transported, this rapturous look on her face, I con-fess to feeling very envious, and she said, "Oh, *doesn't* he run beautifully?" Yet, as I've said, he certainly adored her, too. In Rome, those last few days of the Olympiad, and in London as well—at least for quite a while—they had that *exclusive* quality about them that lovers have. When you were with them, you felt you were intruding. I did wonder, I admit, how much of Ike's involvement could be explained by the fact that Jill took him at his own valuation, but perhaps that was just my jealousy.

Under these conditions, as I've said, Sam accepts Jill, despite what he thinks about women athletes. Or perhaps he's simply shrewd enough to see that it's something he couldn't meet head on. He likes to tell Ike, when Jill's there, "Ike, you have already *won* the Olympic Games. You went to Rome, and you came back with something *better* than a medal." And Ike gives this little, chopped-off smile, then looks at Jill, who's already looking at him, and smiles again—at her. They all know it was just a joke. They all know there's nothing more important than an Olympic gold medal.

We didn't make love in Rome. There was always someone in my room, someone in her room, and anyway, getting into the women's part wasn't that easy. Besides that, I don't think either of us wanted the first time to be one of those hurried things, where you're looking over your shoulder the whole time, listening for someone at the door. I admit there was times when it could be part of the fun of it, but not with Jill and me; I knew it would kill everything.

The whole team stopped overnight in Lancaster Gate when we got back, and I didn't mean it to happen there either; it was the same thing, people in and out of each other's rooms the whole time and sharing. I was sharing with Alan. But it did happen, no planning or nothing, maybe because both of us wanted it so much.

I'd just come up the stairs to fetch something or other— my room was on the first floor—and just as I reached the landing, Jill come down from the second; there was no one else around. We looked at each other; then we kissed, and suddenly it was all too much. I pulled her along the corridor to my room—I knew Alan was downstairs—and when we was inside, I locked the door. And it was great, the best I'd ever known. Her body was marvelous, all smooth and springy, lovely breasts, not big but round, a wonderful shape, and the way she made love; I don't know how to describe it. It was delicate, this gentle touch she'd got, but she knew how to excite you. When she came, she went, *"Oh, oh, oh!"* and squeezed me hard with her arms and legs, you'd never think she was so strong. And I hugged her back; the idea of losing

her, of her going away, well, it was terrible. I heard myself
saying, "You've got to stay; you've got to stay!" and she said,
with her eyes still closed, with this marvelous smile on her
face, "Oh, darling, I'll be back soon; you *know* I will!"

The three weeks she was away up north were terrible
weeks, three of the worst I've ever known. Everything hit
me, then, double hard. I didn't know which was worse, missing Jill or having this whole Olympic thing come back on
me, like I'd been under anesthetic all the time she'd been with
me—which in a way I had. I trained like a bastard then, first
getting the leg right, then back on the Heath; there was nothing else to do, to take your mind off it. I think I amazed even
Sam, though he never guessed the reason.

He was very good, doing his best to cheer me up again,
saying that my next objective must be the world record. He
had to say that, because what else was there to go for in the
next four years? Just a lot of bloody races that didn't mean
nothing, win or lose. I wanted to beat Burke, of course, but
even that wasn't so important, because I'd beat him before,
and if I beat him again, what did that prove? Only that I
could have beaten him in Rome, which took you back to
where you started, what you knew already: that it should
have been *your* fucking medal.

He'd got his gym, now, the one Stan Ling had set up for
him and that Stan went along to himself now and then, him
and a lot of fat businessmen, though quite a few athletes
went there, too. It used to amuse me to see Sam in there,
among all those silver barbells and plush carpets, wearing the
same old tatty jeans and jersey, watching him make these fat
old men grunt and sweat. Alan used to call it the surgical
ward, which was what it looked like, really. Sam hadn't got
no time for that side of it; it was Stan's idea. Sam said, "A
gymnasium ought to look like a bloody gymnasium," and
Stan said, "If it looked like a gymnasium, nobody would
come," which may have been true. I think Sam took it because at least it sort of gives him a headquarters; he never
charged the athletes nothing.

We was going to get married, of course; we'd agreed that
in Rome, and she was going to come down and get a teaching
job in London; she was already teaching in Manchester. I
went up there to meet her family and I quite liked them. Her
old man reminded me a bit of mine, the old trade union stuff;
he was a foreman in a textile factory. There was a couple of

married brothers, and her mother was a bit like Jill, only fatter. Very quiet, bringing in cups of tea all the time. In fact, they were all okay, really, once they'd got over all the cracks about London. They didn't try to stop her coming down; that was the main thing.

When she did come down, she taught at a school near King's Cross. She stayed with us over at Hackney to begin with, which was great, but then she went into a flat with these two other teachers, near Camden Town. I said we ought to take a place ourselves, but she said no, not before we married, on account of her parents. And she trained up at the Heath with me and Sam and the others. He was very fond of her; there hadn't been many girls up there, he wasn't too keen on them, and those we did have never stayed very long, but he liked Jill; I was pleased about that.

> British miler Ike Low is to marry pretty, twenty-two-year-old international sprinter Jill Dailey. They announced their engagement yesterday, but fellow athletes have rumored it ever since the Rome Olympiad. Then Ike, a white-hot hope for the 1500 meters, broke down with a pulled muscle in the semifinal. Jill reached the final of the women's 100 meters.
>
> Sales representative Ike and schoolteacher Jill were often seen together in the Olympic Village. Now their sights are set on Tokyo and the 1964 Olympic Games. Already they are training together.
>
> "I know Ike can get that gold medal," said Jill, who has left her Manchester school to teach in London. "I'm sure he would have won it in Rome, if he hadn't been hurt."
>
> "Jill's a great help to me," said Hackney-born Ike. "It takes an athlete to understand another athlete."
>
> And Jill's own running future?
>
> "We're aiming for a Tokyo double."

Mind you, he had things to say, Sam:

"Jill is a very fine girl, a lovely young woman; it is natural and honorable that you should want to marry her. If I was younger, I would marry her myself! And if an athlete must marry, it is better that he marries another athlete, who will understand his dedication, who will not resent it when he appears to put his sport first, because he knows, and she knows, that there can be no compromise. But you must also consider whether, at this stage, it is fair to you or to herself: whether the demands of running and of marriage can be reconciled. A woman wants a home. A woman wants to have children. These are biological needs. Natural human ambitions. But an athlete's ambition is physical perfection, the transcending of his own possibilities. How can he fulfill both her demands and his? He runs the risk of failing both.

"Marriage is a great temptation to an athlete. You know already that an athlete's life is a lonely life. From outside, it may look a selfish life, but every kind of vocation demands some sacrifice. It is far, far easier to be a suburban husband with a mortgage, commuting each day to do a job with no initiative, than to be an athlete, driving himself daily to a pinnacle of fitness, forever summoning up new willpower, taking decisions in every race he runs.

"Get engaged. By all means get engaged; she is a very lovely girl. But think about all this before you marry."

I did think about it, I thought about it a lot. But I didn't see it the way Sam did. To me, Jill would be a help to me, I couldn't think of nothing better for my running, being trained by Sam and being married to Jill. Besides, she was earning herself, she was going to go on working, and even if I left home, it wouldn't make that much difference. As for kids, well, you could have them when you liked; there wasn't no hurry. I mean, we both *wanted* kids—eventually—but what we both wanted now was to keep on running. At least for the next four years.

> No one actually sprinted up the aisle at St. Jude's-in-the-City yesterday, but it would have been no surprise if they had. For runner was marrying runner; miler Ike Low was wedding sprinter Jill Dailey.
>
> Sam Dee, who coaches them both, was best man, and the congregation included distance runner Tom Burgess and Olympic bronze medal sprinter Alan Bell.
>
> Needless to say, the bride and groom walked arm in arm under an arch of raised spiked shoes. And the reception, just as appropriately, was held among the dumbbells and chest expanders of coach Dee's luxury Hampstead gymnasium.

I think we'd all been wondering how Sam would turn up at the wedding, what on earth he'd wear, but in fact he came in tails and a gray topper, which I suppose was quite predictable if one had really thought about it. The jersey and jeans wouldn't have worked. They'd have been expected for one thing, and for another, the occasion wasn't grand enough to be parodied. Not that the gear in any way suited him, that satyr's face under the topper, it was like putting a pullover on a dog, a straw hat on a horse.

He was certainly the life and soul of it all, springing about in that manic way of his, laughing and grinning, kissing Jill God knows how many times, and putting his arm around Ike. I think anybody who didn't know would have thought *he* was one of the fathers—or both their father—and perhaps that was how he felt. The actual fathers stayed very much in the background with their wives; they all four looked at him as if he were some weird new animal. From his behavior, you'd have thought the whole marriage had been his idea from the beginning, that the wedding was *his* triumph. Until one heard his speech at the reception. Even then, one had to listen fairly carefully; it was largely a question of innuendo.

He stood there with a glass of champagne in his hand—there was good champagne and an excellent buffet; I think his tame millionaire, Stan Ling, had paid for it—and this wicked old smile on his face.

It was a splendid thing to see two fine young people getting married, and when these fine young people were also fine young athletes, it was better still. Jill was a lovely, beautiful girl, and Ike was a handsome, virile young fellow. He'd looked at them during the ceremony, he looked at them now, and he thought what a magnificent couple they made. Some people might say too young, but that was the tendency these days, early marriage; the youth of today was free and independent, it made up its own mind and it followed its own inclinations, and nowhere were these qualities more obvious than in the young *athlete* of today.

He'd said before, and he'd say again, that Ike had won a *greater* prize in Rome than any gold medal (renewed applause, Jill bowing her head). In marrying Jill, who was not only a beautiful girl but a wonderful athlete, Ike had married someone who, he hoped—he *knew*—would help him realize his potential, the potential each and every one of us knew to lie in him, which it was *his* sacred duty to express and *our* sacred duty (looking at Jill, who looked back at him very steadily) to encourage. He wanted to impress on Ike— though he was sure there was no need—that he now had a double responsibility: to his sport and to his wife. Some might think there was a contradiction in this. *He* didn't think so, because he knew Ike and he knew Jill and he knew (another look at Jill, the same look back) that Jill was more eager than anyone that Ike should reach those heights it lay in his power to achieve.

So the two of them were going into matrimony with much, much more between them than the average husband and wife. They entered it not only with a bond of love, but with the bond of a common dedication, a common ambition.

Lots of applause. Thank you very much, and I hope I'll live up to all the things Sam expects of me, both in running and in marriage (same order again), from Ike. Thank you very much, but I just can't make speeches, from Jill, very downcast and demure again. Yet she'd sensed the undercurrents, I was sure; she sensed what was happening, even if perhaps she couldn't find words for it. She was an instinctive person, anyway, rather than a verbal one. But she'd caught the tone of Sam's voice and the look in his eye; I was sure of that from the way she'd looked back at him, calm and querying and remote, as if, having got the message, she was making quite sure she'd got it and deciding what she ought to do. The feminine principle. She was an extraordinary girl to find in athletes, among all those giggling, dowdy, suburban girls, and all those silly words like "aggression" and "competitive." I thought Sam underestimated her.

When athlete marries athlete, who does the housework?

Ike Low, Britain's brightest miler, and his sprinter wife, Jill, have found a democratic solution. "We both do," says pretty, twenty-two-year-old brunet schoolteacher Jill—Jill Dailey, before she was married. "We have a system. In term time, Ike does four days a week and I do three, but in the school holidays, when I'm mostly at home, it's the other way about."

Married last February, the Lows moved into a six-room, semidetached house in Finchley, which is full of cups and trophies that they've won between them. "It's my job to polish them," sighs Jill, "and it takes an age."

At the moment, cooking is her department, too, though vegetarian Ike sometimes brings her breakfast in bed, and she is gently initiating him into the art of poaching eggs: "Nothing too difficult for the moment."

Three times a week she joins him in training on Hampstead Heath, under internationally famous coach Sam Dee. The course, over hill and dale, rain or shine, is so arduous that some runners have referred to it as "Sam Dee's Treadmill." But Jill runs every inch with the men—and keeps up with them.

"She's really terrific," enthuses Ike. "And I daren't slack off, or I know she'll finish ahead of me."

Is there any rivalry between the two?

"Not a bit," says Ike, a sales representative for a Tottenham engineering firm. "After all, we're not going to be running against each other in competition, are we?" And Jill chimes in, "I'm more pleased when Ike wins than if I'd won myself. And you should see how worked up he gets when *I'm* running!"

Now the pair, who got engaged soon after last year's Rome Olympic Games, where Jill reached the final, and Ike broke down with muscle trouble when tipped for victory, have set their sights on the next Olympiad. They hope to become the first-ever husband-and-wife team to land a gold medal double.

And those are two extra medals Jill won't mind polishing at all!

For these two years, these two years up to Perth, I wasn't racing people; I was racing clocks. I was racing for the world record. Of course, you needed people, that was the peculiar thing; you needed people to pace you and to push you; otherwise, it would have been easy, wouldn't it? You could just go out on that old track, and do it on your own.

Like I've said, after Rome the world record was more of a consolation prize at first, but as time went by, it got to be something bigger, something that mattered for itself. Besides, if I did beat it, then I'd prove to everyone what Sam and I believed, that I *was* the best miler in the world, that I *would* have won that Olympic final if I hadn't broken down. Mind you, quite a few people had been on at me since then, getting at Sam, saying he'd overtrained me, I'd been pushed too hard. Ron Vane for one, which you would have expected, and Jack Brady, who'd got an ax to grind as well, and a lot of journalists asking me why had it happened; did I think I'd overdone it? I told them all the same thing, that I hadn't done no more than I did when I won the Empire Games, when I *beat* Burke, but there's a lot of reporters always want to stir it up.

I worked like hell on the leg, though, weights and that, at Sam's gymnasium; we had X rays done, too, and the doctor said there wasn't nothing basically wrong with it. But it still hung over me, the way it had let me down that day, the pain I'd felt and that terrible helpless feeling, which maybe was another reason why I wanted this record, this feeling deep inside that maybe it could happen again, or something like it. For that matter, maybe anything could happen, four years was a long time, you could get ill, you could get run over by a car, but if you'd beat the record, there was *something* to remember you by.

I'd think of Bannister; Bannister never won no Olympic medal, but they'd remember him forever; they'd always remember him as the man that broke the four-minute mile. It didn't matter how many people had done it since, how easy it might seem now; it was him that made it possible. Sam used to say, "Bannister may not have been a great competitor, but he extended the limits of human possibility."

That was a landmark on its own, of course, that four minutes; all the mile records since then had just been, well, just records, but right deep down I think I knew what I was going for, I think Sam knew, too. I wanted to run 3.50, even if it seemed impossible, but even four minutes seemed impossible, before he done it.

But you couldn't do it in the winter, when there was only the indoor, and nearly all of *that* in the States. All you could really do in the winter was train and think about it, but having Jill, being married, made it easier.

We had Alan training with us now as well; he'd retired, but he wanted to keep in condition. He was a great knocker, he loved to take the piss out of Sam now and then, and Sam used to wear this grin; they were a bit like a couple of dogs, circling each other. I think the reason Sam let him train with us was that he realized in a way it proved Alan really believed in his ideas, whatever he might say, and of course, he always had this comeback, that if Alan had carried on with him in the first place, he'd have won a gold medal.

Sam was talking once about the pain barrier, and Alan said, "You mean you want your runners to die in every race." Sam said, "Not die in every race. Surpass themselves in every *important* race."

He used to tease Jill, and all, Alan. I'd tell her that he didn't mean nothing by it, but she never really liked him. She said, "He does mean it. The smile's to make you think he doesn't. Alan's jealous." I said, "Why should he be jealous of me?" and she said, "Not just of you. Of anyone who's happy."

I went to Chicago and run in the Knights of Columbus meeting. Stan was very nice; he paid for Sam *and* Jill to fly across. There was a good field; Driver was there and old Goetz again and a new one they'd found, a boy called Durrant, still at school. I was used to this twelve-lap lark by now, the banking and the boards and that. I still didn't enjoy it, but I knew my way around, not like that first time in New York; they couldn't carve me up no more.

And I won it; I beat Driver. We was both running the same race, waiting for the other to go, and Sam had said if that happened, go on the ninth lap, because in his opinion I'd got a *longer* kick than Driver had, I could sustain it longer so I could afford to break earlier—where usually it's cat and mouse. Which was what I did. Another Yank, Kelly, was ahead when we finished the eighth, and Driver and I were just behind, him in the inside lane.

I pulled out and went past Kelly, and I could feel it had surprised him, Driver—you do feel these things—it was a moment or two before I heard him come after me. By that time I reckoned I must be out at least ten yards in front, and there wasn't no one in the world could pull ten yards back on me, not with only two hundred and fifty yards to go. So I held on, and that was what I won by, just under ten yards. He come up to me afterwards and said, "You surprised me. I'll remember that for next time." I said, "Next time I'll think of something else." He said, "Or Sam will."

I felt like calling him a cunt, but then I thought, *Why bother?* I'd choked him; that was all. Anyway it was typical of him, because he was a snarky bastard, he had this thing quite a few of the Yanks had, this thing they called psyching people, getting an edge on them by passing remarks before a race and that; you just had to ignore it. Beside, I'd heard it before, this digging at me and Sam, especially from Alan. What surprised me was when Jill said something. It was one day after training. Sam had been on about how he'd planned the season for me, which races I should run and which I shouldn't, which I should regard as warm-ups and which ones I could really go for the record, that kind of stuff. In the car on the way back I noticed she was very quiet, quieter than usual, till I asked her was there anything the matter.

She said, "He speaks to you as if you haven't got a mind of your own." I said, "You don't want to take no notice of that. That's Sam. That's just the way he carries on." She said, "He talks as if he thinks he made you." I said, "Well, in a sort of way he did, didn't he? He made me into a miler," and she got angry; I don't think I'd ever seen her like this before. She said, "Rubbish! Nobody made you. He's just brought out what was already in you." I said, "Yeah, but someone had to *bring* it out, didn't they?" She said, "Maybe they did, but it was there already."

I didn't take too much notice at the time, because this was Sam's way of talking, wasn't it? It upset a lot of people till they got used to it. The only thing was, I'd thought Jill *would* be used to it by now. Because Sam would admit all this himself; he'd say, "If the quality is not there, I cannot bring it out. If there is no oil in the ground, you can drill for it forever." In fact, later that night, when I thought of it, I told her, but she said, "He *says* that, yes."

We was lying in bed then; I pushed my arm underneath her and I hugged her, I loved the way she stood by me in everything, even when there wasn't no need, and after a bit she relaxed, she turned her face to me, I kissed her.

"There are two alternative methods of attempting a record. Either can be effective; either can fail. There is the synthetic method, as applied by Bannister, in which a race is deliberately manipulated to assist the challenger. Or there is the actual and genuine race, in which the challenger is pushed so hard in the natural sequence of events that he automatically surpasses himself and exceeds the record.

"In my opinion there is no comparison between the two: It is the difference between an honest record and a manufactured record. A manipulated race prostitutes the athlete to the stop-watch, just as it reduces everybody but the challenger to the level of minions. Records are important, but they are not *all* important. Ideally, they should grow out of the sport, out of competition. In your case, I shall tolerate these manufactured races, I cannot applaud them. I shall tolerate them because I believe you need a goal, because I feel that at this point in your career, the record is important to you as an athlete, that you *deserve* the record, just as you deserved to win in Rome. But it will be far more satisfactory to me if you acquire the record in a true, competitive race, just as I feel it is more likely that you *will* achieve it thus, because you are a genuine, competitive runner."

One thing about these record attempts, one thing Sam never mentioned but he just accepted, was I made a lot of money out of them just when we needed it, just when there was the house to finish furnishing and all. I admit that some races where I was meant to be going for the record I didn't try that hard; I'd win them, but I didn't push myself. I didn't see nothing wrong in being paid, what with these Yanks that were on athletic scholarships when they was thicker than I was, and the Russians all supported by the state, doing nothing else but run. The only difference was that they could get away with it, whereas if they found me out, they'd bloody jump on me.

The record was 3.54.9; it still belonged to Driver, the one he'd put up the year before at Los Angeles, in the American Olympic trials, and personally, inside myself, I thought I'd have to go out to California if I was ever going to do it, there or maybe Australia, somewhere where there was sun and the atmosphere was right, not in England with the gray skies and the rain and the heavy tracks, even if Bannister *had* broke four minutes up there at Oxford.

The trouble was that the *arranged* races had to be run in Britain. There was one at Slough where I nearly did it. I had four of them running with me, Don Maitland, that had been in Rome as well, Jack Newman, Wally Pratt, and Doug Madeley. Doug was actually a quarter-miler, I don't suppose he'd run the mile more than a couple of times in his life, but the plan was to push me over the first quarter. Normally that was the bit that didn't worry me too much, because I had this basic speed, I was always very fast over the first lap, but Sam's idea was that maybe this was the best way to do it, to push your strength, rather than do the more obvious thing, concentrating more on the later part, with somebody pushing you hard in the *last* lap. Which wasn't easy, anyway, because first they'd got to be able to stay with you.

My best time up to then was 3.55.4, that I'd run the year before in Poland. Funnily enough, what happened was that I'd been taking it a bit too easy; then when the last lap come, I found myself too far behind and had to turn it on. If I'd been trying for a time like that, I bet I'd never have made it. In running you can never tell.

The trouble was, the first-lap thing worked a bit too well. Doug went away like the clappers, and I took too much out of myself trying to stay with him, because he ran it like it *was* a quarter-mile, and at the end of that lap, there wasn't more than a few yards between us, and Sam shouted my time at me 55.6, which was ridiculous.

It really left me shattered, that lap, and the result was that I didn't do what I should in the second and third. Jack Newman went away in the second; he was a good club miler, though he'd never broke four minutes, but I found it very hard to keep with him. In fact, it was such hell for a time— the pressure built up in my lungs, the weight in my legs, the feeling I wanted to be sick—that all I could think was, *This is stupid, this is stupid,* because you didn't expect to have to go through the pain barrier in the second bloody lap of a race. Yet here I was, right up against it, the whole world narrowing down to nothing—no stadium, no crowd, no other runners, not even any track, just you, wondering would your legs support you, would your lungs explode on you, every step something separate, an effort on its own, till I did come through it; I survived it, and, passing Sam, I heard him shout, "1.55.8."

The third lap was Wally Pratt, another club miler, and the funny thing was that if it had been Doug Madeley, which it couldn't be, not at that stage, I think I might have done it, because Wally couldn't quite push me hard enough, and by then, after coming through the pain barrier, I needed pushing; it was natural that your body eased up. This time Sam shouted, "2.58.3," and I knew it wasn't good enough.

Don Maitland was okay on that last lap, he really made me go, up to the bend, but that was all he'd got; he was clapped out then, and I was on my own, no one to push me, just Sam's voice and the thought of the record. I finished twenty yards ahead of Don; I nearly fell at the finish; they told me afterward that as soon as I come through the tape, I was shaking my head. Sam come up and said, "A great race, a great race," which to me meant I hadn't done it, but I couldn't ask my time; I was too choked, too exhausted.

Don and Wally come over, then the others, all patting me on the back, all saying, "Well run." I said, "Thanks, lad," or I know I tried to, because talking still wasn't easy; then Sam said, "Very nearly; *very* nearly; let's wait for the official time," and it come over the loudspeakers, a voice said, "The winning time in that invitation mile race: three minutes, fifty-plus point seven seconds." I said, "Fuck it," and I went inside.

Later on, when I'd got over it a bit, it didn't seem such a bad old time, I mean, it was still the best I'd ever done, and if I'd been pushed a bit harder in those last two laps and not quite so hard in the first, I reckoned I'd have done it. Sam said that the next time he'd get a half-miler to make the running in the first lap, but the last lap was always going to be a problem, because there wasn't no one in the country that could really extend me.

Jill thought different from Sam, though; she said, "It's the second and third laps where you really need pushing. You always start well, and you always finish well. If they'd only let you run your normal first lap, you might have done it. I was very worried in that second lap; I thought for a moment you were going to collapse." I said, "I thought I was, and all. I went through the pain barrier," and she looked at me; she said, "That pain barrier." I said, "What about it?" and she said, "Oh, nothing. I've got my own ideas about it, that's all." I said, "You mean you don't believe in it?"

She didn't answer for a bit, till I thought she wasn't going to; then she said, "Sam talks about pain as though it was something good." I said, "Well, it *can* be good. It can be *very* good, if you use it properly." She said, "He talks like some people talk about childbirth, as if it's wrong to run without feeling pain." I said, "Well, you can't have a baby without pain, can you?" and she said, "Yes, you can. I've known plenty who had."

I told Sam what Jill had said about the pacing; we was in the gym and I was doing squats, which I always hated. He said, sort of half to himself, "Thinks that, does she?" and he went across the room to help some businessman with a big gut on him, that was trying to bench-press a barbell. When he come back, he said, "And what do you think?" I said, "I don't know. She might be right. I mean, there's two ways of going about it, aren't there? You can build on your strengths, or you can try and cure your weaknesses."

He had a weight in his hand, a disk, and when I said that, he threw it down, *clink,* into this rack of silver barbells; then he stalked out of the room. I didn't see him again that day.

Next afternoon, while we was running across the Heath, Sam and me and Tom and a few others, he asked, "How many years have I been training you, Ike?" I said, "I don't know. About four, I suppose." He said, "And might I claim by now to know *something* of your requirements and capabilities as an athlete? Just something?" I said, "Yeah, of course," and he said, "Not the requirements of your soul, merely the requirements of your body?" I said, "Yeah."

We ran on for a bit before he said anything else; then it was, "I respect and admire Jill as a woman. I had hoped that she respected me as a coach." I said, "She does. You don't want to get all upset like this. It was a suggestion, that's all. There's no harm in a suggestion."

He didn't look at me; he said, "I hope you're right. I hope I can believe you."

VII

I don't know what the watershed was, what exactly happened, but all at once, I noticed Sam's attitude to Jill had changed. Where he'd been so effusive that it seemed too good to be true, and still was, he'd suddenly grown very *polite,* almost formal, above all, suspicious. He's suspicious by nature, of course, like any self-appointed prophet: suspicious of journalists, suspicious of officials, suspicious of women, suspicious of anyone who isn't a rabid supporter of his theories. And of course, Jill picked it up at once—she was extremely sensitive to atmosphere—and, picking it up, went straight into her shell.

I had the impression that she didn't understand why it had happened. There was a puzzled, miserable air about her now, when she came to the Heath; cautious, too, like a flower that had closed its petals for protection. It had its effect on Ike as well; it was unavoidable. The exuberance had gone out of the whole thing, all that bouncing jollity which had made it a happy triangle, or at least a tolerable one.

Now and again I saw Ike look at Sam, or more often at Jill, rather wistfully, as if he were regretting the good times before the fall. In my opinion, it was stupid of Sam to join battle, whatever the reason—a battle he could only lose—and, being Sam, perfectly inevitable that he should. It was summed up for me by an image I can still recapture, an image of the two of them running together, Jill and Ike, side by side. I'd gone out ahead of the group, on one of Sam's bursts; when he eventually shouted, "Jog!" I looked around, and there they were, together, quite alone, he looking down at her, she looking up at him, like one of those Victorian paintings under which, you felt, was written "Loyalty."

A moment later, Sam's voice, from the dip behind them, shouted, *"Ike!"* and off he went, but it was only a temporary triumph.

Jill began to turn up less and less at the Heath. At first Sam would ask, "Where's Jill?" seemingly concerned, but obviously pleased—*How stupid of him to be pleased,* I'd think—and Ike would fidget and say, "She's training with her club this week"—she'd joined Atlanta—or, "They're keeping her at the school." When she did come now, Sam was friendlier toward her, but Jill was the same, withdrawn and wary—she wasn't a girl who dissimulated—till the time came that she didn't come at all.

"Where's Jill?"

"Gone down the Crystal Palace. Needs the track there, Sam."

Unconvincing.

Then the Wednesday afternoon when Ike came very late.

"Where have you *been,* Ike?"

"Well, over the Crystal Palace. Done a bit of training there with Jill."

"Let me know the next time, will you?"

And Ike full of excuses. "See, I just drove her down, and there wasn't no one else to pace her."

Till it became established that on Wednesdays he didn't come to the Heath.

I told Ike I was sorry she didn't come anymore, and it embarrassed him. "Well, it's not her type of training really, is it? I mean, it's more stamina, this—the middle distance and the distance."

I told her, too, "I'm sorry you don't come." I'd driven Ike home that day, she'd had the car, and he was upstairs, changing. She asked, "Why?" I said, "Because you always brightened my training." She thought for a moment; then she said, "I think it's better for me not to come." I said, "Because of Sam?" She said, "Perhaps." I said, "You felt unwanted?" and she said, "You love asking questions, don't you?"

They have a little, cozy suburban house that she keeps as bright as a button. You'd expect her to; she's incredibly capable, one of those girls who calmly find time for everything: running, teaching, housework, needlework.

It reminds me of the sort of house *I* grew up in—and no doubt the sort *they'd* grown up in—nothing beautiful but everything comfortable, except, of course, that theirs looks so pristine and cared for. Bright, brisk colors, cushions, a cold dining room that's obviously never used, a kitchen that obviously is, very modern—another difference—with a fridge, a dishwasher. A cabinet of cups and medals in the living room, instead of the usual cabinet of china kitsch, a big photograph over the mantelpiece (electric fire) of Ike breaking the tape at Cardiff, in the Empire Games. And the foreign souvenirs, of course, the raffia and the carvings and the ashtrays and the posters and the sombrero and the cut glass and the dolls. All just decoration, though; they don't affect the character of the place, they're the sort of thing you'd expect your parents to buy if *they* went abroad, the sort of thing soldiers brought back from foreign service. In fact, it seemed to me that this was just how you could describe us, us athletes; a sort of nonoccupying army, traveling the world in segregation, seeing everything and seeing nothing, cosseted and cuff off, always traveling with an ulterior motive, so that if we *did* have time really to absorb a new city, another country, it was at the expense of what we'd really come to do.

When I hear athletes talking together, it reminds me of a story about the war, of the soldier who described his travels: "Cairo? Lovely. Smashing canteen. Ham and eggs. Naples? Bloody marvelous. Terrific canteen. Cod and chips." Except that in our case it was, "Milan? Broke the European record there. Athens? Terrible. I pulled a muscle. Stockholm? Smashing. Did a 55.2 first lap." It was the price one paid—if one thought of it as a price. I'm sure Ike doesn't; I don't know whether Jill does. What Ike wants now, what he exclusively wants, is the world record, and wherever he can get it will be wonderful.

After all, that's what Sam has taught him exclusively to want, and Jill wants it for him, too; she speaks about it as reverently as he or Sam does. She asked me once, very seriously, "Do *you* think he'll break it, Alan?" and I said, "Of course he will." It was the wrong tone, I knew, far too casual, but this is the effect they have on one, with their intensity; it's like being provoked out of gentle agnosticism into atheism.

She looked at me suspiciously and said, "How can you just take it for granted?" I said, "I don't take it for granted; I just look at it objectively. Ike's the most talented miler in the world; he's dedicated himself to breaking the record; therefore, sooner or later he's going to break it."

She went on looking at me for a moment as if this didn't

satisfy her—it was too facile a statement of faith—but there was nothing she could quite put her finger on to complain about. I smiled at her—I couldn't help myself—I said, "I *do* believe in Ike," and she went on giving me this steady stare; she said, "Do you?" I said, "Of course. We all do. All in our different ways." And as she looked at me, so pretty and so grave, I saw her suddenly in white robes, a priestess at the shrine of his talent.

I put a frank, searching question to Ike Low this week.

As we sat over lunch in a Soho vegetarian restaurant —Ike hasn't touched meat for the last four years—I said, "Do you really think you can bring the world record to Britain?"

The twenty-four-year-old, six-foot Londoner paused a moment over his Russian salad, before looking me straight in the eye and replying, "John, that record is all I live for. If I didn't feel I was capable of beating it, I would hang up my running spikes tomorrow." And I felt a thrill of patriotic pride at the thought of a British runner with enough guts and will to win the challenge from the subsidized Iron Curtain athletes and the pampered performers of the American college campuses.

At Slough last May, Ike was only .8 seconds outside the record that America's Jim Driver set up in Los Angeles last year. Ike openly admits it was a paced race —"After all, Bannister was paced when he beat four minutes"—and blames his failure on a too fast first lap. Mind you, it was only a relative failure: Ike's time of 3.55.7 was a personal all-time best.

A string of victories in club, international, and invitation races since then has brought him no closer to his dream. At the Northumberland Miners' Gala, he ran 3.55.3: "A bit more pressure in the last lap, and I think I'd have been there." Against Hungary, at the White City, he shattered the opposition with a last lap so powerful that even Olympic finalist Budai was left puffing in the rear, twenty yards behind. Ike's time: 3.56.8.

Already this year he has beaten Driver: at an indoor meeting in Chicago. Next Wednesday he and his pretty sprinter wife, Jill, fly to Los Angeles as members of the small British squad which competes in a major international meeting.

"Driver will be there," says Ike. "That's where he set the record, so he ought to be trying. And Burke may be running, too."

Victory for Ike against this fabulous field would be consolation for the sadness of his Roman summer. But privately he is hoping for more than that. He is hoping for that record.

"In Los Angeles," he told me, "the conditions are right; the opposition is right." A determined look came into his eye. "If I fail this time, it won't be for want of trying."

Flying over, Jill sat on my right; Sam sat on my left. Across the aisle was Stan Ling and his wife, and behind was Ron Vane, behaving like he didn't know Sam was there.

I was worried about the race, I admit it, because there was these two things in it, trying to win and breaking the record, and if you wasn't careful, you could easily come down between the two. Nearly all the races I'd had this season had been one or the other. In the paced races, there was *only* the record, and in the internationals, you'd do your best to win and hope they *might* push you hard enough for a record.

I wanted to talk about it, to get it straightened out, but I didn't know who to talk to, Jill or Sam, because if I talked to one, it looked like I was ignoring the other; whoever I wasn't talking to would just sit there and not join in. It was terrible, really, what had happened, and I just couldn't understand it, my wife and my best friend, the two most important people in the world to me, people I couldn't do without, and all over nothing.

They didn't *argue;* there was nothing like that; maybe it would have been better if they had done, if it could all have come out. They weren't rude to each other either, now and again Sam would say something to Jill, and she'd always answer, or he'd say to me with her there, "Your wife is wearing a very pretty dress." They'd never ignore each other, but it was in the air, like frost, and I didn't like it.

I'd *tried* to put things right, God knows how many times. Sam had come over to dinner, once; he'd talked all evening,

and Jill never said a word. Now and again he'd look at her
like he expected her to disagree, but she didn't, and even
after he'd gone, she didn't say nothing—he'd been quite
friendly when he'd gone; he'd kissed her good-bye and said
it was a lovely meal—she was very, very quiet, till we was
washing up together, and I asked her was there anything
wrong.

She said, "No, nothing," in a way that meant yes. I said,
"Don't you like him, Sam?" She said, "He doesn't like *me*."
She'd said this before, and I'd told her again and again she
was wrong, that he was often asking why didn't she come up
and train no more. She said, "That's to keep you happy.
Those last few weeks, he hardly spoke a word to me." I said,
"It's his *way;* he doesn't mean nothing by it; it's *part* of him."

She said, "You know I don't want to make trouble. He's
been a wonderful coach for you, and you need him; you
need him very badly," and suddenly she started to cry, no
sound, just the tears coming down her cheeks. I said, "Jill,
what is it?" but she shook her head, and when I tried to put
my arms around her, she pulled away. I said, "Look, I need
him as a *coach*. There's nothing wrong in that, is there? As
a *coach!*" And I felt myself being pulled apart, two ways at
once, wanting to go both of them, till I got angry; it was so
unfair.

I started shouting at her, why couldn't I be left alone, why
did she keep imagining things, knowing I was being unfair
to *her,* which made me even angrier. She didn't answer me.
She'd stopped crying. She just went on washing up, wiping
the plates, very methodical, putting them in the rack, and
when she'd done the last one, she let out the water, dried
her hands, took her apron off, and walked out of the room.

I heard her go upstairs to the bedroom and the door lock-
ing, and I felt terrible; we'd never quarreled before; I felt
like walking out of the house and never coming back; then I
felt like phoning Sam and saying, "What the bloody hell do
you mean, going and upsetting Jill?" I picked a plate out of
the rack; I was going to throw it across the room and smash
it, but then I put it back. I went upstairs and tried the bedroom door—still locked. I knocked on it; she didn't answer.
Then I listened—no sound of crying or nothing. I said,
"Jill?" I said, "I'm sorry." Then I heard her getting off the
bed, her feet across the room, she opened the door and stood
there, looking at me; she said, *"I'm* sorry."

I kissed her, and right away we made love. I don't think I'd ever loved her as much as what I did then.

After that we hardly even mentioned Sam. It was like a sort of agreement between us, as though he was part of my job, something that I had to do. I didn't like it, I hated it, it was a terrible strain, like cutting your life in two where before it had been one, but still, it was the only way.

I had a bit of a barney with Sam about going down the Crystal Palace and training with Jill on Wednesdays, her half day. He said, "It disrupts the rhythm of the program I have devised for you." I said, "Look, I'm doing five miles down here, every time." He said, "It is not the same. First, because you are running on a track, not over country; second, because you are not running under *my* supervision." I told him, "Listen, I owe it to Jill, Sam; I get to train with her once a week, that's all." He said, "Jill is welcome here; I have always made her welcome," and what could *I* say, that *she* didn't feel it? I said, "Yeah, but it was too much for her up here; she feels better off there."

For a time he kept on coming back to it—why wasn't I there on Wednesdays; I ought to be there on Wednesdays— but when the season started and things got different, when he and I was doing track work and there was sometimes meetings in the week or trips, he give up. He did say once or twice, couldn't Jill do her track work with us, but I told him she was settled in at the Crystal Palace, and he seemed to accept that in the end.

I'd been to Los Angeles before; I didn't like the place much, nothing but roads and bloody petrol pumps; for me you could keep it, except for the beaches, but for Jill it was the first time. I liked the stadium, though, the Coliseum; it had a lovely fast track.

Because it was an official team, Jill and I weren't in the same room at our hotel, and Sam wasn't staying there at all, he was over one of the posh places at Beverly Hills, with Stan and his wife. As we was leaving the airport, he said to Jill and me, "Remember: Be good!" and then to Jill, looking at her, "Don't forget this could be the race of his life!" Then he squeezed my shoulder, and he was off.

I could tell Jill was furious without looking at her, and when I did, she was shaking. She said, "How *dare* he?" and when I tried to take her hand, she shook it free. So I let it alone, seeing the state she was in, I didn't say the things I wanted to say, because if I did, I knew her, she'd just blow up, with all these people around, Ron Vane and all the athletes, and the reporters, which was worse.

In the cab that took three of us to the hotel she was the same; she still didn't say nothing, but luckily the third was Laurie Keetch, a quarter-miler, who never said much either. I was doing a lot of thinking on the drive myself, thinking Sam was a cunt to have talked like that, but knowing at the same time that he didn't mean it, not the way Jill thought he'd meant it. I mean, he'd said the same sort of thing to me before, half-joking but really serious, and it never bothered me, because I knew he meant it for the best. It was like he said, anyone could be a coach, just concentrating on the running side, but the *real* trainer thought of everything; he conditioned the *whole* athlete.

I tried to tell her some of this when we got to the hotel, but she said, "*I* know what he meant. He meant to insult me. And don't say it's just his way. I'm sick of hearing that—it's just his way. He'll get away with whatever he's allowed to get away with, and you allow him everything!"

I said, "I don't, it's not bloody true!" I was choked, but I didn't want to push too far, because I could see that she was on the point of crying. She said, "Can't you see it's one thing when he says it to you, however bad, and another when he says it to me—and you let him say it?" I said, "That isn't fair!" but she wouldn't let me speak; she said, "What's fair then? To let him run your life? *Our* life? To let him walk all over us? Is that what you always think before we make love: Would Sam approve?"

And I didn't know what to do, I was going berserk standing there listening to her, not able to stop her and afraid of answering back, in case it made things worse. In the end I just went on standing and waited till she'd finished, till she said, "I shouldn't have come. I should never have come. I should have refused selection. Something like this was bound to happen eventually. I'll only upset you here, I've upset you already; I'll only stop you running your best."

I said, "You know that ain't true. You know I always run better when I know you're there. Look, I'll speak to him. I really will. I'll see that he apologizes. Right? I know he didn't mean to get at you." She said, "It's hopeless, isn't it?" and walked away to her room.

Still, I did speak to Sam; I spoke to him next morning

when we was training down at the Coliseum; I said, "That upset Jill, what you said at the airport," and he looked amazed; he said, "What? What did I say?" I said, "You know. About laying off. I mean, I don't mind your saying it to me." He said, "I'll go over and apologize. I'll go over and apologize now." She was across the other side of the stadium with Jack Brady, practicing starts. I said, "No, not now, she'll think I've put you up to it. Later on."

That afternoon at the hotel there was a bloody great basket of flowers for her with a little card: "To the most beautiful girl sprinter in the world from her most crestfallen admirer, Sam." I was with her when she read it; she just looked at me and said, "You talked to him." Just that. I felt like I'd been punched in the stomach.

Next morning at the track he come over to her and kissed her; he put on a great big act; he said, "Am I forgiven? Have you forgiven me? Or must I go down on my knees? I am pre-*pared* to go down on my knees." And he spread his arms wide like some big bird, so that even Jill had to smile; she said, "Yes, you're forgiven," and he lifted his head up to the sky; he shouted, "I'm for*given!*" I don't know what the Yanks made of it.

"Ike, I was wrong and I was stupid. When I made those remarks, I could have kicked myself. No; it is not okay. It was inexplicable. *Knowing* the psychological situation. *Knowing* how delicate it is when one career is overshadowed by another, *however* willingly the sacrifice is made. We will say no more about it. I was wrong, and I admit that I was wrong."

Hi! Brought your dad along again?

Fucking sight better coach than any you've got over here, mate.

We're kinder, Ike. We superannuate ours. We don't drag 'em all over the world when they ought to stay home watching television. Or don't you have television?

Yeah, we got that. We just don't have big mouths, that's all.

That's right. I was forgetting. What you don't have is world records.

Not till tomorrow.

*Just go. Go like the bloody clappers. Don't even think
about the record till the last lap, only the race. Just go.
Christ, it's hot. Stay with that cunt Driver around the first
lap, he'll fade on the second and third, then use Burke and
bang again on the bell. Kill bloody Driver when he tries to
come back. Come on, for God's sake. Start it, start it.*

And there they go! That's Ike Low out in front there, the
British miler, lane number three. He's certainly setting one
fast pace. In there behind him we've got Jim Driver, from
Sacramento, still the world record holder, who set the world
record right here, on this Coliseum track. After that, in the
inside track, it's Marty Green, from Villanova, then a whole
bunch, including the Olympic champion, Jeff Burke, from
Australia. Yes, sir, it sure is a fast first lap; just look at that
British boy go. Looks to me like he may be trying to kill off
the field. Would you go along with that, Mel?

Little early to say, Joe. Ike Low always has been a *very*
fast starter, and so has Jim Driver. They may both pay for
it, later in the race.

Well, as of right now they don't seem in too much trouble;
Low leading Driver into the second lap. What you make that
first lap time, Mel?

I have 55.8, Joe.

Yes, *sir,* a *very* fast lap. Wonder if they can keep it up.
You think they can keep it up, Mel?

I think they'll have a problem there, Joe.

*He's staying with me, the cunt. All right, let him go out
and bloody lead.*

And there's Driver going out ahead, now. Ahead of Low.
Did you expect that, Mel?

No, Joe, this is unusual for Jim. If he isn't way out ahead
on the first lap, he usually likes to hang on, then pull 'em in
the last time around.

Well, he *cer*tainly is putting on the pace, now. And here's
Burke coming up; he's nearly level with the British boy. I
think he's going to pass him.

Burke as well. What's the matter with me?

It's a three-man race now, and I would say Jim Driver, the

world record holder, Jim Driver from Sacramento, is five yards ahead. Mel?

About five yards, Joe.

With Burke of Australia tailing Low as we come into the third lap. The time, Mel?

1.55.9, Joe. I don't know how these three can keep it up.

Would you say we were on the way to a new world record, Mel?

If they can stay on their feet, Joe.

He's kidding, Driver; he must be. He wants *me to go out there with him.*

There's Burke! *Let* him *go. He can do it to Burke. So long as I can stay near them.*

The third lap was in some respects the most intriguing of all, setting as it did a number of puzzles to the connoisseur. Was it Driver's intention to surprise and kill off his chief rivals with his unwontedly fast second and third laps? Would Burke, responding to the challenge, have sufficient stamina to hold off Driver and Low with one of his characteristic bursts in the final lap? And was Low deliberately giving ground, hoping his opponents would devour each other like the two Kilkenny cats, or had the exceptional pace simply forced him into third position?

How do you see it now, Mel?

I don't see it at all, Joe. Just *any*thing could happen. I guess those three out in front are waiting for one or the other to crack.

Could be all three of them are going to crack, Mel.

Could be, Joe. Maybe we'll see a surprise in this last lap, but right now, there's no one within thirty yards of them.

And there's the bell. The time, Mel?

2.56.3, Joe. That was a 1.02.4 lap.

How *about* that? So we're still in with a world record chance here, Mel.

We surely are, Joe.

Now!

And it's Low from London, England, going out ahead! Just look at him move! I don't think anybody's going to stop

him. He's passed Burke; he's level with Driver; he's right out
in front! And something else is happening! Curtis, from
Oklahoma State, Charlie Curtis, has suddenly come into the
picture with a *great* kick; Charlie Curtis who ran his first
sub-four-minute mile just last week at—where was it, Mel?
Tulane, Joe.
Tulane. This is a *great* effort by Charlie Curtis, Mel.
He's giving it everything, Joe.
But still it's Low, with just a hundred and fifty yards left,
Low out ahead, Curtis gaining on Burke *and* Driver; in fact,
Curtis has *passed* Driver, and at the last bend it's Low, Ike
Low, with Curtis behind him.

*I can't, I can't, I'll have to stop, I'm dying. It's too much.
I'll bloody die. Oh, God, I'm through it now; I'm through.*

Low, it's *got* to be Low, with Curtis keeping out Burke for
second place, Low with a *mar*velous final kick, Ike Low,
from London, England. What a race! And the time, Mel?
I make it 3.54.7, Joe.
Which would be a *new* world record, Mel.
If I'm right, Joe, it would be a new world record.
So we wait for the official time, viewers, to see if that's
what we have: a new world record.

Fuck Sam! I'm going to collapse!

You've *done* it, Ike! You've done it, boy!
Oh, Ike, oh *dar*ling! How wonderful!

Her winning and all. What a day.

Then later on that night: celebrating. Stan took us out to
one of these fabulous places they had out there. Hawaiian,
this one was, about a mile long, with bloody great torches
flaming in the dark, outside. Me and Jill and Sam and Stan
and Mary. I don't remember quite a lot of it; I was so happy
for one thing, and I was so shattered for another. For me,
they could stop the clock right there; they could wrap it all
up now. My record. I didn't even care about Rome no more.
My record. Stan talking to the waiters: "You know who this
is? The young man that's just broken the world record."
Even Driver congratulating me after. "I guess I'll just
have to start in on nuts and yogurt."

Stan brought on the old champagne, I had a glass, even Sam drunk some, and the best thing of all, the thing that made me well pleased, was the way him and Jill was getting on. He was talking to her a lot, making jokes and that, and she was laughing. Even old Stan was laughing, old dead pan, that normally you wouldn't get more than a smile out of.

People kept joining us, I don't know where they come from, and in the end we found ourselves in this place, the Keyhole Club, down in the basement of a massive, great hotel, a band and a load of red plush seats and these birds in black stockings showing a lot of tit, that was meant to be waitresses—big girls, all of them. Now and again, one of them would go up and do a turn with the band, dance or sing or something, not too well, and the end of it was that Sam did a turn; he did a striptease.

He went across the floor to the stage, and we was pissing ourselves, the way he was taking off their walk and all, very slow, swinging their tits and kind of wriggling, and the snooty expression on their faces, don't you look at *me;* it was marvelous. The first thing he did when he got to the stage was pick up the microphone and say, "Ladies and gentlemen, I have great pleasure in presenting to you the *new* holder of the world mile record, the man who beat it today in the Los Angeles Coliseum: Ike Low!" and he pointed toward me.

Well, I felt a bit of a twot at first, everybody looking around toward our table; then they started applauding, and Stan said, "Go on, get up!" So I did get up; I give them a little bow; then I sat down again, and Sam got on with his act.

Actually, for once he wasn't wearing the old jeans and sweater, probably because it was so hot; he was wearing an open-neck black silk shirt and a very tight pair of black trousers; we'd had a bit of a barney at the door, to get him in. The striptease that he did wasn't a real striptease, because he didn't take nothing off; he just *behaved* like he was taking them off, poncing around the stage the way strippers do, with those funny, stiff movements, making like he was taking a stocking off, with his leg stretched right out, turning to pull a face at us, then suddenly pretending to throw it at some bloke sitting at a table in the front. I can tell you, in a few minutes the whole place was hysterical; in fact, they played up to him, they turned out the lights and put a spotlight on

him, the band give him rolls of drums and that, and at the
very end, when he pretended to whip off his G-string, then
spun around and turned his back on everybody like he was
embarrassed, well, you should have heard them.

We stayed there right on into the early morning, dancing
and all. Jill was a terrific dancer, things like the twist; she
danced like she'd worked out every movement, almost like
she was on her own, though now and then I'd meet her eye,
and she'd give me a lovely smile.

There was only one thing the whole evening, one little
thing wrong: When Sam was telling some Americans about
the race, how he'd told me to do this, told me to do that, how
it had all been planned, and I saw Jill looking at him, I
thought she was going to come out with something, and I
got hold on her quick. I said, "Come on, let's dance," and on
the floor she said, "You'd think he'd run it, himself." Otherwise, it was all all right. Otherwise, it was fantastic.

Ike, how does it *feel* to be world record holder?

Fabulous.

Did you think you'd beaten the record at the moment
that you broke the tape?

I thought I might have done, yeah.

So it wasn't a surprise?

Well, it was and it wasn't. I mean, you're always *hoping*.

But you and your coach, Sam Dee, had definitely planned
an attack on the record in this race?

I'd planned to have a go at it, yeah. I mean, I was hoping
it would be a fast enough race *to* go for it.

In fact, I believe the pace turned out to be faster than
you'd expected?

The second and third laps, yes. I didn't think Driver
would push it that hard.

Perhaps he didn't think *you* were going to push it that
hard?

Maybe. I don't know.

Did he talk to you at all afterward?

Yeah. He said he was going to start eating yogurt.

Very good! That's *very* good! And now, Ike, now that
you've *got* the record, what ambitions for the future?

I want to keep it.

VIII

I kept it three months, that's all; then a Canadian took it—
before it had even been ratified. Some bloke I hardly knew of
called Terry Cooper; he'd come eighth in the final in Rome.

I remember the evening that I heard about it, the way it hit
me; I felt like I'd been robbed. The phone suddenly went,
and it was Arthur Henry, one of the athletics reporters; he
said, "You've heard all about the new record, Ike?" and I got
this terrible feeling in my guts; I said, "What? What new
record?" Then he told me, this Cooper breaking it in Vancouver; he'd run 3.54.5. He asked, "Can I say you're determined to get it back?" I said, "Yeah, you can say that."
He said, "And that you're surprised?" I told him, "You can
say that, and all."

I was still standing there by the phone when Jill come in
from the kitchen and asked what was the matter. I said,
"I've lost the record. This Canadian's got it. Cooper, 3.54.5."

She put her arms around me and give me a kiss; she said,
"Well, you'll just have to get it back. That's what records are
for: to be broken." I said, "I know, but so quick. I hadn't
hardly got used to it."

Then I rang up Sam, but they'd been on to him as well.
He said, "If he has run 3.54.5, you, by the end of the season,
will have run 3.54. Our intermediate target will be 3.54.2."

But I didn't get it. Not that season. I felt terrible. Honestly,
in some ways, worse than Rome.

It's extraordinary; more and more like a morality play,
Ike as Everyman, Jill the good angel, Sam the tempter. Type-
cast, of course; sometimes I've felt Jill shone with goodness,
quite oppressively, while Sam, the tempter, had most of the
best tunes.

What Sam is tempting him with, dangling in front of him
like a carrot, is the world record. He'd got it, he'd lost it, and

now he had to get it back. And what Jill has seen, it seems to me, is that this is a process which could go on forever; he'd get it, he'd lose it, he'd get it again, and as long as he was involved with it, he'd be involved with Sam. I don't know exactly at what stage she came to realize this; it was simply that I noticed the change in her, whenever I was with them and Ike started to talk about the record in this religious, missionary way, his eyes all aglow like a crusader's. Before— before he *had* the record—she'd been as passionate about it as Ike, but now there was a definite restraint; she made the right responses, but not in the right, crusading spirit, and he noticed it; he'd say, "Don't we, Jill?" "Aren't we, Jill?"— "Yes, of course, Ike"—and at other times he'd dart a look at her, to see how she reacted.

I put it to her once, trying not to tease her, to provoke all her natural suspicion of me. We were at a meeting at the White City—I think it was the British Games—sitting together in one of the front rows of the grandstand, waiting for the mile, of course. I said, "You don't seem quite so enthusiastic now about the record," and she bristled. "Of course I am. I'm just as keen. I *know* he's going to get it back." I said, "I'm sorry. It was only an impression."

She was quiet then, but she was brooding on it, because a minute or so later she suddenly said, "It's just that I don't like him worrying about it."

"Oh," I said, "it's natural enough."

She said, "The great thing is he *has* beaten it. He *has* held it. I keep telling him that." I said, "And what does Sam tell him?" and she looked at me as if she'd suddenly remembered who I was, what I was, and was sorry she'd revealed herself. She said, very curt, "Sam wants him to keep on trying."

That afternoon, I watched him very carefully. I always watched him *closely,* simply for the pleasure of it, the esthetic satisfaction of seeing him move in that consuming, effortless way, all the more fascinating when one knew, as in some great work of art, just what effort had gone into making it look effortless, the work that reinforced the talent.

But now, watching more critically, it no longer looked effortless, merely mechanical, a marvelous robot; what had gone out of it was the delight. Technically, it was as fine as ever: the length of the stride, the piston movement of the arms, the carriage and thrust of the torso, quite enough to win him the race, to get him around in 3.59.6. He went through all the motions perfectly, but that was what they were: motions.

Meanwhile, there they are, the good angel and Mephistopheles beckoning him from peak to peak, target to target, on a self-perpetuating quest, while the poor good angel flutters and anguishes in the rear. Except that my money's still on the good angel.

I don't know what it was, maybe I took too much out of myself in the Los Angeles race, but the rest of that season I didn't run well. I wasn't running well *before* I lost the record, and after that I think maybe something else come into it; maybe I was pushing myself too hard.

Anyhow, I never come near it again that year, the very best I run was 3.56.8 in Berlin. And not being able to get the record back, the races didn't seem to mean nothing, it didn't do me no good if I *won* them. In fact I even lost a couple, one in Warsaw against Poland, when I run like a twot, the other one in Sweden, where quite honestly I wasn't bothering much. The only *good* thing that come out of the record was I'd got a new job. The one with Stan was fine, I'm not denying it, a very soft touch, but this was even better. It was with a French firm that made running shoes and sports equipment, one of the biggest, forty-five quid a week, my own car—a Renault—and just calling on the odd wholesaler and turning up now and then at press conferences; the contract went on till after Tokyo. I couldn't actually endorse the shoes, of course, or I'd be in the shit with the amateur people, but they took care to have me photographed whenever they could, wearing them with the trademark showing, and they give me a great big white leather bag with their name across it, ten feet high.

What I wanted to do more than anything was run against Cooper, because if I beat him, I really *would* have proved something, whether I got the world record back or not, but it never come off. He was meant to come over to the White City in August for an invitation mile, but for some reason he didn't; then there was talk of him doing a Scandinavian tour, but he didn't—he went to Australia.

I had another go at the record in Welwyn Garden City, paced again, but I was so far out in front at the bell that there was never any chance of my doing it, and in the end I run a 3.58.6.

I read everything I could about this Cooper, what he looked like, where he come from, how he trained. I'd be running against him in Perth, in the Empire Games, next year, and I'd got an idea that after them, he'd be the bloke I'd have to beat in Tokyo in 1964. Because, like I've said before, you don't get that many surprises in the mile; it ain't no race for beginners; within a couple of years or so of an Olympic Games, you've got a pretty good picture of who's going to make the running.

Driver I knew I could show the way home now; after Los Angeles, I could beat him any time I liked, and as for Burke, to me he was over the top. There was some other good Yanks coming up, like there always was, they'd got so bloody many of them, and one or two good Europeans, like Glovacki that had beat me in Warsaw, but Cooper was the only one that worried me.

I'd watched him run several times on telly. He was a big man, heavy—about the same height as me, but he weighed more than twelve stone—a typical sort of college boy, hair cut very short, with these steel-rimmed glasses, twenty-two years old. He had a coach called Don McBain that was very big on interval training, which I'd never tried. Sam was dead against it; he said it killed the joy in running, which I'd always accepted, but now I started thinking a bit, because since Los Angeles, *I* hadn't had much joy in running—very, very little.

It worried me terribly; I talked to Sam about it, and I talked to Jill about it. Sam said he'd been expecting it; he said, "I have seen it in your training. I have been waiting for you to come to me. It is a natural reaction of the mind, rather than the body, the mind which has been keyed up to demand the utmost from the body for so long. Losing the record, *tem*porarily losing the record, has reinforced this process. What you require is an immediate change. I shall arrange it."

I said, "That's what Jill says," and he went all stiff, like a cat with a dog. He said, "Says what? What does she say?" and I told him, "That there's too much pressure. That it's piling up on me." For a moment I thought he'd contradict, his lips moved, but in the end he didn't say nothing; he nodded to himself and turned away.

Two days later in the post there was a couple of plane tickets to Majorca. I showed them to Jill, I said, "Look what Sam's sent!" and she looked at them—she didn't smile or nothing, it was strange—she just said; "Is he coming, too?" I said, "Sam? I don't suppose so. He's got too much to look after here, hasn't he, the training and the gym?"

So we went out to Palma; it was great. Sam saw us off at the airport, with a great big box of chocolates for Jill. He said, "Look after him, don't let him get too much sun. See he doesn't worry about the record." He couldn't have been nicer.

When we got there, it was like a honeymoon, not just lying together in the sun, abroad, by the sea, but being together *alone*, without something else on your mind the whole time: the record, your next race, the training day in, day out. It was only the one week, and it went by like a dream. Jill looked terrific; she caught the sun very quick, and she could never get enough of it. She'd lie out on the beach in her little black bikini with her eyes closed and a sort of smile on her face. Often I'd watch her, the tiny gold hairs on her brown arms and legs, the top of her breasts, her stomach with its nice, deep navel moving as she breathed, till it was just too much for me; I'd shake her and I'd say, "Come on, come on, back to the hotel!" and she'd click her tongue and shake her head at me; then back we'd go and make love.

I remember that room very well: the tiled floor, the blinds pulled down, and the little specks of sunlight coming through, onto the bed, onto her, little white splashes across her body. I'd think of what I *should* be doing this time of day, if I was in England, running with Sam across the Heath, and somehow this made it all the better.

She said something funny to me once in there, when we'd just finished making love; she said, "It's the first time I've felt we were properly by ourselves." I knew what she meant, though, because I felt it, too, and I felt bad about it, because after all it was him that had sent us out here, even if he'd probably got Stan to pay it.

Another time she said, into the dark, just out of nothing, "He's like a shadow," and again I knew what she meant; again I felt bad.

Being away made it quite easy to forget the record; I mean, away in a holiday place, where nothing real went on, where no one knew. Jill never brought it up at all unless I did. I asked her once, out there on the beach, "You think I'll get it back?" She said, "Get what back?" Obviously knowing what I meant. I said, "You know, the record."

We was both lying on towels, on our stomachs. Jill was quiet for a bit; then she said, "Does it matter very much?" I couldn't believe it; I sat right up; I said, "Christ, of course it matters." She said, "More than anything?" still with her face in the sand. I said, "What do you mean, more than anything?" and she said, "What I say. More than *anything*." I said, "Of course not. I never said it mattered more than anything." She said, "Well, that's how you behave." It still amazed me; I couldn't understand her; I said, "Don't *you* think it matters?" She said, "Yes. Yes I do." I said, "Then what do you mean?"

She said, "It's doing things to you." She raised herself up on her elbows, but she still didn't look at me. I asked, "Doing what?" She said, "Changing you. Taking over your life. *Our* life." I was really desperate; I said, "Don't you see I've got to get it back?" and she looked at me now; she said, "*Why?* Why do you have to get it back?" I said, "Because I've lost it. What's the matter with you?" She said, "And you'll lose it again." I said, "Then I'll get it back again." She said, "And on and on forever, I suppose, till you're just too old to run anymore."

I still couldn't believe it, not from her, from Jill, of all people. I mean, to me it was something so obvious it didn't need explaining.

I said, "If *you* held the record, the hundred or the two-twenty, wouldn't *you* want to keep it?" She said, "Of course I would, but it wouldn't obsess me, the way it does you. You carry on like it *belongs* to you. It's been terrible to see the way you've been driving yourself. You'll never have rest; you'll never have peace, not even when you've got it, because you'll be wondering all the time will someone take it away from you. You've *proved* what you can do, everyone *knows* how good you are, you may still get it back, but even if you don't, what difference does it make?"

I said, "Look, surely you can see this. If I'm the best miler in the world, I'm going to hold the record, right?" She just give me a look, then rolled over on her stomach again. I stood there looking at her for a minute; then I thought, *Fuck it,* and went on down the beach to the sea.

Among those who attended yesterday's Buckingham Palace lunch were former mile world record holder Ike Low and his sprinter wife, Jill.

Said Ike: "The Duke of Edinburgh seemed very well informed about athletics. He asked me a lot of questions, and he said to me, "You've got to bring that record back to Britain, you know."

What is it like to be a wife who competes in the same field as her husband?

I have been talking to three women: an internationally successful sprinter, a famous actress, and a sculptress whose welded abstracts have just gone on show to a barrage of critical acclaim.

"I think it helps to have a common interest," says pretty, twenty-two-year-old Jill Low, who could leave any man standing in a race for the bus and whose husband, Ike, is Britain's best miler. "It must help if a wife can take a really constructive interest in what her husband's doing, and vice versa. Most wives must get as bored hearing their husbands talk about the factory or the office when they come home, as the husbands do when their wives go on and on about little domestic problems."

But didn't she feel her own career had been overshadowed, I asked. "After all," I told her, "you had been a well-known sprinter in your own right, long before you married the man who was to break the world record."

"Not at all," replied this spirited brunet schoolteacher with the top model figure. "Ike and I *help* each other. We do a lot of training together. In fact, I think I've become a better runner since I married Ike. Of course, I recognize that Ike is a greater athlete than I'll ever be, just as you have to accept that male athletes have higher standards than women's do.

"But I haven't sacrificed myself or subordinated myself or anything like that. It's just that being a woman, one's obviously pulled in other directions, too."

Like children, I suggested.

"Certainly we both want children eventually," she replied, "but for the moment, running comes first."

Ike's running or her own, I asked.
"Our running," she answered, firmly.

I done a lot of thinking, that winter. In a way, I wished
I could just dig myself a hole and go to sleep until the spring
come, like a squirrel or something, because winter was dead,
winter left you hanging. In a different way, it was as bad as
the winter before, even worse, because at least then I'd got
the world record to go for, something definite, something
that I'd never had, whereas now I'd had it and I'd lost it, and
if I did get it back, like Jill said, I could lose it again.

Even Sam didn't talk about it as much as before, he was
more on about the Empire Games, but the Empire Games
weren't for another bloody year; you might just as well start
thinking about the Olympics, which weren't for another
three, because let's face it, that was what mattered; com-
pared with them, even the world record was really rubbish,
something to prove to yourself you could do it, when the
time come.

I got hold of a picture of Cooper; I cut it out of a news-
paper and stuck it up over the bed. When Jill saw it, she
said, "What's this?" I said, "It's to remind me."
"Well," she said, "I hope he's got a picture of you over
his bed, that's all." I asked, "Why? Because I'm better-
looking?" and she said, "No. I just hope he's as worried by
you as you seem to be about him. If you go on like this,
he'll have you beaten before you start." I said, "I know what
I'm doing," but I thought over what she said, and in the end,
after a week, I took the picture down. I kept it in my wallet.
I mean, there was no use letting him get on top of me.

When Sam talked about him, he'd always knock him,
saying who's he ever beaten, what big races has he ever won,
breaking records is one thing but winning races is another,
which sounded fine while he was saying it, like everything
did, but then when you were on your own, you thought,
Whatever he says, the other fellow's got the record.

I told Jill, "If I could just run against him soon, just beat
him once, even indoors." She said, "I don't think it's a good
idea," and I said, "Why not? What do you mean?" I was very
tense all during this time; I'd get angry with her when she
disagreed with me; I needed confidence, and to me it seemed
like she was letting me down. Yet later on, when I'd cooled

down, I might think, *Maybe she's right; maybe it's me that's wrong*— or even Sam, because there were some things where they disagreed so much that one of them had to be wrong. I suppose in the past I'd just take it for granted he was right, what with me being so young, his planning my career, and nearly everything turning out like he said it would. One thing I couldn't help thinking was if the world record was that unimportant, why had he been on about it so much, especially after I'd lost it? Last winter it had all been world record, and this winter it was all Empire Games. I supposed if I screwed *those* up, the winter after, it would be all Olympics.

The trouble was that one thing led to another. I'd think, if he's wrong about this, *if* he's wrong, he might be wrong about other things, too—the food, for instance, maybe even the training. Because there was so many different methods, everyone you talked to seemed to have different ideas. There was Cooper, with his interval training; in Australia they ran up sand dunes; in New Zealand they was on this jogging lark. Then some people had this idea you didn't *have* to train that much, that it was bad for you, that you could easy leave it on the track. Once you started to compare, there wasn't no end to it.

I said to Alan one day when we was running across the Heath, with the ground all soggy underfoot and the sky that terrible dead gray color, "Christ, I hate the bloody winter," and of course, he made a joke out of it, the way he always had to; he said, "Now is the winter of our discontent." I said, "It's all right for you, doing all this for fun, you can *afford* to laugh." I said, "I don't know *where* I fucking am, world record one minute, Empire Games the next."

He said, "What's this? You're not beginning to experience religious doubts?" and I was sorry I'd spoke; I should have remembered how he loved stirring things up. I said, "Oh, fuck off," and he said, "Now, now. You're growing up, that's all. These are simply growing pains."

A lot of times I was going to have it out with Sam, get things straight, but I don't know, whenever it come to the point, I could never find the words, I was afraid he'd take it personally. I even thought of writing him a letter once, which was ridiculous.

Toward the end of the year, an invitation come through to run in Madison Square Garden, just after Christmas, and

I was very excited; I thought Cooper was bound to be there, or at least he'd be *asked*. I phoned up Phil Jenkins, one of the athletics reporters, could he find out, and that night he rang me back and told me yes; Cooper *had* been invited, and they expected him to run.

Well, that settled it; I mean, to me there was no question of would I go or not, I *had* to go. Sam had seemed quite keen on it when he heard about the invitation, but I hadn't even told Jill. It was only after I spoke to Phil that I couldn't keep it back no longer. When I come into the room, she said, "What are you smiling at? What are you so pleased about?" and when I told her, she said, "Ike, don't go."

I said, "Christ, don't let's have that again. Don't go? Why shouldn't I go? What do you think's going to happen?" She said, "You need this rest. You're not in the right mood to run; you don't really want to run; you're only going because of this Cooper." I said, "Well, what if I am? That gives me an incentive, don't it? That *makes* me want to run. That's what I need, an incentive." She said, "It's the wrong kind of incentive. It's the wrong kind of race. He's probably been running indoors, all winter."

I said, "All right; so maybe he'll be stale and I'll be fresh. Why can't you think of it that way? Why have you got to be so bloody pessimistic? Anyway, you don't have to come if you don't want to."

"Oh, yes," she said, "I'll come."

There was a couple of weeks before the race, and I took it very serious. I went down to the air force place at Cosford with Sam, to get used to this twelve-lap touch, again. It wasn't easy, planning the race, because we didn't know too much about Cooper. When he beat the record, he'd done a very fast first lap, 56.1, he'd fallen off a bit in the second; in fact, by the end of it he was nearly two seconds behind what I'd done in Los Angeles. But then in the third lap he'd pulled his finger out, and in the fourth he'd just gone like a bomb all the way. Jim Driver had been in it, and he'd kept with Cooper till the back straight, but then apparently this Cooper had gone off like he was on his own, which was worrying in a way, because he'd done his time without even being pushed over the last couple of hundred yards.

Sam said, "There is only one thing to do: You must run your *own* race; then *he* must adjust his style to *you*." So we worked it out that I'd aim for a very fast beginning, something like 56.8 for the first three laps, which took some doing with those bends, a faster second lap, which meant the next *three,* of course, than I'd normally go for, a bit like Los Angeles, hold on for the three, after that, then with four laps left, really *go,* which took a hell of a lot of stamina, but Sam thought I could do it.

He drove me very hard over the old Heath; there was days I could have cursed him. We'd go around what had become more or less the normal course, him pushing me, making me sprint and do a lot of hills and that, until I'd think, thank God we're getting to the end; then just before we did, he'd say, "Right around again!" and we'd do maybe half of it another time, or else he'd take me around a new way, with as many ups and downs as possible. Still, by the time we left for America, I felt as fit as I'd ever done through the summer.

There was a bit of trouble with Ron Vane before we went; he had the dead needle because he hadn't been invited, which was crazy when me and Laurie Keetch, the quarter-miler, were the only ones from Britain that were going. There was the usual thing at the back of it, of course; he was furious because he knew that Sam was bound to go.

Alan said to me, "Ron can just about forgive one one's successes if he can participate at secondhand, but with Sam in the way, he can barely participate at third hand." And he got real nasty about it, Ron did, he rang me up and said, "I've sent New York a cable; either I accompany you as your manager, or you don't get permission to go." I said, "I think that's diabolical," and he said, "Oh, you do, do you? Well, let me tell you, young man, the standard practice was laid down long before *you* started running, and it will go on a long time after you've finished." I said, "Maybe for teams." He said, "Never mind teams! When you travel to meetings abroad, you travel as a representative of this country, and it's our responsibility to see that you conduct yourself properly. I'm prepared to believe you'll do your best, but there's a lot that's left to be desired in some of the influences around you, Ike, a lot, and it's been reflected in your form."

When he said that, I felt like telling him to stuff himself and slamming down the phone, but I was afraid that if I did, he'd go ahead with this ban, because he *could* stop me going. So I just said, "What do you mean? What are you talking about?" He said, "You know what I'm talking about. I'm not going to mention any names. The sort of people who keep you up in night clubs till the small hours of the morning. One of these days, Ike, you'll look back and realize that we've always advised you in your own best interests. I only hope that by then it won't be too late."

I couldn't help it; I said, "Too late for what?" but he ignored that; he said, "And another thing. You be careful, Ike. I don't like the sound of some of the things I've been hearing. This job you've taken." I said, "What about it? I'm a salesman. I work for a sports equipment firm; what's wrong with that?" He said, "You know as well as I do; there's a very narrow border line. And another thing. You've been running at a very large number of minor meetings, Ike. Jack Watling pointed out to me the other day you ran on average three times a week, through July and August." I thought, *Him, is it? He's been making the bullets for old Ron to bloody fire.*

I said, "I don't have to get permission every time I run in England, do I?" He said, "Just take it as a timely warning. It wouldn't be very nice if we had to suspend you before the Empire Games. Not for any of us."

When I put the phone down, I shouted, "Fuck him, *fuck him!*" and Jill come out and asked, "What's wrong?" I said, "That bloody Ron Vane. First he wants to stop me going to New York; then he's on about suspending me." She said, "What for?" She looked very worried. "For taking money?" I said, "Christ, nearly everybody does, one way or another. How the hell do they expect us to live? It's like Sam says, they don't bloody well care. They'd sooner keep us poor so they can order us about."

She gave a little sort of laugh, bitter; she said, "Maybe I'd better talk to him. He says I'm a good influence." I said, "Who, Ron? When did he say that?" She said, "Oh, once or twice. Coming up to me at meetings, putting his arm around my shoulders and saying things like, 'I'm glad he's married someone like you, Jill, because I think you're going to be a good influence.'" I said, "Who's the bad one? Sam, I suppose," and she gave a shrug; she said, "I suppose so." I said, "Bloody hell, why can't I just out and run; why can't I be left alone?"

In the end what it come to was that the International Club took it up. Alan had a lot to do with it; he was on the committee now. There was protests and all that, articles about it in the papers, and in the end, Ron had to back down; he got around it by saying that business commitments wouldn't allow him to go, and in the circumstances, he was prepared to waive the practice. I got a letter from him saying he couldn't understand my behavior after the way he'd supported and encouraged me throughout my career, but nevertheless he wished me success and hoped I'd remember I was carrying the colors of Great Britain.

> Get the bit between their teeth,
> Think they bloody know it all.
> It's experience that counts,
> But they find that out too late.
> They're exploited by some coach,
> Who'll just use them for his ends.
> Not like us, who love the sport,
> Never stand to gain a thing.
>
> *Never give the sport a thing.*
> *Parasitic, everyone.*

Miler met miler in the Garden last week, and when miler toppled miler (literally) the crash could be heard anywhere between London's White City and the Los Angeles Coliseum. And might have reached, come to think of it, the University of British Columbia campus, where world record holder Terry Cooper churns around the track on his interval training kick.

Cooper came through at the Garden to win in a chugging 3.58.8, but the question of whether he or Britain's Ike Low is currently the world's fastest miler is still hanging around, right now.

For Low's fifty-eight-year-old coach, Sam Dee, a kind of Sindbad the Sailor who throws up theories the way a Manhattan subway entrance throws up commuters, there was never any doubt from the beginning: Ike Low is the greatest. He was saying so before the race, loudly; he was saying so just as loudly afterward, when Ike had limped in a bruised and bitter fourth.

Low flew into New York with the kind of entourage that usually goes with a boxer, rather than a runner. There was his wife, Jill, a pretty brunet who tripped the light fantastic herself in the last Olympics. There

was Sam, of course, and there was a guy called Stan
Ling, in a camel's hair coat, giving an impression of
Edward G. Robinson giving an impression of a ward
heeler, who'd come along with his wife, just for the
ride.

There wasn't any press agent, but maybe that was just
as well, because if there had been, he'd have had a
tough time getting in a word ahead of Sam. Everybody
does. The first thing Sam told an openmouthed press
corps was that Cooper's world record had to be some
kind of a freak, because Ike Low was still the fastest
miler on two legs. The second was that Ike would crack
3.57 in the Garden, and if Cooper could beat that on
boards, he'd like to be around to see it.

Well, Cooper couldn't, but then neither could Ike,
who was too busy getting someone else's legs tangled
with his own, midway through the third lap, and going
down with the crash we were telling you about.

Sam also had quite a lot to say about Cooper's interval training, about which, one gathered, he was very
far from keen. Cooper and his coach, Don McBain,
wouldn't join the battle. "If that's how Sam wants to
train his men, that's okay with us," he said. "We think
it's a little out-of-date. He thinks *we're* a little out-of-
date. I guess there has to be room for both of us."

On Saturday night there was only room for Cooper.
A tall, pale, crew-cropped, spectacled, Ivy League figure, renowned for never losing his cool, the twenty-two-
year-old marine biologist had approached the race as a
problem, rather than a challenge. "Ike's got to be good,"
he said. "I saw that Coliseum race on television. It just
bugs me a little that the first time we come in contact
has to be indoors."

When the two of them met for the first time, at lunch
in Toots Shor's—where else?—both appeared to like
what they saw. "Ee seems a right nice fellow, Terry,"
said Ike, whose diction would have intrigued Professor
Higgins. "I mean, e's modest, ain't e?" Terry dug Low
because, "With Ike, you don't get any of that psyching
that goes on all the time among American milers."

"You don't have to," said McBain. "Not as long as
he's got Sam around."

Both runners had a plan. Ike's, which turned out to

be academic, was a flat-out first three laps, a fastish second three, a holding action in the next three or four, climaxed by an all-systems-go.

Cooper, who runs with the tireless consistency of a man programmed by an IBM computer, and has the finishing kick of a Ferrari to go with it, planned to stay with Low through the Britisher's now-famous fast first quarter, then open out a big enough lead to nullify Low's equally famous finishing kick.

"We knew Ike runs a wonderful first quarter-mile," said Don McBain. "We know he comes on very strong in the last quarter. Where we reckoned Terry has it over him is in the second and third quarters, and that's where we planned to attack him."

The attack, as it panned out, came from a different direction; from a chunky, twenty-one-year-old physical education major from UCLA called Tom Bannion. No one but Bannion saw Bannion, who made the U.S. track team for the first time only last year and only in one meet, as anything but a pacemaker. Bannion's view was that he was in the race to win. "I got tired of reading just two names every time I opened a paper," he said afterward. "Like the rest of us had no right to be running on the same track."

So when Low and Cooper took off at the gun, Bannion stayed right with them, in the inside lane. And on that fatal third lap, when Low tried to go outside him around the steep banking, there was what looked like a flurry of legs and elbows, and Low came down.

"What does the guy want?" asked Bannion, who proceeded to run in second. "Do I have to lie down and let him walk over me?"

"Ee tripped me," said Ike, laconically. "That's all there was to it. I was tripped."

Dee, predictably, thought there was a lot more to it. No boxing manager could have defended his meal ticket with more passionate eloquence. "It was a piece of calculated aggression. That runner should have been disqualified. If my athletes can't be guaranteed protection from this kind of thing, I shall never bring them to New York again."

Since this sort of thing has been going on ever since Adam chased Eve across the Garden of Eden, what

happened in the Garden of Madison Square couldn't
have surprised Sam as much as it seemed to. What it
did do was spoil a race which may now have to take
a rain check till the summer.

Which left me just where I was before: not knowing.
Worse than before, in a way, because however he'd done it,
Cooper, he'd won; it was his name went in the record books;
they didn't write nothing there about how someone tripped
you up and you fell. So it had given him this edge on me,
just because he *had* won, and even *because* I'd lost it in the
way I did. I couldn't help thinking something was always
going to happen when I run against him, like I'd got that
pulled muscle in Rome.

He was very nice at the end; he come up and said,
"Tough luck, Ike. I was surely disappointed." I said, "I was
disappointed and all," but this other bastard, the one that
done it, *he* didn't come up and apologize.

He'd already blocked me, the very first time around that
bend, which let Cooper go ahead. The second time around,
when there was maybe four or five of us, he had his elbows
going like bloody windmills. I kept out of the way, and
Cooper just got clear of him around the banking. It had
balled up my plan for a fast first quarter, and on the
third lap, with the three of us out there, I decided I'd
have to get past this twot. He was about five yards behind Cooper, and I reckoned that he'd blow up any moment, but I couldn't let Cooper build too big a lead, and
at the banking, I tried to pull outside this Bannion—who
pulled out again and blocked me.

I give him a bit of an elbow, there was nothing else for
it, he give me one back, which I managed to deflect;
then, as I start shoving past, he trips me, and Christ, I
come down a wallop, bang on my left knee; I thought at
first I honestly wouldn't get up again. By the time I did, I
was last in the field, and when I started to run again, it
was agony. It did wear off a bit after a while, but fourth
was the best I could manage; I was really choked.

I said to Sam, "That fellow's an animal. They never
ought to let him on a track," and he was talking about
official protests and the rest of it.

Before we left, they invited me to the Knights of
Columbus meeting again, but Cooper wasn't going to be

there; he was off on some expedition to Greenland or something, and when I found that out, I refused; what was the point?

I must say I quite liked him, though; he was very interesting about his training; he said that maybe my way *was* better, but he didn't get the time for it with his studies; he needed something more intensive. In fact, he said that for him, running was a relaxation, which sounded daft to me. The only thing was, it made me start thinking about training again; did you *have* to slog away, the way Sam made me, year in, year out, summer and bloody winter? I didn't even mention it to Sam—he'd only hit the roof—but I mentioned it to Jill after we'd got back, and she went very quiet, even quieter than usual; then she said, "Do you really want to know what I think?"

I said, "Of course, I want to know what you think. I wouldn't have asked you, would I?" She said, "Not necessarily. Sometimes you do want to know what I think; others you just want me to say what *you* think, especially where it's Sam."

I said, "Look, okay. I want to know what *you* think." She looked at me then in this way of hers, very serious, and she said, "Yes. I think you need a change." I said. "A change from the training?" and she said, "Sam only knows one kind of training."

For a time we both sat there saying nothing; there was too much to think about; then I said, "He can vary it a bit, can't he? I mean, if I ask him. A bit of cross-country and that. Maybe less concentrated." She kept on looking at me; she said, "No, he can't, Ike; you know he can't," and I looked back at her; I said, "You want me to leave him, don't you?"

We had another of these long silences, her looking at me, not speaking, me waiting for her to speak, until she said, "It's not a question of what *I* want."

I got off the sofa; I just couldn't keep sitting there; I said, "Look, he's done everything for me. I mean, what would I be? I can't just say thank you very much and walk out." She said, "Oh, I know it's not easy. *He's* seen to that." I said, "Could *you* do it? Could you walk out on him?" She said, "I don't call it walking out on him." I said, "Then what *do* you call it?" and she said, "Standing on your own two feet."

So what it turned into was a row. I started shouting at her, I told her, "He's my *coach,* for Christ's sake; that's all he is,

my bloody *coach*," and she said, "He doesn't think so." I
said, "How do *you* know what he bloody thinks? You just
want to stir it up. *I've* never asked you to give up *your* running; why do you always want to interfere with mine?" She
said, "Is that what Sam told you? That I want to interfere
with your running?" I said, "Never mind what he told me;
you are inter*fering*," and she got up to leave the room. She
said, "It was silly of me to answer you in the first place,
wasn't it?"

I did talk to Sam. A few days later, up at the gymnasium,
I said, "About this interval training." He said, "*What* about
it?" I said, "Well, I was thinking, that's all. I mean, maybe
just for a change." He said, "Why do you believe you need a
change?" I said, "Well, I'm stale, aren't I? I mean, I haven't
been running well for months." He said, "And this you at-
tribute to your training? You have decided, after five years,
that the training program I have devised for you is mis-
conceived?"

I said, "No, not that. Not that at all. It's just that maybe I
need to vary it a little." He said, "But why suggest interval
training? Because Cooper does interval training? Because
Cooper *temporarily* holds the world record? Because Cooper
defeated you in a race where you were tripped and fell? Let
us forget for the moment about *my* methods of training—
which have enabled you to beat the world record and become the fastest miler Great Britain has ever possessed. Let
us forget that I am in any way concerned in this. Let me
simply say that in imitating Cooper's methods, you would be
surrendering to Cooper. You would be admitting Cooper's
superiority. You would be trying to become like Cooper;
therefore, you would always be beaten by Cooper, because
Cooper is himself, and you would be merely a copy. I understand your reaction; it is a perfectly normal one. You are
disappointed; you are suffering from a transient loss of confidence. In situations like these, it is natural to look for a
magic formula, a new solution. It is equally natural to believe it has been found by whoever defeated you. It is natural,
but it is irrational. Ike, if you want to take up interval training, do so. But you will never do so under me, first, because
I regard it as a monotonous drudgery which turns the athlete
into a machine, second, because I see it as a betrayal. A betrayal of your own self-respect."

I said, "Well, not necessarily interval training then. Maybe a bit of cross-country racing, or cut down on the amount just a little. " He give me a very long look; then he said, "I am always prepared to discuss changes in your program. Your program is and always has been an individual one. It was devised for you, and you alone. It may be that your needs have altered, though I personally do not believe it. What I do believe is that you are suffering a reaction which will pass. If in a month's time you feel the same, then we shall proceed to analyze what is being done and in what way it might be altered. In the meantime, you must allow yourself this month. It is the least you owe to either of us."

So what could I do? I let it go a month. When I told Jill, she just nodded, like she didn't care no more. I said, "A month. What the hell's a month?" She said, "You're quite right; what's a month?" and I said, "Come on, out with it, for Christ's sake." She said, "I'm agreeing with you, Ike; what do you *want* me to say? A month is very little." I said, "All right, I know. You think I've let him con me into it."

She said, "He didn't need to, did he?" and went out of the room. I followed her into the kitchen, I was angry again, and the way she went on made me angrier, washing things up and putting things away, like I wasn't there. She's got a very stubborn streak in her, Jill; it was something I'd noticed right from the beginning; there's times she'll go back in her shell like a tortoise, and nothing you can do will bring her out.

So the less she'd answer me, the more I went on at her, till I was saying a lot of things I didn't mean. I said, "There's things Sam's done for me that *nobody* could do for me; there's no use being jealous of him," and she spoke then; she said, "Me? Jealous of *him?*" I said, "Well you don't think he's jealous of you, do you?" but she didn't answer. It ended up with me saying I was sorry. She said, "Why say you're sorry?"

We was in the bedroom, she'd just pulled her dress over her head, and I was watching her; she did everything so graceful. I said, "Because I am. I am sorry." I went up and put my arms around her; I kissed her shoulder; I said, "I really mean that—about the month. You wait and see." She said, "If only it was all so easy." I said, "It can't be easy. How can it be easy? You're trained by a bloke for five years; he puts you on top of the world—" and she sighed. I said, "What's the matter?" and she said, "Oh, nothing. Just that so long as you feel like that, you'll never break free," and I found it coming up in me again, this anger, although I tried to fight it down. I said, "I'm grateful, aren't I? That's all. What's wrong in being grateful?" She said, "Nothing," and she broke away from me. She turned her back on me in bed, and she lay awake a long time; I could tell from the way she was breathing.

Well, the month went by, and things didn't get better, they didn't get worse. At the end of it, Sam didn't say nothing, and I didn't say nothing. Nor did Jill, though I was wondering if she might. The thing was, I'd decided to let it go until the season started; then, when I saw how I was running, how I *felt* about running, I'd be able to get a clearer idea. I didn't tell Jill that, because I knew what she'd say, that I was just putting it off again, which wasn't true, because how could you decide in the winter when there wasn't nothing happening? It was natural that you got depressed in winter, with the bloody miserable weather, the rain coming down day after day, and the feeling everything was dead.

It was a strain, though, because although Jill never said nothing, it was in the air like something between us, the one thing there'd ever been, and I was holding things back, things I'd normally have said, about my training, about what Sam had said, because I knew how she'd feel about them.

IX

By the start of the summer it was plain to me that there was only one way Sam could hang on to him, and that was through a stupendous victory. It might be a victory over Cooper, who'd become the official antichrist; it might be another world record—whose effects would last until he'd lost it again. The irony of it is that so long as Ike continues in this state, it's most unlikely that he *will* win anything stupendous.

He grumbles a lot now, which is something he didn't do before; for the first time, there's an air of coercion about his training. He'll even ask me what I think about other methods, such as interval training—"Cooper does it; Sam doesn't reckon it"—and I tell him quite truthfully I don't know. At this point in time, it seems to me that all kinds of training are equally good or equally bad; it's simply a question of how they are packaged and presented—like so many soap powders. Another comparison occurs to me: They're like medicines which depend on the doctor's personality. Given the right suggestive force, some doctors could cure you with a phial of colored water.

I can imagine what must be going on at home. Jill would do it, if at all, with hints and silences, and I am sure she is ready for a long campaign; there is that stoicism about her. Now and again, I've seen Sam look at Ike, sometimes when we were running, sometimes when we weren't. It was a wary look, an anxious look: Is he loyal to me? The sort of look which would have been as inconceivable six months earlier as Ike's attack of questioning.

I suppose poor Sam is wondering what he can do. After all, he sent Ike to Majorca, and *that* hadn't worked.

Toward the end of winter, Ike began to miss the odd training session, which was like a novice missing Communion. He'd have excuses—illness, the need to go somewhere for his sports firm—but it was obvious Sam didn't accept them.

If you asked, "Where's Ike?" which I'm afraid I invariably did, you'd get a snarl: "Says he's *ill*." I think Sam regards any disease that keeps one away from training as psychosomatic at the best.

In a sense, it's becoming like a bad marriage; you wish for both their sakes they'd have the courage to split up. But Sam will never let go, there is too much ego capital involved, and in Ike's case, I suppose, too much guilt, too long a history of dependence. Time is on Jill's side, and I suppose she knows it. She can afford to be stoic.

I write this in June, the period of the phony war. Meetings take place, but nothing real is happening; the great confrontations all lie in the future. Ike has won all his races—without great effort or distinction. Three or four times he's been over four minutes. There have been no more paced attempts on the record; he finds them, he says, a useless exertion. "If I do it, Alan," he once told me, "it'll be in a race, like I done it in Los Angeles. These people here can't push me hard enough, and the ones that can won't do it." Which may simply have been a rationalization, but I think he's right.

When he asked me, "How do *you* think I'm running?" I answered, "Not very well," and he thought a moment; then he said, "I suppose you've got to go *through* these periods." I said, "Of course," thinking, *How long does a period last?* He never directly asked my advice and I never offered it; it was none of my business; I was simply a voyeur. Besides, it was obvious where things were going; nothing I told him could make any difference.

Though he did once canvass me, indirectly. He said, "I've had this offer." I asked, "What offer?" and he said, "An athletics scholarship. From this American university, in California." I said, "Why don't you take it?" It seemed fine to me: an escape from Sam without tears, recriminations; a lot of sunshine. He said, "It's a long time, isn't it, three years? And Jill's not all that keen." I said, "A marvelous climate. You can run day in, day out. They'll even give you a degree —of sorts." He said, "Yeah, I ought to think about it," but he obviously thought about it already—or she had.

Another change was that he ran fewer races, went to fewer of those little, unimportant meetings which mattered because of the backhanders they paid him. He said, "I had to cut down, Alan; races weren't *meaning* nothing," but these were palliatives, and I'm sure he knew it, like a man with cancer who cuts out smoking.

I can't recall when he first mentioned Giesemann to me, but I've an idea it was one Monday, when he might well have been suffering from a post-Saturday race depression. He asked me, "What do you know about him, this Giesemann?"

I said, "Not much. He trains Koppel, doesn't he?"—a German who'd just set a new European record for the 400 meters. He said, "That's right," and his eyes shone, like a seeker after truth who's just been told about a new prophet. "He's at Nuremberg," he said, "interval training," and I said, "I know that." Everybody did. Interval training was the man's gospel. I'd seen him once or twice; solemn, German, a believer. Gray, curly hair, a small mouth, and an aura about him of easily hurt feelings. Much, much quieter than Sam.

I said, "You're not thinking of switching allegiance, are you?" He was so quick to deny it that he obviously was. "Oh, no," he said, "no, no. Nothing like that. I mean, it's just that I'd *heard* about him, that was all."

I've thought about it since, and it's occurred to me that perhaps this is the only way he *could* do it, exchanging one guru for another, one totalitarianism for another. And if Jill's encouraging him—I assume, at the very least, that she's not *dis*couraging him—is she wise? Won't she simply be perpetuating the situation, merely changing its terms of reference? She's awfully shrewd; I'm sure she must have thought of it—or *felt* it; she's one for the emotion, rather than the concept. She couldn't for example, really tell you why she's wary of me, except that she obviously senses in me what I see in myself, the tendency to stand outside and enjoy watching. Perhaps she's simply desperate, reckoning that the gamble's worth it, or perhaps she reckons that once Sam's hold has been broken, Ike won't need another Svengali, that *she'll* become the unchallenged center of his life, or should one say the principal satellite?

It fascinates me; I'd love to talk to her about it, but she'd just clam up; she's not much of a formulator anyway. I'd really like to help her, too, just as I'd like to help Sam, who's beyond help. Yet for all his hubris, I feel sorry for him, knowing what's being prepared, knowing he's already sensed it, like a jungle animal at the water hole. When it does happen, he'll never understand, of course; like the Old Testament God, demanding nothing short of total commitment. I think it could be quite traumatic for him; after all, he's never had an athlete like Ike, and I don't suppose he ever will, again. Ike's the *raison d'être* he must always have been looking for, the runner who could prove to everybody that he's right, that all his theories work. One may be skeptical; one can't actually disprove it.

I wish there were some way of preventing it, the nemesis, but it *is* like a Greek play, there's no stopping it at all, even if one *were* prepared to get oneself involved. Which, I suppose, is how I shall eventually console myself.

With Kurt, it was his being in Germany as well. I mean, going there, having to go, was a dead bore in a way, yet in another way it meant you'd got this distance between you; there was none of this getting on each other's wick. He just sent you the instructions and you did the running, he trusted you enough, it was as easy as that, and then of course, there was Jill to run, too; it meant that *she* could play quite a part.

Those weeks before finally deciding were terrible; I'd never have got through them without Jill. Knowing how Sam would feel, knowing what was bound to happen. I never made direct contact with Kurt, never wrote to him or nothing, but I admit that one of the reasons that I run in this meeting at Frankfurt was that I reckoned he'd be there; I wanted to talk to him, because quite honestly I was desperate; I didn't want to train, I didn't want to run; nothing. Even if I'd never gone to Kurt, I could never have kept on like I was.

After Frankfurt, where I didn't run well, I won in 3.40.1, Jill and I stopped with Kurt at his sports center, just outside Nuremberg. It was a wonderful place; we hadn't got nothing like it in England; very modern, lots of glass, and facilities for everything—basketball, gymnastics, a swimming pool, a lovely little outdoor track. They'd put it up with money from the pools. Kurt was in charge of what they called the department of sports physiology; I spent a whole day there just being tested, blood pressure, urine, what they called electrocardiograms, strength machines, and at the end of it, he said, "Your physical condition is quite perfect. I myself would make certain variations in your diet and your training." It was very stiff, his English, but we could get along all right. He told me he thought I was devoting too much time to training, and that probably this was what was the matter; he said, "At the moment, you have not the desire to run."

The night before we left, I asked Jill what did she think I ought to do: Should I leave Sam, should I go to Kurt? I said, "It's right, what Kurt says. I can't go on with Sam's training." She said, "Are you sure you'd get on well with Kurt's?" I said, "It's worth trying, isn't it?" and she said, "Then try it." I asked, "Is that all you've got to say? Try it?" and she suddenly turned on me; she said, "What am I supposed to say, Ike? Leave Sam? So that when you do, it's me that made you? I think it *might* work. I think it *is* worth trying. How can I be sure? Just *try* it!"

I took a lot of notes home with me, instructions Kurt give me, and I started in right away at the Crystal Palace, whenever I went there with Jill. I told Sam I wanted to go training with her two or three times a week now, and he give me an old-fashioned look, I thought we was going to have an up-and-downer, but in the end he just nodded.

And I liked this interval training; there was something very cut-and-dried about it, you could get a lot done in a little time, and you could even do it on your own; all you needed was a track and maybe a stopwatch; you didn't need no one up your arse the whole time. One thing was obvious, though; you couldn't mix the two. I found I was more and more reluctant to go over the Heath, and when I did go there, it grated on me; it was a bigger effort than ever to go through with it.

It couldn't go on, and I kept thinking to myself how can I tell him, how can I break it? I said to Jill, "He's done so much for me." She said, "And you've done so much for him." I said, "Me? What have I ever done for Sam?" she said, "You've made him famous." I said, "Come off it. What would I have been without him?" She said, "What would he be without *you?*"

One afternoon I turned up at the Heath, and he had this paper in his hand, this magazine; he looked really choked. He said, as soon as I got near him. "You never told me this," and there was this article, about Kurt, the runners he'd trained, and a paragraph that said how Jill and me had stayed with him in Nuremberg.

I said, "Well, it was just a couple of days, that's all, after the Frankfurt meeting." It was a lovely, sunny day, I remember that, the whole Heath looking so lush and green that for once you didn't mind the idea of running over it for the five thousandth time.

Sam said, "There is one thing I have always insisted on, and that is total honesty. The relation between the athlete and his trainer must be absolutely frank, or it becomes impossible. You have not been frank with me, Ike!" I said, "Bloody hell, Sam, just *staying* with him."

He said, "Precisely. Staying with him! Staying with a coach whose ideas are in total opposition to my own. And staying with him to what purpose? What other purpose could there be than to deceive me? To embrace his methods and betray my own!"

Now and then I tried to interrupt, but it was hopeless, there was just no stopping him:

"If you felt you could progress no further under my guidance, then the manly thing was to come to me and say so. To have discussed it openly. To have allowed me the basic courtesy of defending my position. You are free to come and go as you please. You have always been free. I have never charged you one penny. I have asked nothing from you but your loyalty and your dedication. I am disappointed in you, but I do not wholly blame you. I know the pressures to which you have been exposed. The envy, which disguises itself as sympathy. The hatred of the small for the large, the failure for the successful, the weak for the strong, the corrupt for the honest.

"You have held out, but now you have succumbed. Like Samson, you have at last been undermined from within, by friends rather than by foes. I shall not attempt in any manner to dissuade you. Nor is there any object in your coming back, once you have gone. Once a relationship like ours has been disrupted, there is no piecing it together. It is better for both sides to make the breach clean and complete. You have been going through a bad period, as every athlete must. The test of the great athlete is to *use* these periods for reappraisal, as a springboard to something better than before; I would have regarded it as my duty to show you how this could be done. You, on the other hand, prefer the easier course, the solution of blaming other people for your failures. I am willing to accept that blame. I have been, I still am, prepared to show you it was wrongly attributed, but *you* are not prepared to give me that chance.

"There is no point in your procrastinating. Your behavior has confirmed this. I can't pretend that this is easy for me. It is not. It is bitterly difficult. You have been more than an athlete; you have been a son to me. I have taken joy in your career. I had hoped that I would be there to guide you at the end, just as I guided you at the beginning, but you have decided otherwise. Under my tuition, you have developed into a great runner, but your full greatness lies ahead of you, and may now never be realized. In my opinion, you are only at the start of your achievement; my plans for you would have ensured the eventual reaching of your full potential. These plans you are rejecting. Very well. You have a free choice, as I have told you. I shall not attempt to influence it. I believe that what you are doing is wrong and that you will live to regret it. It will be no satisfaction to me to see myself proved right. But I repeat what I said: There can be no turning back. A relationship like ours can never be repaired. It is absolute, or it is nothing."

When I saw them, they were standing on a hill—Mount Sinai?—and I stopped; it was too perfect a cameo to interrupt. Sam on the crest, all declamatory gesture, Ike a little way below, head bowed—the penitent.

He was being cast out; there was little doubt of that; I couldn't hear the words, but one didn't need to. I wondered if Sam had deliberately chosen that hill, that mound; with his sense of the melodramatic, I wouldn't have put it past him. *Trust Sam,* I thought, *to get the last ounce of personal satisfaction even out of a defeat.*

Now and again, Ike's mouth would open, and he'd try to speak—to explain, I supposed, to placate—but he hadn't a hope. I waited for the last grand gesture, a hand thrust into the air, a finger pointing—"Go!"—but it didn't come; I should have credited Sam with a greater sense of style. The end was all diminuendo, Sam's head downcast as well as Ike's, bowed with the weight of disappointment. And when the last words were spoken, Ike turned and came very quickly down the hill.

As he passed me, I saw he was crying.

The news that Ike Low, perhaps the finest miler we

have ever had, and Sam Dee, his coach, have parted after more than five fruitful years saddens more than it surprises. The nature of the coach-athlete relationship is such that breaches of this kind are inevitable, and in this case, there had been signs for some time that Low had outgrown the need for an athletic father figure.

As he said to me himself, last week, "Sam's fantastic, but he wants you body and soul. I'd never have been anything without him, but there comes a time when you want to make your own mistakes."

For Low, that time may have come when he lost his world mile record last August to Canada's Terry Cooper. Talking to him, a lively, handsome young Londoner, with a sharp taste in suits, one has the impression this may have been the moment of truth. "When I couldn't get the record back," he said, "I started thinking. Something seemed to have gone out of me; I'd lost the will to run."

Every athlete knows this feeling and dreads it, just as a writer fears a writer's block. Sometimes he temporarily abandons running, hoping that a rest may give him back his edge, sometimes he deliberately steps up his rate of training; sometimes, as Low has done, he turns to another method.

Low himself took a holiday in Majorca toward the end of last season and has subsequently reduced the amount of his training, but it hasn't worked; these have turned out to be no more than desperate expedients to postpone the parting of the ways between a remarkable but dominating coach and an athlete who, now married, has been maturing as a man as well as a miler.

The pity of it is that there has never been room for compromise, and no one who knows Sam Dee and his approach would hold out any hope for it in the future. Dee is an absolutist, who expects his runners to do as they are told and regards the least deviation as treason. He discovered Low as a junior quarter-miler of average possibilities, turned him into a world-class miler, and has pushed him through five years of the most relentlessly demanding training any athlete can have undergone since Zatopek. There are great differences, it is true, between the systems, but each involves driving the runner to the limit of his possibilities and even beyond.

Unlike Zatopek, who just went out and ran and ran, Dee's routines are cunningly devised. He believes, as I do, that an athlete must force his way through what he calls the pain barrier, and not only in his races but also, under artificial pressure, in his training.

Now Low, who is married to the former Jill Dailey, herself an Olympic sprinter and thus intimately aware of the problems a top-class runner must face, has clearly had as much as he can take. He has opted for the less demanding, more concentrated, though still highly taxing interval training, as practiced by Professor Kurt Giesemann, of the Sports Institute at Nuremberg.

It has plainly been a colossal wrench for him, just as it must have been a massive blow to Dee. One can only hope that Low will find his old form, and Dee, perhaps, a new protégé.

For nights afterward I couldn't sleep, and when I did sleep, I had these dreams. He was in all of them. Jill told me I kept shouting in the night; one night I sat up in bed and yelled, "I'm falling, I'm falling!"

The reporters were after me the whole time; the phone kept going; things kept appearing in the papers: what Sam had said (how he only hoped I wouldn't live to regret it, and that), what I was meant to have said. Even my mother got on to me about it. She rang me up and said, "Are you *sure* you're doing the right thing, Ike? I mean, he *was* very good to you." I said, "I know he was very good, Mum, I *know* that, but there's a lot of things involved you don't understand." She said, "I know he had his funny ways, I'll never forget the first time he come here, what a shock we had, but he always meant well." I said, "He did, Mum, I know he did, but a lot of things have changed; it isn't easy to explain. It's just that with this other fellow, I think that I'll start running better." "Well," she said, "as long as you feel happy about it," meaning that she didn't agree with me, but I mean, you couldn't *tell* her.

When I'd come back that night, Jill took one look at me and she said, "It's happened, hasn't it?"

I just nodded, I was still too choked to talk. She said, "Did he blame me for it?" like she took it for granted. I said, "He was on a lot about this Samson stuff," and she said, "I suppose I was Delilah!" I said, "He said it was like losing a son," and she nodded, like she'd expected that as well.

After that she didn't say much; she could see the mood I was in, and she was always good at that, not talking when you didn't want no jabber. In fact, the next few days I hardly talked at all; I had too much to think about; I kept turning the words round and round inside my head, the things he'd said to me up at the Heath.

Every day I went down to the Crystal Palace track with Jill—she had her holidays—and I trained till I bloody near dropped, just to stop thinking. I run a couple of races, and I was awful, one intercounties at the White City that I nearly lost, another up in Birmingham, and both times I was over four minutes. When I run, it was like I had this weight on my chest.

Ron Vane come over to me at White City, and he said, "Ike, I want to tell you how relieved and delighted we all are." I went on like I didn't know what he was on about, I looked him straight in the eye and said, "About what, Mr. Vane?" and that shook him for a moment; then he said, "About the way you've seen good sense at last. You should have done this years ago, Ike. You should have listened to us. That man was exploiting you for his own purposes." I said, "Is that what he was doing, Mr. Vane?" He said, "Definitely. I'm quite convinced of it." Then I suppose he must have realized I was taking the mickey, because he nodded at me; he said, "You stick with Giesemann, a much healthier influence," then buggered off.

Every time the phone rang, I was on to it like a flash, thinking I suppose it might be Sam, though it never was, it was generally another bloody reporter, and when Jill was there, she'd watch me; I could tell what she was thinking. Several times I nearly phoned him; once I actually dialed the number but hung up before anybody answered.

In the end I wrote him a letter, telling him how grateful I was for all he done for me, how much I owed him, couldn't we still go on being mates, but he never answered.

One day Jill said, "Why don't you go to Germany for a while?" I said, "Germany, here—what's the difference?" She said, "He told you you were always welcome, didn't he?"

So I went, and she was right; it was what I needed. Kurt

was wonderful; it was the first time I'd had him really concentrated, on my own. He never made a song and dance, but he was always one step ahead of you, planning the next move, knowing what you wanted.

The first day or two he wouldn't let me train at all, it was things like swimming and basketball; he had this saying, "Variation is essential." One afternoon, he even took a whole bunch of us out in the country, into some woods, men *and* women; we jogged along a mile or two; then we had a picnic. He said to me, "You are in a state of toxemia, primarily psychological, and first you must be detoxicated." So when we started the interval training, it was quite gentle at first, just one-minute quarters and that, gradually building up, till when I'd been there a week, I was aiming for under one minute, and mixing it with two hundreds. At the end of every one, I'd lie down and Kurt would take my heart and then my pulse. Always very, very quiet, completely different from Sam, none of this voice dinning in your ears the whole time, driving you on, telling you what to do.

There were still times I missed Sam, though; I've got to admit it. In a way it was like having your arm cut off; you kept on wanting to use it, and it wasn't there no more. I'd heard from Alan he was bitter, which I'd expected, knowing Sam; I suppose from his point of view you couldn't really blame him. Alan said, "Your name is more or less taboo; it's liable to set him off; he sounds like King Lear," and he did quite a good imitation of Sam, waving his arms around and saying, "I did everything for that boy. I expected no reward; I did *not* expect to be betrayed."

Other times, apparently, it wouldn't be me he'd be on about, but Jill; Alan did that, too: "Never underestimate a woman's power to corrupt. You can resist a man, a man will oppose you directly, but a woman will destroy from within."

This was the only thing that got me; I said, "It's diabolical, blaming Jill," but Alan said, "It's far easier than blaming himself. Besides, you know how Sam feels about women, especially women athletes."

Kurt was always very nice to Jill, very polite. When I'd been out there a couple of weeks, he got her an invitation to run in a meeting I was running in, at Frankfurt, so she could come over and stay. We met her at the airport, and he brought her flowers; it was great seeing her again. The first thing she said was, "You look *so* much better!" I said,

"That's Kurt," and he smiled, this little, pleased smile he had; Alan said once, "It's like a famous chef accepting the congratulations of an American tourist."

I asked Jill later on, "You like him, don't you?" She said, "I think he's been good for you." I said, "Yeah, but he's okay, isn't he; you like him?" She said, "I like anyone who's good for you." She was always very slow to take to anybody; this northern thing of hers.

But it was true I was feeling better; I really wanted to train now, and I wanted to run; only in a way I was afraid of actually running; I was afraid I wouldn't feel as good as I thought I would, because out at this place with Kurt, I'd suddenly begun to feel free, in a way I hadn't done for years. I mean, the training was hard, you were running against the clock the whole time, whereas with Sam I suppose in a way there was a bit more variety, even if you did have to put in a lot more time. Maybe it was partly that I'd done it now, I'd actually made the break after all this waiting, and now I'd got somebody helping me instead of *telling* me. Before, there was the clock *and* Sam, but now, there was only the clock.

They had quite a good field in this race: Erhardt of Germany, Boissy of France, Budai of Hungary, and a Czech called Kuna that had done some very good times this summer, but *they* didn't worry me; if I ran to form, I knew I'd skate it. It was me that worried me, how I'd be when the gun went. It worried me so much I hardly slept the night before, and Jill didn't either. She put her hand out once and squeezed mine. She was a marvelous girl.

Right up to the start, I was frightened how I'd do, but once I was off, I just hadn't got no worries. I was going like a bomb; this old feeling was back that I hadn't had for God knows how long: of me just being there, and the body doing all the work, the *flying* feeling, like sitting in a car and only having to put your foot down.

I hadn't planned the race. If I went well, I wouldn't need no bloody plan, and if I didn't, a plan wouldn't make no difference. I think Kurt realized this, because *he* didn't try to give me one, the way Sam always used to; he just told me one or two things about the people in the race who I didn't know and he did, like Kuna had a terrific finishing kick, so it was best to try and leave him before the bell; how Erhardt could go on running forever, but he was all one pace, more of a three-miler.

So I just went; no plan, no fucking pain barrier, nothing. In fact, I think that made more difference than anything else, not hearing, day in, day out, about the pain barrier, trying to go through it in training, being afraid you might have to go through it in a race. When I'd asked Kurt what he thought about it, he'd smiled; he'd said, "Pain barrier? There is no pain barrier. Only what a runner can do, and what he cannot do."

I led that race from the start to finish. Kuna came after me at the bell, but all he did was push me a bit faster, he was still twenty yards behind at the tape, and I won it in the best time I'd run all season, 3.37.8. Old Kurt was beaming all over his face, and as for Jill, she was dancing up and down. She won *her* race, too, the hundred meters, so it was a wonderful day for both of us.

That night Kurt took us both to one of the beer cellars, where they all put on these funny hats and sing songs. I don't mind telling you I knocked back a pint or two, poison or no poison.

When Britain's Ike Low broke the world mile record in the Los Angeles Coliseum last year, it was, though he didn't know it then, the end of an old song. When he equaled it last week, again in the Coliseum, it looked like the start of a new one.

Miler Low set the record under coach Sam Dee, an ancient Briton whose eccentricities made the wildest Village beatnik look like a man in a gray flannel suit. Dee fed his athletes on fruit, nuts, and vegetables, trained them on a heath, yelled them on from the track side when they competed, ran a one-man public relations service louder than the loudest Hollywood press agent, and showed up everywhere, from sports stadium to royal reception, in the same beat-up jersey and jeans.

This time Ike brought as his coach Professor Kurt Giesemann, a German physiologist who practically takes your pulse rate every time he shakes hands with you. The twenty-four-year-old Britisher changed horses, or coaches, in mid-season, back in early July, because he felt he wasn't getting any place, which meant getting any place faster than Terry Cooper, Canada's world record holder. Grumbled Dee: "The only thing I could never teach the boy was patience."

Giesemann, in Dee's view, can't teach Ike anything at all. "This interval training of Giesemann's," he's gone on record as saying, "isn't for runners; it's for robots." Which prompted the crack from a strictly nonaligned American runner who heard about it, "Sure, we're robots, the whole bunch of us. It's just that some robots run faster than others."

Last Sunday, in the California sunshine, nobody ran faster than Ike Low, who resents the definition anyway. "That isn't fair, what Sam said," he protested to a sportswriter. "If anything, I get more freedom with Kurt than what I did with him. You can discuss things with Kurt."

Giesemann, a tanned gray-headed fifty-five-year-old, with baby-blue eyes, a Peter Lorre accent, and the permanently hurt expression of a man who's just heard his wife has gone off with his best friend, runs the physiology department of the Sports Institute at Nuremberg, Germany, the place they hold the rallies. When the Nazis made a film about them, they called it *The Triumph of the Will,* which is just about all they had in common with Giesemann and his philosophy of track. He, too, believes that victory represents the triumph of the will.

"A coach," he says, "must prepare a runner not only in the body but the mind. I do not believe in all this talk of pain, but it is true that a runner must be prepared sometimes to suffer. In the last moments of the greatest races, only the runner who can surpass himself will win."

Which doesn't sound a whole lot different from the pain barrier Dee talks about and Low no longer wants to know about. When he broke the tape after a 56.1 last lap which left everyone but Russia's Lev Semichastny strung out like beads on a wire, Low looked fresh enough to run a lap of honor.

"It's all in the mind," he said. "It's like Kurt says: A barrier's only there when you think about it."

The only possible barrier to his Coliseum victory, after three fast laps which he led all the way, was Semichastny, a twenty-one-year-old Red Army sergeant who exploded at the bell like he'd just received a Kremlin ultimatum, overhauling Low around the first bend and staying out ahead of him all the way, up until the back straight. Then the Britisher came through with a finishing kick that was good enough to give him the race— and half the world record.

The one thing that spoiled it for him was that Terry Cooper of Vancouver, who holds the other half, wasn't around when he did it. He was at home, recovering from a pulled muscle.

"There's always something comes up when he's meant to run against me," said Low, suspiciously. "Once he had to go to Greenland; this time he pulls a muscle. And the only time we *do* run against each other, somebody knocks me over [issue of January 21]. Looks like I'll have to wait till Perth before I nail him."

Perth is where the British Empire Games take place next November. That ought to be a mile worth going quite a few miles to see.

I've stopped training with Sam. It was simply too much; too sad, too paranoiac. He'd always had these black moods of bitterness, of feeling shunned, tricked, unappreciated, conspired against, but they'd only been sporadic. Now they're predominant, while the old, manic moods, the clowning and the parody, are barely even sporadic. He's getting older, too, which doesn't help. The only immediate help was for Ike to come crawling back as the prodigal son, begging to be forgiven, to be taken in again, and there wasn't a hope of that. Not now, when he'd got his world record back, and was winning every race he ran.

That must have been the hardest thing for Sam to bear, that, and all the periodic quotes and interviews Ike was giving, praising Giesemann, which he countered with interviews of his own, damning Giesemann and rebuking Ike.

Needless to say, Sam's rationalized it all; he'd *told* Ike this was going to happen, he'd told him he was only in a trough, a period of incubation, and now he'd been proved right—only for someone else to grab the credit. Oh, he'd expected it; he'd had to fight this sort of thing all through his life, this jealousy and this conniving.

There was one other remedy: to train a runner capable of

beating Ike, or at least capable of eclipsing him over another distance; but where to find him? Sam knows that he's on trial; he knows what people have been saying: that he'd been lucky to find Ike, who'd have done just as well without him. I'm sure the subconscious fear of this was one reason why he was so anxious to hold on to Ike till the end of his career. As I've said before, so long as Sam was training him, no one could prove he hadn't made him. But now, Giesemann was training him; the boot was on the other foot. *Post hoc, ergo propter hoc.*

And Giesemann was playing it so cleverly, much more cleverly than Sam: deprecating what he'd done, saying Ike was such a great *natural* athlete, yet every now and then putting in a little barb, an allusion—that Ike *did* need very carefully graduated training, that an athlete *should* be encouraged to feel that he's his own master.

Is he, though? I trained from time to time now down at the Crystal Palace, with Ike and Jill, and when Giesemann came over for the Britain-America match at the White City, I made sure I was there. I could see why Ike should have turned from Sam to him: so quiet and calm, such a contrast; withdrawn, almost; very precise and scientific, his stopwatch never out of his hand. Yet why should he remind me, more than anything else, of an animal trainer who does everything by kindness? I *preferred* Sam. With all his monstrous egotism, exhibitionism, his shouting and his showing off, his publicity hunting and his intransigence, he was human, even a parody of human. He may have bullied Ike and dominated him, but he dominated him like a father with a son, not a trainer with a tiger—or an inventor with a machine.

For this is how Giesemann speaks about Ike—with great admiration, colossal seriousness—but as though he were discussing a machine or a splendid animal. "His lung capacity is exceptional. Also he is unusual in the rate of his heartbeat, which is much slower than the normal. His recovery rate is also outstanding, and it is even improving." Seriousness is his essence; everything matters. One hardly ever sees him smile. If you make a joke, it's ignored, like a car inadvertently squashing a dog.

It's round the track and lie down, round the track and lie down; lie down exhausted, heaving, like a body pulled out of the sea. Then Giesemann stoops over him, one hand on Ike's heart, the inevitable stopwatch in the other, frowning, anxious—would the machine hold out? was the tiger dying?—till at last he'd nod, Ike would get up, and the lapping would begin again, sometimes with Jill beside him. What a cameo of loyalty that was!

Sometimes, when she trained with him, she'd run the first few laps, sometimes every other lap, very grave, that vestal virgin expression, participating in the religious rite; but now there was a new priest.

I asked her, one day, "Do you like him?" She said, "Who, Kurt?" and gave me that devastating child of nature look, the kind which overwhelms one—or is meant to overwhelm one?—with its innocence. Perhaps I'm being unkind to her; perhaps it was simply her legitimate defense against mischievous questions. "Yes," she said, "I do," which left no loophole.

If she doesn't like him, then too bad for Kurt; what she'd done once, she could certainly do again, and this time, from a position of strength. I assumed she'd let things take their course as long as she thought he was good for Ike, that Ike needed him or needed someone like him.

Meanwhile, Ike has found the will to run, again; you can see it in every stride. On the Crystal Palace track he's like a greyhound, waiting to be slipped, to hunt, to prove his power. And when he races, he looks unbeatable; there's a surging confidence about him; so much so that when someone passes him, as Driver briefly did in the American match, you feel that he's allowed it, just to make the race more interesting, to create an artificial challenge. In the end, he just walked away from Driver, as he did from Curtis, the other American, not to mention George Collins, the British second string.

If we were to have the Olympic Games this year, instead of in two years time, I'm sure he'd win; there's only Cooper at the moment who could live with him, and the way he's running now, in all the euphoria that's come with change, he'd beat Cooper. But there we are; the Olympics are two years away, and God knows what will have happened by then.

Whisper it not among the nut-cutlet set, but one of Britain's best-known vegetarians is going back on the beef standard. After five years' total abstinence, joint mile record holder Ike Low is happily carnivorous.

"I felt a bit guilty to begin with," said twenty-four-year-old Ike, "especially when I found myself enjoying meat so much. But then I got used to the idea, and to tell the truth, I realized all I've been missing."

Ike's change of diet coincides with a change of coach. Sam Dee, who discovered Ike and trained him till this summer, is a confirmed vegetarian who persuaded Ike to eat his way. His new coach, Germany's Professor Kurt Giesemann, believes a runner needs the proteins that come from meat.

One person who's delighted is Ike's wife, Jill, the international sprinter. "It makes life so much easier," she says. "I no longer have to plan two different menus."

X

Until that happened, everything was wonderful. I suppose I should have known it was going too well. The only thing I had on my mind was Cooper; he was like a shadow. Sometimes I've wondered, will I ever run against him anymore, is he avoiding me deliberately, keeping out of my way till Perth, not giving me a chance to beat him?

When I talked to Kurt, he said he didn't think so, he said I'm reading too much into it, and so did Jill. Maybe I have been, I don't know; but I'd still like to beat him before Perth; otherwise there's going to be too much at stake there.

Part of the trouble's his being Canadian; we never run against Canada, but there's still all the invitation miles, and whenever he's invited to them, there's always something. When he *has* run this season, he's done good times, only twice over the four minutes, a 3.55.4 in San Francisco, a 3.55.8 in Toronto, but nothing as fast as my time in Los Angeles. Kurt's analyzed him, he's got hold of his time *and* lap times for every race he's run over the last two years, and he thinks to beat him, you've got to do it early on, before the middle of the third lap; if you let him open out a lead, he can hold up to the bell; you'll never catch him. He says, "You must be stronger than he is. I think perhaps maybe *you* must try to lead all of the way." Which I don't think any miler likes to do, not in a race where there's anyone he's really worried about; you're afraid of what's he's doing there, behind.

Other than that, it couldn't have been going better. I'd pop over to Germany maybe once a month, sometimes for a few days, sometimes for longer; otherwise, I'd use these training schedules Kurt sent me; there was pages and pages of them, every session broken down into laps and half-laps, every lap timed, building up when there wasn't a race, tailing off when there was one, what I ought to eat, now I'd gone back to

meat again, how many hours I ought to sleep, especially
traveling abroad; he was dead hot on that, he'd done a lot of
research on the effect of flying on the human body. There
was nothing he didn't think of, nothing.

I was running well, too, winning at the White City against
the Yanks, beating Driver again, which I always like doing,
and winning in Moscow, too, against Semichastny. After Los
Angeles, I knew he'd be after me, and he'd fancy himself
out there on his own track.

I always liked going to Moscow for the atmosphere; they
really go for athletics there; they'd always have eighty-odd
thousand in the stadium, shouting their heads off, and by this
time it always helped me, whether they was shouting for me
or shouting for the others. The thing was, at least you'd got
the background.

This Semichastny was a strong-looking fellow with a crew
cut that looked like a prison barber had done it. He was built
more like a sprinter than a miler; I would have thought he'd
have done better over the half-mile, but he'd really gone at
the bell in Los Angeles, and he did it again in Moscow, only
this time I was ready, and I stayed with him. Kurt and I had
reckoned if I did that, he might crack, which he did. In the
end I left him on the final bend, and he finished up twenty-
five yards behind: I did 3.38.6.

Then I went home, on top of the world—and walked
straight into this, right out of the blue.

I know a lot of people have blamed me since, the way I
went on, and I'm not saying I behaved that brilliantly, but
what I do want to say is this: that there *was* this agreement,
this understanding, to wait at least till Tokyo, and after that,
then we was going to see. And I'm not saying it was her fault,
because I know that; I know it wasn't, even if she often said
this to me, "You behave as though it's my fault." But she
could have seen it more from my point of view; when it
happened, she could have *tried* to put things right. Okay, it
wouldn't have been nice, it would have cost her something,
but not doing it cost *me* something; it cost us both something.

Anyway, as soon as I got home, I smelt something funny.
She opened the door, and I was full of it, I was really excited,
and normally she would have been as well. She hadn't been
in the team for a few matches, they'd put this Scotch girl in,
and as soon as I saw her, I kissed her; I said, "All right, then?

3.38.6! I skated it!" and she said, "Wonderful, I was so pleased," smiling, but a *tired* smile; it was like she'd been learning what she ought to say.

It must have been about ten at night. She'd made some sandwiches, she made a pot of tea, and we sat there in the kitchen, talking. I said, "Well, you'll be going to Perth anyway; you're bound to go for England," because in the Empire Games, all four countries send a team.

It was then that she said it: "I won't be going to Perth." It didn't sink in for a moment; I said, "Don't be silly, of course you'll go. They'll pick you for England, won't they? You'll probably be back in the British team by then, and all; this other girl ran terrible."

She said, "It's not a question of being picked. I won't be able to go. I'm pregnant."

Well, it hit me like a bomb. I sat there dazed. In the end all I could say was, "What do you mean, you're pregnant?" She said, "I wasn't sure. I had tests. I got the results on Friday."

I said, "What are we going to do about it?" It was the first thing come into my head. She said, "What do you mean?" all sort of cold, and I said, "We can't *have* it." It was when she didn't answer that I realized, that the penny dropped. She looked down at the table, she didn't answer, and I knew what it meant; I knew only too well. She was disagreeing with me. She wanted to have it.

I said, "So you want it?" She said, "Yes, I do," not looking up. I said, "After all, we agreed. Everything we'd planned." She said, "I couldn't help it." I said, "Of course you couldn't, I know you couldn't help it, but now it's happened, we can *do* something about it."

She said, "I don't want to do that." And I admit I did my nut; I shouted, "Christ, of all the bloody times! As if I haven't got enough on my plate between now and Tokyo!" She said, "You needn't worry. There'll be nothing on your plate. I can easily go home." I said, "That's fine! That's wonderful! You go home, and what happens to me? And where's the money going to come from, especially when you have to stop working? I might just as well pack up tomorrow!"

She said, "As you like," then got up and walked out of the room. I didn't follow her upstairs; I sat about until I thought she'd be asleep, thinking what a fuck-up it was, feeling bloody furious with her, wondering what the hell to do. I knew one thing: I'd never make her change her mind; there wasn't a hope of it. When she made up her mind to something, that was it. She wouldn't even argue, she'd just go very quiet, and the more you went on at her, the more she'd dig her heels in.

I honestly thought of leaving her, I was that choked about it, I thought of going over to Nuremberg and staying there; Kurt had told me I could come whenever I liked, for as long as I liked; he'd said, "This also is your home." Then she could do what she bloody well wanted; she could sue me for desertion, if she liked. Next moment I'd be thinking how wonderful everything had been up till now, why the hell this had had to happen, how bloody unfair it all was. Till I finished up doing something that I never normally do, getting the bottle of whiskey out that we kept in the cupboard and drinking three straight off, neat.

When I did get upstairs, the light was out, but she wasn't asleep. I could feel it; I could feel her lying there and watching in the dark. I didn't talk to her, though; I pretended I thought she was asleep; in fact, I wished to God we had another bedroom so I didn't have to sleep beside her, the way I felt.

When I woke next morning, she'd gone off to school. Usually if I woke up late, she'd leave my breakfast in the oven, but this time there wasn't a thing. I thought, *Right, that bloody settles it then, don't it?* and I went to the phone and I rang up Kurt in Nuremberg; I said, "I'm coming today." He said, "For how long?" and I said, "I don't know. Indefinitely."

I packed my suitcase, and I left that afternoon. I wrote her a note that said I'd decided to go to Nuremberg and she'd be hearing from me. Because I had to get away: from her and from the whole thing.

England will not, after all, be sending a husband-and-wife running team to the Empire Games, in Perth, Western Australia.

Pretty, twenty-four-year-old sprinter Jill Low, wife of world mile record holder Ike, has told the selectors she does not wish to be considered. She is expecting a baby.

Ike, meanwhile, is living outside Nuremberg where he is in training at the Sports Institute under famed coach Professor Kurt Giesemann. Says Jill: "I'd be the very last to stand in his way. I know he's set his heart on that gold medal."

Which provides, at last, a clue. It's all been very mysterious. Going down to Crystal Palace a few weeks ago, to find Jill training on her own.

"Where's Ike?"

"In Nuremberg."

Just that. Then actually running off and away from me, around the track. I ran after her and caught her; she wasn't going to get away with that.

"For how long?"

"I don't know."

Then running off again, right off the track, this time—"I must go now"—after which she'd not turned up there since.

I'd phoned once or twice and had the same, bitten-off replies. "I don't know. I've no idea. I couldn't tell you."

It's been puzzling me and even worrying me. Not simply out of morbid curiosity, though there's that as well, but out of a sudden anxiety for her, for him, for what could have happened to them. Had there been another battle, and had she lost it this time, lost it to Kurt? I couldn't believe it. Yet she obviously didn't want Ike to be away, and he'd equally obviously defied her. *How stupid of him,* I thought; *how shallow and egocentric.* Putting his needs as an athlete first, or, rather, what he thought to be his needs, because she was worth ten times more to him than Kurt—and his damned stopwatch.

But now I can see why she was so anxious for him to stay. Or I think I can. Morning sickness, all the rest of it. Or is there something else? Could it have been an accident; was that behind it? The more I think about it, the more I'm convinced it *was* an accident. On his part.

She'd been there before, Helge, but only like for a day or two, and anyway I hadn't been in the mood I was now. She'd sort of smiled at me now and again; I'd thought maybe she fancied me a bit. She had this way of looking at you like she was sizing you up, very cool, but like I say, I hadn't done nothing about it.

She was a smashing-looking girl, very tall, taller than I was, with these long legs, strong, but not big and bulky, like a lot of the German girl athletes. Her hair was black, and she wore it very long. The first time I remember her was in Belgrade, winning the 400 meters at the European Championships where I won the 1500, all this hair flying out behind her.

Her old man was an industrialist in Frankfurt, he was loaded, and she used to drive this red Ferrari that went like a bomb. She'd got a mind of her own all right; you had the feeling that whatever she wanted, she'd always been given, on top of which she'd been to university and that; she was clever.

The morning after I got to Nuremberg, she trained with me and Kurt; we did some lapping together, and she could certainly move, with those long legs. In fact, on about the third lap we did; it turned into a race; she ran on ahead of me; I thought, *I'm not going to have this,* and I went after her.

When I did that, she started going faster, and she turned around and laughed at me. Kurt was calling to us, "Slower, slower!" but we didn't take no notice; it was like a challenge, both of us flat out, and in the end I just got in ahead of her; I finished up maybe a yard in front, but I'd really had to shift.

Kurt come over looking very sad, shaking his head; we both lay down to have our pulses taken, and she turned her head to me and laughed again. She laughed at Kurt, too, when he started talking to her, something in German, and she said something back, what it was exactly I don't know, but obviously disagreeing. Then to me he said, "It is useless to race. Training is not for racing," and I didn't answer, it was true, but she'd begun it, and I couldn't let her get away with it.

That evening she drove me into Frankfurt. I hadn't been too certain at first, but she said, "Sure you come! I get you back in time; I drive you back. You don't miss any sleep."

The way she drove frightened me to death. We went along the autobahn; we could never have been under eighty, and sometimes over a hundred. Every now and then she'd look at me and smile, and I don't know how I managed to smile back, the risks she was taking, weaving in and out, overtaking every car she could.

When we got there, to Frankfurt, she took me to quite a fancy restaurant where you could dance. Walking in, looking at the waiters, hearing the music, seeing the way the customers were dressed, I got a shock, and it must have shown, because she said, "Don't worry. I will charge it to my father."

She was like Jill; she danced well, and she loved it; the difference between them was that where Jill had this way of sort of dancing on her own, very graceful, very rhythmic, but a *solo,* Helge danced with you; she'd keep smiling at you, teasing you almost. She was wearing a bright-green trouser suit, and she looked fabulous all that hair flying about.

While we was having dinner, she said, "Now you eat meat, but before I think you don't." I said, "That's right, I was a vegetarian," and I wondered what she was getting at; she'd got this smile on her face again; it made me uncomfortable. She said, "I think you give up a lot of things to run." I said, "You have to. Don't you give up a lot?" and she shrugged; she said, "Not so much. Running is not my life." We looked at each other, her with this expression; I reached across the table for her hand, and she squeezed mine hard; she had very strong fingers. She said, "You like jazz? I have at home the *Modern Jazz Quartet.* I asked, "What about getting back?" and she shrugged again; she didn't care. She said, "I ring Kurt and tell him that the car has broken down. It is often breaking down."

She had a fabulous flat; she lived there on her own. Very modern, tiled floors, a lot of rooms, rugs, paintings on the wall I couldn't make head or tail of, and this metal furniture, all angles. When we got in the door, she said, "I think you can kiss me." The *she* kissed *me,* pressing up against me, putting her arms around me, squeezing; it was like a python winding around you.

We was in bed inside five minutes, this great big double bed she had with a fur rug across it, white, and on top of that a whole bloody line of toy animals: teddy bears and dolls and that. She swept the whole lot of them off with just one movement—bang!

And she was great, with her long legs, this fantastic body, doing everything and loving it, things I'd never even thought of; she made love like it was some kind of game, saying, "You like this? And *this?*" When she lay back and I come into her, she shut her eyes, and she went, *"Ummm!"* like she'd just swallowed something that she liked.

By the time she got around to phoning Kurt, it must have been midnight—and that was only after I'd got on at her; she said, "I don't know why you worry." When we got back next morning, he didn't say nothing, just looked at us and nodded in a sort of hurt way, but later in the day he got hold of me alone and said, "An athlete must make certain sacrifices. I cannot instruct you, only advise you. Your heartbeat today was on average five percent higher."

So after that, I'd make her drive me home earlier; sometimes I'd drive myself; I felt safer.

I'd been there a week before I wrote to Jill. I hadn't heard a word from her. I couldn't bring myself to phone her, first because of the argument, second because of the thing going on with Helge. I didn't feel so angry now, just that I didn't want to talk to her about all that, the baby and all; I wanted to stay away from it, which may have been wrong, but it was how I felt; I'd have felt like that anyway, Helge or no Helge. I needed time to get over it.

Still, I did write in the end; I told her I was sorry I'd gone in such a hurry, that it was just on an impulse, I just suddenly felt I had to get off alone and train; I'd have explained to her if only she'd been there that morning. I apologized for how I'd behaved, too, the things I'd said to her; I told her I'd been tired and it had come as a big shock to me, which it had, but that as soon as I got back, we'd talk about it again. I said I needed a bit of time to think about it. Not that there was much time to think about anything, between Kurt and Helge.

Kurt didn't like what was going on, he still kept dropping remarks—about my heartbeat, my pulse rate—and one day he come up and said, "For a woman, running can never be so important as for a man." I knew what he meant, I knew he was right, that I was jeopardizing my chances, but the way I was still feeling then, it was the best thing for me; it was what I needed; if I hadn't had something like that, I'd have gone mad.

Once, when we was lying in bed, Helge said to me, "I've seen your wife in Belgrade; she's nice, I think." Then she got hold of me under the covers, so I was feeling one thing and thinking another. It was just like her, this. I said, "Oh, yeah?" casual, like. She said, "You don't like to talk about your wife?" and I said, "There's times, aren't there?" and she laughed.

When a week went by without an answer from Jill, I began to worry, until one evening I rung the house, and there was no reply. Next morning I rung again, early, around about half-past seven; still no answer. The only thing I could think of was maybe she'd gone home; maybe she'd be in Manchester, so I rung there.

It took a long time getting through, and in the end it was her mother that answered, very cautious, "Yes, who is it?" and when I said, "Mrs. Dailey, it's me; it's Ike," she said, "Oh, yes," very cold. I said, "Is Jill there?" She said, "Yes. She is," like, what do *you* want with her? I asked, "Can I speak to her?" and after quite a bit, she said, "I'll see."

God knows how long I waited; it seemed like an hour. It was probably less than a minute; then at last Jill come on and said, "Yes?" even colder than her mother. I said, "Get my letter then?" She said, "Yes, I got your letter." I said, "Well, I thought you'd have written." She said, "What was there to write about?" I said, "Well, at least you could have told me you were going to Manchester." She said, "And you could have told me you were going to Nuremberg."

"Look," I said, "if you want me to admit I was in the wrong, okay, I admit it. I said so in the letter, didn't I?" She said, "What good does that do?" I said, "It means we can talk about it all again, don't it? At least we can *talk,*" but she wouldn't give a bleeding inch, she said, "I know how you feel. Talking won't make any difference, will it?" Which really got me; I started shouting down the phone; I told her, "Of course it bloody would! You mean it won't make no difference to *you!* You just want to get your own way!" She said, "It's pointless going on like this," and hung up the phone.

I stood there shaking; I thought, *Fuck her, I'm* never *going back.* When Helge arrived—she was coming almost every day now—she said, "What's wrong, Ike?" I said, "Nothing much, nothing special," but that night we told Kurt that the car broke down again.

Outside the ancient city of Nuremberg, with its medieval castles and cathedrals, stands a large, low building which is a shining contrast in modernity.

It is here that Ike Low, Britain's brightest miler, is quietly but intensively preparing for what he knows will be his toughest-ever race: the final of the mile in the Perth Empire Games.

There, the twenty-four-year-old, London-born sports goods representative will almost inevitably meet and have to beat the man with whom he shares the world mile record: Canada's brilliant Terry Cooper.

Said Ike, when I talked to him last week beside the Sports Institute's red asphalt running track, which cost £10,000 to lay (the money comes from football pools): "In a sense, I have been preparing for this race for over a year. I have been preparing for it ever since I heard that Cooper had beaten my world record."

Tall, tanned and tautly determined, his body a muscular miracle of ruthless, even brutal, conditioning, Ike plans to reach peak fitness only in Perth itself. Under his coach, world-renowned sports physiologist Professor Kurt Giesemann, nothing has been left to chance. Ike's weight, pulse, heartbeat and recovery rate are checked and chronicled every day.

Together, the two have watched films of Cooper's races and have analyzed them lap by lap. Grinned Ike: "By the time I get to Perth, I reckon I'll know more about Cooper than he does himself!"

They even have a film of the one race in which Ike and Cooper *did* meet: an indoor affair at New York's Madison Square Garden, where Ike was tripped and fell in the third lap, Cooper romping home an easy winner. "It doesn't *tell* me much," says Ike, a glint in his eye, "but it reminds me."

For six weeks now he has been living and training at the Sports Institute, following Giesemann's demanding program of interval training, a system to which he turned last June, after five years of very different stamina training under fiery, unorthodox British coach Sam Dee.

"Sam was wonderful for me," says Ike. "But I think I'd got as far as I could with him. Maybe it's just that after five years of any kind of training, you need a change."

I asked the former junior quarter-miler, who ran his first four-minute mile when he was only eighteen, whether he was still in contact with Dee. A frown crossed the ruggedly handsome, almost Hollywood-idol face before he replied: "No. I wish we were. Sam took it very hard. I think he's a great coach. It's just that at this stage of my career, I think Kurt has more to offer me than Sam."

The quiet, courteous Giesemann, a complete contrast with the flamboyant Dee, explained, as he watched Ike lapping the track, side by side with Germany's glamorous, Wagnerian brunet, 400 meters European record holder Helge Walter, "Each athlete needs not only the right coach, but the right coach at the right time. Ike and I luckily found each other at the moment I think I can help him. For me, it is a privilege to work with so talented a runner:"

Ike's only regret is that his wife, Jill, the British international sprinter, can't be with him in Nuremberg—or in Perth.

"She's expecting a baby next spring," he told me. "At the moment she's living with her parents in Manchester."

But, as Giesemann says, "Every athlete must be prepared to make sacrifices."

Sam demands pain, and Giesemann wants sacrifice. I suppose Ike finds some difference between them; to me, they seem indistinguishable, in the last reduction. Two early Christian hermits, preaching salvation through the mortification of the flesh. I can see all their pupils, one day, in a pantheon. St. Ike of the Running Spikes, St. Emile of Prague, St. Roger of Iffley, beaming down upon us from Olympus, leading us on to higher things, faster times, greater renunciations.

Not that Ike's renunciation was total: There are too many pictures of him training with his Valkyrie, yet she, too, must have her place in the hagiography: the temptation, sent by the Devil, succumbed to, denied, and finally overcome. "Oh, God, give me the strength to resist temptation, but not yet."

Is it sour grapes? Merely that I know if I'd made greater sacrifices, mortified the flesh a little more, it would have been a gold medal, not a bronze? At this point in time, do I regret it? In a sense, yes, certainly; I regret not having won the gold medal, not having it hanging on the wall or in a glass case, not having my name on that steadily receding roll of honor. After all, what's left of what I did with my time, instead of using it for self-mortification? A few vanishing memories. Should one always strive for the permanent, what one can keep, what one can show, what is likely to outlive one? I don't think so. I've no great ambition to leave anything behind, not even children, and isn't any man the sum of his moments? Youth's surely for enjoyment, not self-flagellation. No, I don't think on the whole I'm really sorry. Who's to say, in any case, that I *would* have won the gold medal? I might not even have won the bronze.

Two days ago Ike phoned me. From Nuremberg. "It's Ike." Very embarrassed he sounded. "I don't like to ask you this." Would I talk to Jill? "Just phone her. She's up in Manchester. I mean, I'll pay for the call and all." And tell her what? More embarrassment.

"Well, she's pregnant; you know that. Yeah, well the thing is, she wasn't that keen on me going back to Nuremberg."

"Were you surprised?" I asked him. No, he said, he wasn't surprised. "The thing was, she sort of sprung it on me. Just when I'd got back from Moscow. It come as a bit of a shock."

So I'd been right. I said, "And now?"

He said, "Well, now I've come around to it, haven't I? I accept it. I mean, if it's got to be, it's got to be."

I asked him, "Can't you phone and tell her yourself?" He said, "I don't know how she'd take it. I mean, if it came from *you*. Someone that knows us both. That could tell her I really *meant* it."

I said, "Are you sure I'm the right person? I've always thought Jill was rather on her guard with me." No, no, he said—rather too quickly—she liked me; it was just at times she didn't know how to take me, whether I was joking, and this, to me, was the measure of his desperation, for he knows as well as I do that this isn't true.

He said, "Before Perth. I want to get it all straight," and before I could help it, I found myself replying, "So you can go into battle with a clear conscience? I know. I'll drive up there, Ike. Telephones are no good for this sort of thing."

He said, "Will you?" with enormous relief; obviously it was what he'd been hoping for. He said, "Maybe it's best not to let her know you're coming. They can be a bit funny, her family. You know what they're like up there."

So I arrived out of nowhere, out of space; in that dull little street, with its semis, my white Lotus must have seemed almost as exotic as a space capsule, and I to Jill, at the door, as unexpected as an astronaut.

After the moment of amazement, her face set hard, and she said, "Did Ike send you?"

I said, "Not exactly, but I've got a message from him." She said, "I don't want to hear it."

I said, "You're not going to send me straight back to London again, are you?"

For a moment, I wondered whether she might. Poor girl, she'd obviously had a wretched time. Her face no longer had that high-toned wholesomeness about it. It was thinner, though the body was fatter; she looked as if she weren't sleeping much, and that fine inner stillness she used to radiate had given way to sheer sadness. In the end, she said, "You'd better come in," and stood aside to let me in. It was a poor man's home, mine again, God-fearing working class, another of those live-in-the-kitchen homes where the parlor was the shrine, all gloom and polish, a sort of inanimate sacrifice to the gentility principle.

Her mother came into the parlor, wearing an apron, going gray and a little fat, but with the same fine, steady eyes. When she heard who I was, she wasn't quite sure how to react to me, whether to regard me as friend or foe, and she settled for being cautiously polite, asking me would I like a cup of tea, which in these homes is no more than a Pavlovian reflex.

When she'd gone out, when Jill and I had sat down, I told her, "He rang me from Nuremberg two days ago." I knew it was going to be awfully difficult. In her present mood, any plowshare can be turned into a sword.

"He rang you," she said, and I rattled away about desperation, last expedients, while she watched me with this fixed, hostile look, obviously incensed, humiliated, that he'd brought me into it at all, and wondering just what I knew. Finally she asked, "Then what's the message?"

I didn't say, "That it's got to be." I paraphrased and told her, "That he's changed his mind. That he agrees with you."

"And he sent you to say it," she said.

I began, "Jill, listen—" but she wouldn't. She said, "You can tell him that if he's got anything to say to me, he can say it himself." I said, "I will." She was quite right. I said, "Jill, I want you to believe one thing. I know you don't like me very much." She didn't deny it. "But I did truly want to help. I thought this might."

She listened without looking at me; there was one more hiatus, then she said, "I'm not blaming you." Which I suppose was the most that I could expect.

When I got back to London, I phoned him and told him he'd have to come over himself.

How remote it seems, now, how ironic; the image, the tableau, he and she, running side by side. I suppose it was always too romantic to last.

XI

I didn't see her before we left for Perth; to tell the truth, I was afraid. Not of her, but of the effect it might have on me if we quarreled. Taking all that with me twelve thousand miles, or however far it was, and having to live with it, having it preying on me, night and day.

I did ring her, after Alan had rung me, and if she'd been friendly, if she'd give me any encouragement, *then* I'd have gone up to Manchester. But she didn't; she was just cold again. I couldn't understand it; I said, "Look, I *want* it. If you want to have the baby, you can have it. I *mean* that." All she said was, "Very well, Ike."

I said, "Is that all you've got to say: very well?"

"Yes," she said, "yes, it is." It sounded like she was going to start crying; then she put down the phone. No how are you, how's it going? So when I come to London, to join the team, I didn't even ring her again, which I admit was wrong, but like I say, I was frightened.

I did write to her, though, saying how I really *had* changed, and I loved her, and if I hadn't come up to see her before I went off, it was only because I was in this funny state you get in before something as big as this was, and I reckoned she'd understand that better than anyone, knowing me and knowing these events.

I didn't go back to the house—I couldn't have faced it, not without Jill there—I just stayed in Lancaster Gate with the team. I was sorry Helge wasn't going; I could really have done with her, though in another way, of course, it was just as well.

The last couple of weeks she hadn't trained no more at the Sports Institute. She told me Kurt had been getting at her, telling her to lay off, that I'd got this important race coming up and she ought to think of other people. She said, "I told him you are not a child, that you know too about this race. I told him I do not force you to do anything. I say, 'You may tell him what to do, certainly not me.' " So she stayed away; it was better, really; I'd go into Frankfurt on my own now, or else she'd pick me up somewhere on the way, in the car. That bloody car. She said to me once, "You know what I think Kurt would prefer. Not man or woman, just machine, so he may measure everything, and when we are not running, he may switch us off."

Kurt was the same as Sam, in a way; from outside everything looked different, a bit nutty, and although Helge *was* a runner, although she had trained with Kurt, it wasn't the same even with her, it couldn't be for a girl, and in any case, for Helge, running was just a hobby. You had to be right inside before you could understand.

That was a hell of a long trip to Australia, even by jet: taking off and touching down, taking off and touching down. As soon as you'd get to sleep, they'd be throwing you off the plane again.

There was the usual argument, this time about how much say the captain ought to have. I didn't want to get involved with it; I had enough on my mind.

I knew I'd have Ron Vane after me some time on the journey, and in the end he caught up with me after we'd left Los Angeles. The usual stuff, how pleased he'd been with my results; he said, "What did I tell you, Ike? Wasn't I right? You see: as soon as you changed your coach. You should have done it long ago." I just sort of nodded; there was no use talking to him.

Kurt was going to be there in Perth, but so was Sam, which was one more worry. He'd been coaching a couple of the lads in the team, Jack Scott, a hurdler, and Ronnie Black, that run the 880. I'd trained quite a bit with Jack, but the other fellow was new to me. They wouldn't speak to me much, just looked at me and exchanged remarks I couldn't hear; I could imagine what Sam must have told them.

When we got there, it was like Cardiff all over again. Not the weather, of course, nor the people, the Aussies, but the atmosphere, completely different from an Olympic Games, more like a kind of party. We all lived in bungalows; I was sharing with Peter Carson, the other miler, and in a way I envied him. He didn't have no chance, so he could join in all the fun, whereas until we'd run that final, that was all I could think about.

My first day on the training track, with Kurt, Cooper was there; he was very friendly. He come over with his hand out and said, "Hi! I hope neither of us falls over this time."

I shook hands, and I said, "*I* hope not, and all." He asked did I want to jog a few laps with him, but I said no, thanks, I was training with Kurt. He smiled and said, "Okay, take it easy," and went off on his own. He was a nice enough bloke, but even with him you never knew; you always had to watch it before a race like this. He probably means nothing by it; on the other hand, he might have been hinting I was over-trained, I should have eased off by now, whereas he was confident. Or again, if I *had* run with him, it might have been just a doddle, or he could have done like some of them do, go like the clappers over a couple of laps and leave you behind and shake *your* confidence.

The third day what I was afraid of happened. Sam was there.

Up to this, I'd managed to keep out of his way. He'd been at quite a few of the meetings I'd run in, but I don't think he was any keener to talk to me than what I was to talk to him. Once, over at the White City, I'd nodded to him and said, "All right, Sam?" but he'd turned away, and I'd thought, *If that's how you want it, then bollocks.* But this time he was out for blood; I could tell it. I could tell from the way he stood there looking at us, Kurt and me, with his chest stuck out, one hand on his hip, and this stare, this sort of grin.

I nudged Kurt, and I said, "There's Sam." He looked, too, and he said, "I have no quarrel against him." I said, *"You* may not."

Jack and Peter was on the track; Sam had them doing his stop-go sprints. We had to pass him, going up to the start. I said, "Good morning, Sam," but instead of answering me, he turned to all the people around, there was quite a few of them, and made this sort of speech.

"Ladies and gentlemen. You now have the opportunity of watching two opposed types of training in action. One is the interval method, employed by Professor Giesemann, whom you see here, a method which, in *my* opinion, turns runners into robots. You will see Professor Giesemann's methods at their most characteristic; this is *all* he does. *My* methods, as you may know, are not slavishly confined to the track. They demand the use of spaces, where an athlete can run free, preferably in beautiful and inspiring surroundings. They demand trees and hills and grass. Here, my two runners, Jack and Peter, are merely putting the gloss on what has already been done in London.

"But this is as it should be; or as *I* think it should be. A properly prepared athlete has no need to drive himself immediately before a race, but Professor Giesemann's methods are mechanical. The treadmill can only work at one pace, and in one way. That is not to say that the athlete he is training, Ike Low, will not be successful in these games. He has had the benefit of five years of my own training, and he cannot lose that in a few months.

"If he wins, there are those who will say that it was despite my methods, rather than because of them, that it was thanks to the training of Professor Giesemann. This will amuse me, my friends. I have long ago lost all respect or appetite for public acclaim; my rewards lie in the achievements of my athletes, even when they fall into the hands of my rivals and denigrators. I know and they know who is really responsible for their success. I bear no malice toward them when they leave me; I am merely sorry for them. Sorry that they should give up a kind of training which has been rationally devised for the athlete, for one which makes a cypher of the athlete.

"There you see a man who could have been the greatest miler that the world has ever seen. Look how beautifully he moves. I taught him to move. If he is honest, he will admit that. But I fear that now he will never realize his true capacity, and I shall never train him again, even if he were to return and beg me. There can be no turning back. Once an athlete has left me, it is irrevocable. There is more to our relationship than physical preparation; just as there is far, far more to it than mechanical conditioning.

"Watch him; you are watching a great athlete who has betrayed his possibilities."

And then, on top of that, the very next day, her letter.

DEAR IKE,

I have thought for a long time whether to reply to you. Dozens of times I've begun, only to stop after a line or two. It's so hard to put into words what I feel, and just as hard to write them down when I do think of them.

I'm not going to go into a lot of reproaches over how you've behaved. I've realized now that it isn't really your fault and that you couldn't have behaved any differently. I've even realized that we all of us, and I include myself, helped make you like this.

That wasn't how I felt to begin with, I admit, but up here there hasn't been much else to do but think, and I've been thinking such a lot. I didn't mean to tell you about the baby at first, and certainly not the way it happened, immediately you'd got home from Moscow. It was very wrong. I meant to get rid of it, I honestly did; that was my first reaction, because I remembered as well as you did what I'd promised, what we'd both agreed. But when it came to the point, I couldn't face it; I wanted it so much, and most of all, believe it or not, because of you. Because I loved you, and it would be yours.

I don't expect you to understand this. But I couldn't just have it killed and washed away, Ike, because it would have killed *me*. I'd never have been the same.

It was cruel of you, though I suppose you didn't mean it, to send Alan to see me, instead of talking to me yourself. How could you have done it? How could you *tell* him things which should only be known between you and me? I've never trusted him. He makes me feel like a monkey in a cage being looked at through the bars, and I still think he's jealous of you; I still think he doesn't like me, whatever he may tell you. I think he'd be glad to see us split up, though he was quite kind when he came to see me.

Ike, I hope you win your race, I hope it with all my heart. I know how important it is to you, more important than anything on earth. I realized that before I knew about the baby, but in a detached sort of way. When it really came home to me that night, it hurt terribly. Goodness knows *I* want you to win, just as I want you even more to win in Tokyo, but now, with this baby inside me, I can't help it, Ike; I can't think there's nothing else in the world.

When you got away from Sam, I was so pleased and so relieved, because I felt you'd find yourself and *be* yourself, which he'd never allowed you to do. But it seems to me that nothing has changed. Kurt doesn't bully you like Sam did, he doesn't seem to resent me like Sam did, but *he* seems to want you body and soul as well, in his own particular way. That's why I sounded strange on the phone last time. I'd been thinking, and I still think, what's left for me, and what will be left for the baby when it's born?

I know you say that you've accepted it, but you say it as if you were making the best of a bad job. And I can't pretend that when the baby's born, I can give you all the attention that I used to. I'd give you as much as I possibly could, but I have this awful feeling that it wouldn't be enough.

I do still love you. I'm praying that you win. But I'm frightened for us, Ike. Be patient with me.

That was all I needed.

Ike, we had your old coach, Sam Dee, on the program, and he seemed to think you'd made a mistake, changing your training.

Yeah, well, he would do, wouldn't he?

You think you were right?

I wouldn't have changed if I didn't, would I?

Can you tell us something about the difference between Sam's system and the one you follow now, with Professor Giesemann?

Well, one's interval training, isn't it? Giesemann's. You do laps of like four hundred meters, two hundred meters, with an interval after every one.

And Sam's?

Sam's is more sort of cross-country. Up and down hill at different speeds; not a lot of track work.

And why did you decide you'd change, Ike?

I'd been with Sam five years. I was running bad, and I felt I needed it.

Sam seems to think Professor Giesemann turns his runners into automatons.

Into what?

Robots. Would you agree with that?

Yeah. You can see the wire coming out of me head.

How do you feel about this race? Confident?

I think you've got to be confident; otherwise, you've got no chance.

Your main rival's Terry Cooper, isn't he? The two of you share the world record.

That's right.

Have you any plan to help you beat him?

Yeah. Run faster than what he does.

The start of the mile final. Ike Low, England's great hope. You can see him there, looking very tense, as well he might.

Look at him there; I don't know how he stays so fucking calm. He probably isn't. Wants to con me.

And there—Terry Cooper. Joint holder with Low of the mile record, the man he'll have to beat if he's to retain the title he won four years ago in Cardiff. Cooper looks very, very calm. Twenty-six years old, a marine biologist from Vancouver.

Where's Sam? Thought I saw him there; by the track. I hope to Christ it wasn't.

Low ran the fastest time of anybody in the race this year, when he equaled Cooper's world record in Los Angeles. Never run against each other outdoors before. Just one meeting at Madison Square Garden, where Low slipped and fell early in the race, Cooper going on to win. Both qualified easily in their semifinals, without having to break four minutes. So it's wide open. Cooper in lane number two, Ike Low in lane four.

That feeling in my guts, like water. Thought I was over that.

There they go, and *what* a start by Low! He's running as though it were a quarter-mile. And Cooper's going right after him. Cooper has accepted the challenge. A *tremendous* spurt by both men.

Christ, he's still there! Fucking take over then!

And as you can see, Cooper has actually passed Low. Around they come, with hardly a yard between them. What did you make the lap time, Cecil?

I made it 54.2, George. An incredible lap. I don't see how either of them can hope to keep it up.

Grogan of Australia lying third, a *good* twenty yards behind. He can only hope they're going to crack.

Sod him, he's conning me; he must slow down.

A really amazing pace. Inevitably slacking off a little now.

I should think so. Let him bloody stay in front now.

And how did you time that second lap, Cecil?

I made it 55.4, George.

Not as fast as the first lap, but still a *very* fast time.

A remarkable time. If they keep this up, there could be a new world record.

Now Cooper seems to be pulling away again; he's opened up a gap of about five yards. Low certainly can't afford to let it get much bigger.

I don't believe it. Moving like he could go on forever.

Yes: Low *is* closing that gap—and just in time for the bell. This ought to be a sen*sational* last lap. How did you time that third lap, Cecil Partridge?

At 57.3, George.

A slow one.

A relatively slow one. I think that was inevitable after the pace they set in the first and second.

And it's still a two-man race, with both Cooper *and* Low setting a *tremendous* pace, again.

Now! I've got to catch him now!

They're both *flat* out, Cooper moving superbly, but Low still right on his tail. Into the back straight; still no change. Now Low is gaining slightly. They're shoulder to shoulder!

The pain. I can't go on. Let him win it; let him fucking win it!

Around the last bend, into the home straight, *still* neck and neck!

Through, *I'm through!*

And Low very slightly ahead! With fifty yards to go, he's just about a pace in front! Now they're level again! Now Low's in front!

Give up, you bastard!

And Low has won! At the tape, Low finishes a yard ahead of Cooper. What a finish! What an astonishing finish by the English boy! Cecil Partridge, can you give us the final time? 3.54.7, George. Just two-tenths of a second outside their joint world record.

But what a magnificent race! And what a wonderful performance by the twenty-four-year-old London sports goods representative! So it's another gold medal for England, won by Ike Low in what *we* reckoned to be a time of 3.54.7.

Which would be a new Empire Games record, George.

Which, as you heard Cecil Partridge say, would be a new Empire Games record.

I'm dead. For Christ's sake, leave me alone; I want to be sick.

There's Cooper shaking hands with Low; a great sportsman, this Canadian.

Yeah, well run, Terry.
Don't know where he finds the strength.
Thanks, Kurt.
Sam there; looking at me. With that smile. Think what you fucking like then.
Ta. Well run yourself.
I thought I'd die then. I honestly thought I'd die.

Sam came out afterward with a curious statement, one that claimed the credit, of course: "He won because I had taught him to overcome the pain barrier."

And suddenly I had a revelation—Sam's language is catching—the corollary of what I'd thought before. For it seems to me that what Sam's after, even if he doesn't know it, is a kind of rebirth through suffering. The athlete passes through the valley of the shadow of death, through the pain barrier, and is born again in the holy spirit. I'm sure it's that, or something like that, something mystical, and I'm sure the runners themselves must have some inkling of it, or they'd never submit to it.

As for Giesemann and the rest, with their morbid talk of sacrifice, they're after more or less the same thing. It's the ascetic, dedicated life, the purification through pain. Good God, must we all be initiates now, before we can win an Olympic medal?

Miler Ike Low, England's gold medal hero at the Perth Empire Games, was welcomed home at London Airport yesterday by his wife Jill, the girl who might have won another gold for England. But Jill, who is expecting a baby next April, had to drop out of the team.

"I didn't mind so much for myself," said the twenty-three-year-old brunet sprinter, "but I so much wanted to be there to see Ike win. I was sure he would."

But there are hopes of an Olympic double in Tokyo, in two years time. Says Jill, "When the baby is born, I certainly hope to compete again. After all, lots of mothers do."

XII

It was the best thing I could have hoped for and the last thing I expected; it staggered me. Through the door of the customs hall, where they was all of them waiting. I couldn't believe my eyes at first; then she smiled at me; it was wonderful really; I don't think I've ever been so pleased to see her smile.

Now I was sure it was her I waved to her, and she waved back; she said something, but of course, I couldn't hear.

It was just perfect, the perfect end to everything. It's true I'd had a cable from her, CONGRATULATIONS DARLING, but that could mean anything or it could mean nothing; I hadn't let myself build too much on it. Besides, to tell the truth, I was having it off then with this South African bird, this fencer; she was dark with a fantastic little body; she reminded me a bit of Jill.

But there she was, and I couldn't have been more pleased; we kept on smiling and waving to each other while I waited for this twot at the customs to go through my case; he said, "No gold medal?" and I said, "I flogged it." It was in my pocket; I showed it him; then I got out at last and I kissed her. I didn't care about the bloody cameras. We stood there I don't know how long, kissing, like we both wanted to make up for something, what we'd been missing, all the time we hadn't been together.

She had the car there, and I drove us home. We didn't talk much on the way, just smiled at each other now and again, kissed at traffic lights and that; then, as soon as we got home, we went to bed and stayed there; it was terrific, both of us still making up for things, to ourselves and to each other, something you couldn't say in any bloody letter, or in words, and when we weren't making love, even then we didn't speak; we just lay there holding one another, now and then looking at each other, smiling.

We started to go training together again, and I liked that, too, though she only watched me now. She'd got her job back at the school, but whenever she could, she come down with me. We talked a lot about her coming to Tokyo, running for Britain again after the baby was born; I was getting used to the idea of the baby. I don't say I was mad about it, but I could see it now; I could see how the whole thing could work. We'd never been closer, the two of us, and when the baby arrived, it didn't *have* to make that difference; there was ways *round* it.

I went over to Nuremberg about once a month now, and I'd speak to Kurt on the phone like every ten days or so. I was a bit worried going back the first time, what with Helge; I was hoping she wouldn't be there, I was afraid that if she found out *I* was going to be there, she would be, but when she didn't turn up, the funny thing was that I missed her.

Next time I went out, she phoned me. She said, "What's the matter, you don't call me now?" and something come over me when I heard her voice, a sort of shock, something I'd been hoping wouldn't happen. I told her, "Yeah, well I wasn't here for long, the last time," and she laughed; she said, "Anyway, congratulations on your win," making the whole thing sound a bit of a giggle, which was another way of hers.

The trouble was that I knew now I couldn't turn her down, not just because I wanted to go to bed with her again, which I did as soon as I'd heard her voice, but that no matter what excuse I made, she'd only laugh at me and make me feel a right idiot.

So when she said, "Come into Frankfurt tonight," I didn't say no, which I'd like to have done; I didn't say nothing at all, I didn't *know* what to say, and I think she could tell that, too, because she laughed again and said, "Okay, I pick you up at the same place, around seven," which was a bus stop about a mile outside Nuremberg.

Over the next few hours I must have changed my mind a dozen times. I'd decide not to go, definitely not to go, and then I'd think, *If I don't, she'll only come after me again,* because she wasn't like other birds; they'd take it as an insult, but to her it would be a joke.

So I was there when she drove up, with the hood down and her hair all flying, looking fantastic, and once I'd seen her, there was no going back; I felt about her like I always done.

When we was in bed, she smiled and said, "So now you are with your wife again."

I said, "Yeah." I'd never liked talking about Jill to her, even when Jill and I was quarreling. She said, "And that is why you are so timid?" I said, "Maybe," and she said, "Were you so timid in Australia? I don't think it!" and she laughed. She hadn't got no sense of right or wrong. Like I've said before, she just took what she wanted, and when you was with her, she made you feel the same; you did what you felt like, and you didn't care. Which helped in a way, because it meant that the whole thing never seemed quite real, it was like a kind of dream, not just because you was abroad, though that helped, too, but because of *her,* the way she made you look at things and feel things. You'd leave home, which *was* real, go into this sort of dreamworld with her, then go back to what was real again.

Once she asked me, "Does your wife know about us?" I said, "No, I don't think so." She said, "You mean you don't *hope* so," and I got the idea that she'd have been pleased, she'd have got a kick out of Jill knowing.

Now and again I'd think Jill guessed; when she'd ask me about Helge, the times there was something in the paper about her, the way she'd look at me, the tone she had, but nothing ever direct. I'd tell her, "I told you Helge ain't training there no more," and she'd look at me like she wasn't sure whether to believe me.

Now and again I'd meet Helge actually *in* Nuremberg, which was a place I liked, the old buildings, the churches and that. She took me to a museum where there was all these paintings by some German, which I quite liked, the colors and these gnarled old faces, but half an hour was enough. Which amused her, of course, like almost everything else; I could see she *wanted* me to be bored by them, so she could take the mickey, again. She said, "Only running, nothing in your life but running!" I said, "That's not true," and she said, "No, no, also this!" and grabbed me. She didn't care what she did.

And so they're back together, brought together, I'm convinced, by the gold medal, by the mutual euphoria of it all. Terribly ironical, when one remembers how it seemed to be precisely the gold medal, the *pursuit* of gold medals, which was pulling them apart.

They've even reestablished the loyalty tableau: the two of them going down again to the Crystal Palace track. I've trained there with them only once; there was something in the air, a coldness, as if part of the new bargain involved a scapegoat: me. I know too much, I've been invited too far in, and now they're anxious to be rid of me. I embarrass them. Not that they weren't polite, but there were undertones. There always have been with Jill, but they're new in Ike. I'm sorry, but I think I understand.

And is it malign of me to wonder if the newly rebuilt structure is strong enough to last, to stand up against the baby, the approach of the Olympiad?

About Tokyo: Sam's already crying doom. I saw him at an indoor meeting.

"By Perth there was not sufficient time for my work to be undone. There was no time for him to be corrupted, to be turned into a zombie. But the Olympic Games are still two years away, and in that time even the foundation I established can be gradually destroyed."

I said, "Wouldn't it be awful if he won in Tokyo, Sam?" but it's impossible to rile him. He answered, "Not at all. I should be overjoyed to see him win in Tokyo, for his sake and for his country's. But at present, I see no possibility of his doing so. His only chance would be to return to me in time, and as I have explained before, that is out of the question. In these two years, Giesemann will strip him of his will to run. He will transform him into a runner of laps, not a runner of races. An athlete's capacity cannot be measured in the laboratory and calculated on instruments. You cannot weigh and measure the human spirit.

"These are *Teutonic* methods, and Ike is not a German, he is an Englishman."

He may be right, I think; right to the extent that Ike won't win the Olympics. Two years *is* a terribly long time, interval training *can* be a deadening thing, but then, Ike was sick of *Sam's* training; something one hardly mentions. The farce of it is that if the race were run now, I still doubt if there'd be anyone to touch him. I don't think Cooper's going to beat him again—not at the highest level. A miler who loses a race like that one is rather like a heavyweight boxer, beaten for the world title. He may not lose by much, but he's taken such a beating that he'll never be the same. A physical beating, of course. In a runner's case, the physical beating may be less—or less obvious—but the psychological beating's worse.

I'd like to go to Ike and say, "Retire. Quit while you're ahead; be a father; bring up a family," and I'm sure that in her heart of hearts, Jill would, too. But of course, it would be futile.

. But would you say, Mrs. Low, that there *was* a conflict between being a mother and having a career as an international athlete?

No, I don't think so. I think it's good for a woman to do other things, not just stick inside the house all day.

But surely an international runner nowadays does have to do an enormous amount of training and a great deal of traveling?

Quite a lot, yes.

How do you manage it all?

I take baby with me. To training, anyway. I think he enjoys it.

He enjoys it?

Yes.

I see. How splendid.

He seems to, anyway. Gurgling away to himself there.

But if you're running abroad, you can't very well take him with you.

Oh, I wouldn't run abroad until he's bigger.

And if you did?

I'd leave him up in Manchester with my mother. Or maybe in London with my mother-in-law. I think there's going to be a bit of rivalry!

As long as you don't have to give a judgment of Solomon!

Oh, I hope not!

Mrs. Low, your husband is a very famous runner. Do you think this has helped your own career?

People are always asking me that. I think it *has* helped me. I train with him.

Really? How often?

Every day, when I'm not teaching. That helps. And then the more he achieves, the more it makes *me* want to do.

So in a sense it makes you compete with him?

No, no. Not compete with him. We're neither of us competing with each other. It just encourages me.

You don't think intense competition of this kind tends to make women *over*competitive?

No, I don't. After all, they're just as competitive in other ways if they don't run, aren't they? Who's got the best fur coat, who's got the nicest home, and that.

Would you like your son to become a runner?

Oh, yes, but I'd never force him. He probably thinks we're daft as it is, just running around a track all day.

It was worse than what I'd ever been afraid of. Changing everything, disrupting everything, pushing you onto the outside. Mind you, I should have been warned, the way she'd been over the last two or three months. It was like she wasn't really with you; she'd go off into another world, this little smile on her face; you'd talk to her, and she wouldn't hear you.

She didn't seem to mind about swelling up, turning this shape, carrying all this weight about. She give up the teaching job, of course, which didn't make things no easier, and naturally she couldn't come training no more. What I didn't understand was the way she obviously expected me to be happy, too; she'd come out of these sort of dazes and smile at me. It was sometimes all I could do to smile back. If it wasn't for going over to Nuremberg, and Helge, I reckon I'd have been up the bloody wall.

It was hard, the training, very hard on your own, having to drive yourself every day, through all these lap schedules he sent over; just you and the watch, timing yourself, plugging around the track until your shins got sore, the same old track, day after bloody day. Still, I was *doing* the times he wanted, even though he made them faster and faster, with less recovery time. I'd send him back the schedules, all the times filled in, every lap—he insisted on it—and back would come another batch.

What kept me going now was Tokyo, but it was such a hell of a long way off, and there was days when I'd wake up and see the rain come down the windowpane that I'd think, *Fuck it, I'll stay at home today,* though I never did. These were the times I admit I missed Sam, somebody to talk you into it, when this remote-control thing didn't work so well. I did have Jill, at least there was her to talk to, but she'd keep going off into what I called her trance, and it was never her that raised the subject now, running; it always had to be me. She'd talk about it then, all right, but not in the way she used to, like she wanted to get back to thinking of something else.

It's Tokyo or bust for twenty-four-year-old world mile record holder and Empire Games gold medalist Ike Low.

"I'm going all out to win the Olympic 1500 meters there in 1964," the six-foot, London-born sports goods representative told me, "but even if I don't make it, I shall still retire. After all, it will be my second Olympiad, and standards are getting tougher all the time. People don't realize what sacrifices an international athlete has to make."

She woke me up at four in the morning. I was in the middle of a dream. I was flying again, with Sam and Kurt both looking up at me from below, and Sam saying, "Of course, he's on the automatic pilot." Then feeling a pain where my right wing joined my body, thinking I can't go on, I'm bound to fall, then waking up, because Jill was shaking my shoulder.

She said, "I'm sorry, darling, I've had the pains two hours," so I got up and drove her to the hospital, over at Barnet. They were very nice to us there, give us a cup of tea and that; then, when they took her away and she went out with this expression on her face, half like she was saying sorry to me, half like she never expected to come out again, I had a funny feeling in my stomach; I was frightened. I stood there kind of dopey till a nurse come up and said, "Now, there's nothing to worry about, Mr. Low," and I wanted to say, "No, not for you there ain't."

I went down to train that day because anything was better than hanging around the house, but my mind wasn't on it, and I must have phoned them half a dozen times; you could tell they were getting right sick of it by the finish. I'd rung my mother, and I'd rung Jill's mother; they were both well pleased; they neither of them seemed that worried, but *I* was worried, because after all, you could never be sure; things *did* go wrong.

I put off and put off phoning again, grinding out the laps,

though I just couldn't settle down to time them; they were the hardest bloody laps I've ever done, wondering what was she going through. Then, when I finally come off the track, I went straight to a phone; I didn't even bother to change; and it was a boy. The nurse said they were both of them fine.

I put the phone down, and I thought, *Thank God for that, she's okay,* and then, *Thank God it's a boy.* The funny thing was I'd been reckoning on a boy, I suppose fathers generally do; thinking of what I'd teach him, what I'd like him to be.

I went to see them that evening; she looked beautiful, Jill, against the pillows, happier than I'd ever seen her, with this lovely, beaming smile. Not that she'd never smiled in the past; she had, a lot, but there'd been something, I don't know, like something held back about it, a kind of sadness, but now there wasn't nothing held back.

Then I looked at the baby, in a little cot beside her, and I don't know what I'd been expecting; I mean, I'd seen enough babies before, but somehow they'd been nothing like this—maybe they'd been older—this little white monkey thing, with a squashed nose and its eyes screwed tight—all red around the eyebrows, and this tuft of hair on its head, like a red Indian. Jill said, "Isn't he lovely?" and I said, "Yeah, lovely," and when I got outside, I felt a bit strange, sort of empty.

It wasn't just the baby; it was something to do with *her,* her smile. I mean, I was included *in* the smile, me *and* the baby, but it was *about* the baby, and I was expected to join in and feel like she did. It took the baby to make her smile like that.

Not that I wasn't fond of the baby; I was. I'd do anything like get up in the night to him, walk him around and pat his back when he'd got the colic, things like that, but when I'd look at them together, her playing with him, her smiling at him, well, I'd wonder where did *I* come in.

It mightn't have been so bad if at least we could have made love, but of course, that was out, and there was times when I felt terrible; I'd lost Sam, I seemed to have more or less lost Jill, and Kurt was over in Nuremberg. There was days down there on the Crystal Palace track that I could have cried, bashing along in the rain, my shins hurting, clocking myself at the end of the lap, resting, belting on again. It was worse than old Sam's pain barrier, this, this being on your own, this flogging yourself.

It was all too much for me, I couldn't take it, and I started spending more and more time in Nuremberg. I'd go over for a weekend and find myself spending a week, or I'd go for a week and I'd stay for two. Kurt was there—and Helge was there. I admit I'd feel bad about it at times, but what could I do? If I'd just stayed in London, I'd have gone mad.

Then the season got going, and it wasn't quite so bad, except that in a way it was a crap season, one with nothing to go for; you could lose a lot, but you couldn't prove nothing. If you won, well, you was expected to win, and if you lost, you was a twot. Even the world record, there wasn't the same incentive to break it now that you held it or, anyway, half of it. You was more concerned with someone else coming along and breaking it, which they did. This Keita. In July.

XIII

Poor Ike. First it was Cooper, now it's Keita; the usual African police sergeant with eighteen or nineteen children; a noble savage, an unspoiled primitive without a motorcar, a runner who has been running all his life, simply to get from one place to another. He's knocked a second and a quarter off the record, and there's only a few weeks for Ike to get it back before the season ends, leaving him a whole winter to worry. And he won't get it back, at least, not this year; he simply isn't running well enough, and he knows it—3.54.8 is the best time he's done all season, and he's lost a couple of races, one here and one in Sweden.

The joy's gone out of his running again; he's a circus horse, prancing around the ring, plumed and splendid, but doing it under duress. For Kurt: the kind animal trainer.

Not that it's all Kurt's fault. There's the baby behind it, too, as one had thought there would be. It's rare that one ever sees the tableau, loyalty; after all, her loyalties are divided— and he simply can't bear it. There must be a new tableau, now, one that doesn't include him: motherhood. Jill would look splendid in that, as well, with those fine, grave eyes. I'm not even sure that, purely as a tableau, it isn't superior. The other had just a tinge of bathos.

When there's not a meeting here, he seems to be in Nuremberg, where he's got everything: Kurt, his Valkyrie, perpetual attention. I don't know how long Jill will stand it.

He's had me out training with him again, *faute de mieux,* no doubt. He phoned me one day, early in the summer, rather sheepish, and said, "Alan, don't you come down the Crystal Palace no more?" He knew as well as I do why I didn't, but the appeal was clear enough, and I trained with him.

Very sorry for himself, he was: "There's times I feel like packing the whole thing in."

I said, "Doesn't every runner?"

Around and recover, around and recover. He said, "How would *you* fancy it, day after day?" I said, "I'd hate it."

"It's bad enough with him," he said, "out in Nuremberg. But on your own." And then, "Especially when some of the people you've been relying on don't help you no more."

I suppose if Sam can be a prophet, Ike's entitled to be a martyr. At times, one conjures up ridiculous images of him, crucified, say, on the hands of a stopwatch.

Then . . . Keita.

We trained together the week after it had happened. "First one and then the fucking other." Like Hydra heads. "And Kurt can't get the lap times," he said. He sounded desperate, almost in tears. "They don't seem to *keep* no bloody records in them countries."

I sympathize with him. The unknown enemy's always more frightening. "Done it in bloody *Tunis,*" he said. "To me, the whole thing looks bent."

So I've a new role now—no longer that of go-between, but comforter, *her* old function. I make the expected noises, the requisite, stock responses, give no advice, because he doesn't want advice, merely reassurance. The advice I'd like to give —retire!—is the last he'd ever want to hear. When he's not complaining about Jill, he's talking about Keita, denigrating him. "Never won nothing that matters. An Olympiad's different"—true enough—"there's no substitute for having *been* in one."

There is, of course: sheer talent, native temperament— and Keita may well have both. Being an illiterate policeman —which I assume he is—in a backward country has marvelous advantages. You're shielded from so many of the pressures: the press, the prying microphones, the television cameras. Though actually I've seen him on the television; so has Ike. He's tall and very slim and moves divinely. No one's ever taught him; you can see it. He simply seems to *glide,* quite effortless. No rigidity—which means no complexes— no obtruding theory.

He's *got* a coach, some Englishman or other, but the fellow sounds modest and sensible, more of a district commissioner who loves the natives. No doubt some American college will grab him in time—Keita, too—and turn him into another pundit.

Ike said, "Moves well, don't he?" then, "He don't look strong."

It's true in the conventional sense he doesn't, but I'm sure he is. We always seem to want the outward and visible signs of strength, looking for these rather than for viability, evolutionary *rightness*. How strong is a bird? How strong is a fish? Would a salmon swim better if it did weight training? Keita has evolved through generations of people who have had to walk and run. When his country ceases to be underprivileged, he'll grow obsolete. So Ike, poor devil, worries about Keita, but I'm sure Keita doesn't worry about Ike. He's probably never even heard of him.

He'll come out onto that track in Tokyo—I can already see it—cool as can be, the way these Africans are, quite expressionless, closed in an envelope of calm, and when the gun goes, he'll be off like a gazelle. He may not win, but that's how he will be. While Ike will be sick and tense, his muscles knotted, full of thoughts of pain barriers and sacrifice, lap times whirring in his head like wasps, conscious of What's Expected of Him, conscious that he's Running for His Country, before the Eyes of the World—and all the thousand shabby clichés.

He *might* still win. I don't believe he will.

Ike Low, Britain's brightest hope for gold medal glory in Tokyo, isn't thinking about Kwame Keita, the man who took away his world mile record: yet.

"I don't suppose we'll run against each other till Tokyo," the tall, twenty-five-year-old Cockney told me, briefly interrupting his skintight training schedule, down at the Crystal Palace Recreation Center. "There's no Empire Games coming up this year, and he's never run in Europe. Mind you, if there's an invitation mile here or in the States, that would be different, but I'm definitely not looking for him. I think you can worry too much about another runner. Let him worry about me."

I asked the Empire Games gold medalist whether he was going to go all-out to recapture his world record before Tokyo.

"No," he told me, "I'm not going to make any special effort, paced races or things like that. If it comes, it comes. But my object is Tokyo; everything else is secondary. I want to arrive in Tokyo in the best possible physical and mental condition I can achieve. Concentrating on the world record, even if I beat it, could throw everything out of gear. I can't afford to risk getting stale."

"But this was just what some people believed you were last season," I reminded him. "That you were jaded. That the blazing will to win, the vibrant ambition, which had driven you irresistibly around the world's tracks had disappeared, albeit temporarily."

Ike paused before replying, "It's true that I've had better seasons. But an athlete isn't a machine. People forget that. And remember, Tom, how long I had to stay tuned up for the Empire Games. A race like that" —Ike beat Canada's Cooper in an unforgettable fighting finish—"takes more out of you than you realize at the time, emotionally as well as physically."

Did he think,—I asked the Cortina-driving London representative of a world-renowned French sports goods firm—that his present training methods could have anything to do with it?

"Some critics," I pointed out to him, "have said that the form of interval training you practice under Nuremberg's Professor Kurt Giesemann can have a deadening effect on a runner."

"That's a load of rubbish!" he snapped. "When an athlete's not running well, people always blame it on his training. They said just the same when I was coached by Sam Dee"—the eccentric individualist whose athletes run on Hampstead Heath—"whose methods are totally different. Kurt certainly puts me through a tough schedule, but so did Sam. Every athlete knows that to stay at the top, he must make sacrifices."

One of them is to spend most of his time between now and Tokyo at the Nuremberg Sports Institute, away from his pretty wife, Jill, herself still a possible for the British sprint team—and his fourteen-month-old son, Neil.

"Do you still intend to retire after Tokyo?" I asked him. "Win or lose?"

"Yes," he replied firmly, then added, with a smile, "Of course, it will be much easier if I win!"

It had to come, the blowup. The wonder was it didn't come no sooner.

She hadn't *said* nothing about me being away so much, nothing about Helge, but every time I come back, I could feel it; it was in the air. The way she never seemed to speak now unless I did. The way she never smiled unless it was at him, at Neil. Not that I'd got anything against *him*, of course; he was a fine little kid, happy all the time, smiling, hardly any trouble, with these blue eyes and chubby cheeks and fair hair. But it was him and her now; I was on the outside; I didn't even ask her to come training no more, because I knew what the answer would be. Too busy.

One Sunday morning I couldn't stand it no longer. I'd come back to run at the White City against France. I'd won all right but in a bad time, 3.59.8, and I was sitting there looking at the papers, most of them knocking me. She hadn't even been there, the kid hadn't been well, and that didn't help; that gave me a lot of encouragement.

She was feeding Neil in his high chair, burbling away to him, and suddenly I just couldn't take it; I said, "I might as well move out altogether, mightn't I?"

She turned to me and said, "Yes, you might." Like that. Changing completely. Not smiling when she looked at *me*. I said, "All right, I will. I will, then. I'll move out to Nuremberg."

She said, "Why not? You can live with your girlfriend all the time then, can't you?"

This was the first she'd ever mentioned it, and it shook me. I said, "What do you mean?"

She said, "Oh, Ike, you know what I mean," and just went back to feeding Neil, like I wasn't even there.

That made me mad. I got up and grabbed her arm; I said, "What are you *talking* about?"

She shook free, she picked up the baby and went out, chatting away to him, telling him not to mind. I sat down again at the table; I was completely choked. You couldn't *be* more choked than what I was.

She come back after a while; she said, "He's settled down. I don't want us quarreling in front of him." I said, "Oh, yeah, always him." She looked at me like she didn't understand me; she said, "He's a baby, Ike. He's still completely helpless."

I said, "What's all this about my girlfriend?" and she give

a little sigh; she said, "Oh, Ike, don't bother to bluff it out. I've known for ages." I said, "Who from? Who's been telling you?" She said, "Everybody knows. You didn't keep it very secret, did you? You'd be surprised how glad people are to tell you things like that."

I said, "Well, what do you expect? The way you've turned away from me. The way you've ignored me."

She shook her head; she was smiling again; she said, "*I* haven't turned away from you, Ike. It's you that's turned away. You ask more than anyone can give."

I said, "I don't ask no more than what you *used* to give me."

I got up and left the room. There was only the one case to pack.

XIV

Last night he turned up on my doorstep and said, "I've left Kurt," with the tone and expression with which a man might say, "I've left my wife." Except, of course, that he *has* left his wife; she and the baby have been in Manchester for weeks.

I asked him in and offered him a drink, a reflex action, but he took it, gulped it. He looked distraught, utterly lost, and one felt for him. Quite adrift; no wife, no father figure. For when he'd left Sam, at least he'd had Jill, at least he'd gone to Kurt, and now . . . he could only come to me.

I said, "I'm sorry." He said, "I'm not sorry. Pounding that fucking track, day after day. I should have done it long ago. Got no bloody *shins* left."

"What'll you do now?" I asked.

"Christ knows," he said. "Christ bloody well knows."

"You won't go back to Sam?" I said, as if it were the last thing one imagined, to which he said, "Fuck Sam. Fuck all of them. You do the running; they take the bloody credit."

"I could have told you that," I said.

He said, "Well, why didn't you?" and I, "Because, my dear Ike, you'd never have listened."

He got up and started moving about; he's as nervous as a racehorse and in the same way, full of such animal energy that he can never sit still for long. "First Jill," he said, "then this," like a young King Lear, a young Sam. "That's all I bloody needed in Olympic year."

"Well," I said, "I think it could make you or break you," and when he asked me what I meant, I told him, "You're on your own, aren't you? For the first time," and he brightened at that; he turned to me and said, "Yeh, a mature athlete don't need no coach, do he? Poncing on him, ordering him around. Look at that Belgian fellow; I was talking to him over there. Give his coach the boot, and he's never run better.

That's one of the things decided me. He said to me, 'A coach! What for do you need a coach?' "

I said, "Well, certain athletes do. At certain stages."

He spoke about the scene when he told Kurt that he was going to leave him. I could imagine it only too well, all the head shaking, the tearful incomprehension: "But this I do not understand."

He said, "I told him, 'Look at my times this season; nothing better than 3.57.2. I don't *want* to run,' I said, 'that's what you've done to me.' " He said, "You remember how old Sam went on? About this flying thing? How when things was really going right, you didn't seem to *make* no effort, you felt like you was flying? Well, I can't remember when I felt that last. All this season, I've *known* about every step I took. I used to look forward to races; now every one's a job of bloody work."

"So now you'll train yourself?" I asked, and he turned to me again, pathetically, I thought, "You'll train with me, won't you, Alan?"

"Of course I will," I said, "if you think it'll be any help."

"It *will* be," he said. "It gets so fucking lonely on your own."

Then he became euphoric, like a genie escaped from its bottle. "You don't know what it'll be like without those bleeding schedules to slog through, lap after bloody lap, like some bloody engine going around and around."

"Oh, yes," I said, "I think I can imagine."

"And him with his hand on your heart between the laps," he said, "and that expression on his face while he does it, like you were fucking dying. I mean, there's not *that* much to training, is there? Not when the season's on. A bit of stamina work, a bit of speed work. Maybe a little cross-country."

I was waiting for him to mention Jill, wondering if he'd send me up there again, and eventually he said, "Jill, you know; that's finished."

I said, "I'm very sorry."

"Oh, yeah," he said. "Well, she found out about Helge, and that done it. That and the kid. She changed when she'd had the kid."

"Women tend to," I said.

"But after what we'd *had* together," he said, as though he still couldn't credit such a gross betrayal. "After the things we'd *done*."

He said he'd had no contact with her since they'd parted again, and he'd let the house, "I couldn't stay in it, not now." The few times he's been back, for meetings, he's stayed with the team, in Lancaster Gate, at that friendly, flyblown way station. I told him he could move in with me if he liked; there was a comfortable divan.

So that's what he's done. I've an idea that it will only be temporary, that sooner or later he'll be on his way to Manchester, to Canossa; or is Canossa Hampstead Heath?

Only two months away from the Tokyo Olympics, British miler Ike Low has decided to go it alone.

Henceforth, I can reveal, he will no longer be trained by Germany's Professor Kurt Giesemann, foremost exponent of the rugged interval training method, at the £250,000 Nuremberg Sports Institute.

This is the second time Low, who has been living in Nuremberg most of this season, has parted company with a top-level coach. Two years ago he ended a five-year partnership with fast-talking vegetarian Sam Dee, announcing that he no longer believed in Dee's unconventional methods.

Instead, he put himself in the hands of Giesemann—and went on to strike gold for Britain when he won a majestic mile at the Perth Empire Games.

Now, after a disappointing season in which he has failed to recapture the world record he once held from new wonder miler Kwame Keita, he has decided to break with Giesemann and carry on without a coach.

"I don't think I need one now," he told me. "I'm not saying that I didn't learn a lot from Sam and from Kurt, but I feel it's time I stood on my own two feet. If I'm going to win in Tokyo, and I still think I can, there's only one way to do it; the way it has to be done on the track. Alone."

Ike, a lot of people seem to feel that coaches claim too much credit for their runners' achievements. Would you agree with that?

Yes, I think I would.

Would you agree with it in your own case?

Well, up to a point, yes. I mean, I'm not saying that they

haven't helped me, Sam and Kurt, but sometimes I've wondered, "Blimey, who was running this race?"

Is that the reason you've decided to do without a coach, in future?

Partly, yes.

It seems a pretty bold decision, so close to the Olympic Games.

That's why I done it. *Because* they was so near. Because I knew I was running badly.

You think it was because of the effects of interval training that you weren't running well?

I do, yeah. It was taking the edge off of me. I didn't want to run.

And now you do?

Yeah.

But when you switched from Sam Dee's form of training to interval training under Professor Giesemann, you said very much the same thing.

Did I?

Well . . . more or less. Yet soon after making the change, you had that magnificent victory in the Empire Games mile at Perth.

I think at the beginning interval training did help me. I mean, it was a change. I'd been training Sam's way for five years. This was something different. Maybe because of that.

And how will you train between now and Tokyo?

Well, sort of a mixture. Some track work, some cross-country. I'll mix it up. When I get bored with one, I'll go on to the other.

Won't you find the tremendously tough schedules a world class athlete has to follow pretty hard without someone to supervise you?

No, why should I? I done a lot of training on my own when I was under Kurt. He'd send me the schedules, and I'd run them.

But he drew up these very meticulous schedules, didn't he?

Well, now it'll be me draws them up, won't it?

I'd been back a couple of weeks before I went up to see Jill. Since the day I walked out, we hadn't spoke to each other, hadn't written, nothing. But I wanted her back; I just had to have her back; it was pulling at me.

I knew what a lot of people thought, that I'd behaved like

a shit; my own parents did, though they never said it in so many·words, just hinted, Mum shaking her head and clucking the way she did, saying what a pity it was, what a nice girl Jill was, what a shame about the baby, because I couldn't hide it from them, not after I'd gone ahead and let the house, and anyhow, I reckon she'd guessed for a long time.

I could see why they all blamed me, because they could only see one side, the obvious side, which was her side, and I'm not saying I was in the right, that it was all one way. What I am saying is that we was *both* wrong, Jill *and* me, her from my point of view, me from her point of view, but like I say, hers was the one everybody saw: the obvious one.

The funny thing was I missed the kid as well, he was a lovely little boy, and if things had been different, if I hadn't got so much at stake, I'd have liked to be more with him. But the way I saw it, there was time for that; there was time after Tokyo; I could be with them both then.

I didn't know just what I was going to do. Probably stay with the firm, only doing a bigger job, maybe sales director for Britain or something. The only trouble was that when I put it to them, they were always a bit evasive; they'd have to see, they weren't quite sure what plans they'd got for the English side, till gradually it sunk in. If I won in Tokyo, I'd be all right. If I didn't, as far as they were concerned, I could get stuffed. And I wondered what would happen to the job I *had* got, if I didn't win and then I retired; would I keep it, or would even that go, too? It wasn't a very nice thing to have on your mind.

I drove up to Manchester; I'd got so much to think about, I nearly had a couple of accidents. I knew how she'd be when I got there, I knew it wasn't going to be easy, but I just hoped I could get through to her, make her see *my* point of view.

When I did get there, it was her mother opened the door. From the look on her face, I thought for a moment that she'd slam it on me. I said very quick, "Can I speak to Jill?"

She said, "If she'll speak to *you*, which I doubt." I said, "All right; ask her then."

She give me another look, but then she called upstairs, "Jill, it's Ike," like she was saying, it's chicken pox, and I heard *her* say, "Ike?" Then I could hear little Neil in the background, and honestly it did something to me, in the stomach; I'd just got to see him; I called, "Neil," and he called back, "Dadda!" Then I could hear them on the landing upstairs, her talking to him very softly, then coming *down* the stairs, and waiting then was like waiting for a race, for the gun to go; the water in your guts.

When she did turn the corner, you couldn't have seen two expressions more different, him, the baby, laughing all over his face he was so pleased, flapping his little hand at me, but her all closed, the old thin red line touch. At the bottom of the stairs she stopped and just said, "Yes, Ike?" while Neil was still bubbling over, so I talked to him, not her; I didn't mind; at least it was a start.

So I didn't rush things. We went into the living room, and I sat there with Neil on my lap, playing with him, making him laugh, and what could she say when he was enjoying it so much? When her mother got up and said she'd go out and make some tea, I knew I was in, all right.

Jill looked at me and said, "What is it you want, Ike?" I said, "I want you back."

"No, you don't," she said. I said, "For God's sake, Jill, why do you think I've come?" She said, "I did come back. Look what happened." I said, "Look, it's *diff*erent." I started to get up, and she held out her hands for Neil. Always Neil. I let her take him. She said, "Nothing's different," and she hugged Neil close to, like I wanted to take him away. She said, "The only difference is that you've left Kurt. Don't worry. I expect you'll find somebody else." She was really putting the boot in.

I said, "I've left him; I've left her." She said, "Did you let them know? Or did you just walk out on *them,* too?" Then she started bouncing Neil up and down on her knee till he was laughing again; he'd gone all quiet and serious, almost like he realized what was up.

I said, "You know what your trouble is? You won't make no allowances." She said, "And *your* trouble is you expect everyone to go on making them."

I didn't answer that. What I'd told her was true, though; I had left Helge, the same time, really, as I'd left Kurt. To me, she was part of it, part of the whole Nuremberg thing, even though she and Kurt hadn't got no time for each other. He was one side, she was the other, and they was both wrong, both no good for me. It wasn't only the sex thing with Helge, though I'd been getting worried about that, too—it was the way she knocked things, the way she laughed at me training so seriously. She said once, "So if you lose in Tokyo, what do you do? Do you shoot yourself? Yes! I think maybe you shoot yourself with the starting pistol, no?" which didn't seem funny to *me*.

Besides, she was bound to be out there herself, running for Germany, and that was all I bloody needed in Tokyo, her undermining me in every way, in *and* out of bed.

Jill's mother brought the tea in, and what with one thing and the other, it wasn't till she'd bathed Neil and put him to bed that we really got to speak. By then her father was back, and he was the same as her mother was; he'd hardly speak to me. I wanted to get her out of there to talk to her, I asked her why didn't we go for a drive, but she wouldn't; she didn't want to leave Neil, she said; he'd been waking in the night, so it was back to that living room again.

I told her, "Listen, I can get the house back quick enough, if that's what's worrying you." She said, "That doesn't worry me," and I said, "Well, what does then? Come on, tell me what does, and I'll put it right. Don't you think I love you? Is that what it is?" and she shook her head from side to side like it was all hopeless.

I said, "Of course I bloody love you; why do you think I come up here? I took hold of her hand; she just let me hold it. I said, "Don't go telling me you don't love *me!*" And she looked at me then; there was tears in her eyes; she said, "I don't, not now. I'm cold, Ike, I don't feel anything. That's how it's left me. And if you did it again, if I let it happen again, I think it would be the end of me."

I tried to kiss her mouth; I was kneeling in front of her. She turned her head so I only kissed her cheek. I said, "It won't happen again. I can promise you that, darling."

She said, "Oh, no, you can't, Ike. You may mean it now, because you're worried and lonely, but it's not in you to change. I knew that, and I still came back to you; it was my own fault. But not again. Never."

I said, "Bloody hell, Jill, I'm going to re*tire* straight after Tokyo, you know that, win or lose." She said, "That's another thing you say now. I don't think you'll retire. Not if you don't win."

I said, "Look, if I promise you? If I swear to you that after Tokyo I'm giving up, whatever happens?" But she shook her head; she said, "It's finished, Ike. I could never trust you. I hope you do win in Tokyo, because I know it means more than anything else in the world to you. And

that's why, Ike. Don't you see? That's *why* I can't come
back."

Training these last few weeks with Ike, I begin to be more
aware of the dangers inherent in coaching, a little more toler-
ant of the way Sam and Kurt and the rest have succumbed
to them. For now I can see the temptations, can see how
awfully easy it is to find oneself playing God, by tacit request.
For the athlete himself encourages it; he *wants* to be
treated as a child, to be told what to do and when to do it, to
have his injuries coddled and commiserated, to feel that in
the background, constantly, there's some great, looming
figure who cares, who can convince him that all his pain is
good, who can, if necessary, induce the pain himself.

And there's no doubt about it: Ike *is* running better; it's
concretely evident on the stopwatch, in the results he's getting. "You've done a lot for me, Alan," he says. I tell him,
"I've done nothing at all," and know it's true; but how easy
it would be to believe him! When one knows that this is
simply the effect of the wind of change, the charge he's had
from breaking with Kurt, which may last no longer than a
few weeks, a few races.

He's staying with me still; he's let his house; he can't abide
the thought of going back to his parents. I don't mind having
him, part of the God syndrome perhaps. He's forever con-
fessing to me, forever demanding reassurance. He drove up
to see Jill and came back with a flea in his ear. Apparently
she told him she'd never come back to him, because he'd
made his order of priorities too plain.

Fair enough, but didn't she help establish it? Didn't she
feed the fantasy?—loyalty? The high priestess. Perhaps it's
simply that she's changed cults; from Mercury's acolyte to
Juno's. Not that I tell him any of this: I merely make sympathetic noises. I've been drawn in once, disastrously, and
that was enough.

So I train with him virtually every evening at Crystal Palace, I drive out with him to Richmond Park, which we've
decided we like, and sometimes to Regent's Park, for the
stamina stuff. At least it's pleasant in the parks: deer in one,
Nash terraces round the other, so different from the no-
man's-land of the tracks, with their functional anonymity,
bleak amphitheaters of sweat and toil, almost as bad as the
gymnasium, to which he goes for weight training. But there

I draw the line; I tell him he must go alone to those ugly, fetid places.

The change in him has been astonishing, clearly psychosomatic; we athletes must be among the most neurotically suggestible people on earth. Within a week, a matter of days, the tension had gone out of his body. "Alan," he said, "I've got that *flying* feeling again"—his face suffused with joy— and when he ran against the Russians at the White City, he ran superbly: a 3.55.8 mile which left Semichastny looking like a cart horse.

In the meantime, Keita's knocked another tenth of a second off his own world record, but Ike takes it almost casually. "It was in California," he says, "we've all set records in California. We'll see when the time comes. We'll see, in Tokyo."

I've had to promise him I'll be there; God knows how, with the expense. I'm investigating possibilities, package tours, the sort of thing which encompasses Buddhist shrines, a fortnight in the Olympic Stadium and a visit to the Kabuki Theater.

Ike alternates between states of manic confidence—"I know I'll do it; I know I'm going to win it; I just feel it"—and the need for reassurance: "Do you think I'll do it, Alan? No, but do you really think that? I don't think Jill does. She talked about my not retiring if I *lost*."

That seems to have upset him dreadfully. After all, I suppose, she was once the great believer, and I can't offer him that sort of blind belief; I simply *hope* he wins it. I've got no stake in his success, the way that Sam or Kurt had. For them, it was a vested interest, a justification. They had to believe in him, as much as he had to believe in them. But I feel the same as I've always felt, that he won't win, that his moment passed in Rome. Keita hasn't formed or influenced that view; he's simply the outward and visible manifestation of it at the moment, one's apprehensions made flesh.

"This Keita, Alan, I mean, it's *known* blacks are mainly sprinters."

"Or marathon runners."

"Yeah, all right; marathon runners. But not middle-distance runners. They never *done* nothing in middle distance."

Poor fellow. He needs a far more passionate preceptor than I can ever be.

Olympic gold medal hope Ike Low powered his way

to a 3.54.9 invitation mile triumph at the White City and flung out his challenge: "Now I'm ready for Keita."

The six-foot, twenty-six-year-old Low, now carrying on without a coach, left behind a field which included three of the men expected to challenge him in Tokyo: Canada's Terry Cooper, Hungary's Pal and West Germany's Blattler.

Said Ike: "I took a gamble when I decided to go it alone, but now it's working out. I'm approaching my peak at just the right time. Keita, here I come!"

Disappointed at the 3.40.8 in the 1500 meters which was good enough to win him only a second place behind Hungary's Zoltan Pal in Budapest, Ike Low said, "I just couldn't get going. I'd had some stomach trouble before the race, and it seemed to weaken me."

XV

HAMPSTEAD HEATH. *An afternoon in early September.*
Autumn is not yet here; the trees are still a deep, unblem-
ished green; the sun is gentle, the sky a little hazed.
    Like a pilgrim, or a penitent, IKE LOW *ascends the crest of*
a small hill, and casts his eyes about the Heath. He wears a
soft, pale-blue woolen jersey, open-collared, over a second
jersey, maroon and polo-necked. His trousers, blue, are cut
fashionably narrow, without turnups; his black leather, lace-
less shoes come to an emphatic point.
    Far away, from out of a copse, three tiny, white, running
figures appear. IKE *watches as, alternately, they vanish, then*
reappear, growing steadily larger on each reappearance,
swallowed by dells and declivities, to be revealed again by
the brows of shallow hills. In time, it becomes clear that they
are wearing white briefs and singlets. One has white hair;
one is dark; the third is blond. As the men approach—it can
*be seen now that they are men—*IKE *seems to grow increas-*
ingly uneasy. Hands in pockets, he pivots first right, then
left, as if he were about to go. But at last, with anxious, mani-
fest resolution, he straightens his shoulders, hands still in his
pockets and, statuesquely, waits.
    The three men do not advance steadily or regularly. Every
now and then the blond man or the dark man dashes for-
ward, as if invisibly pursued; the one left behind then rushes
to catch him. The white-haired man moves always at the
same speed, the others occasionally slowing, to allow him to
rejoin them.
    Now they are only a few hundred yards away, and they are
recognizable. The white-haired man is SAM, *bronzed and*
corded, his lean body still carrying the very minimum of
flesh. The dark man, tallest of the three, is TOM BURGESS, *the*
distance runner, his forehead lined now; his face, taut with
effort while he sprints, set, in repose, in an expression of

faint, perpetual surprise, as though something has gone wrong, but he is not sure what. The third blond man is RONNIE BLACK, *the international hurdler.*

IKE'S *own face, now, is transformed by apprehension. His eyes snap, his mouth twitches a little, but the position of his head is consciously maintained, like that of a guardsman, conditioned to stand firm under fire. The* RUNNERS, *when they are two hundred yards away from him, turn suddenly and sharply to the right. He opens his mouth, as if he were about to call them, but closes it again, without a sound.*

SAM'S *voice can now plainly be heard.*

SAM: Go Tom!

TOM BURGESS *obediently sprints.*

The tension slowly leaves IKE'S *face, giving way to a wan satisfaction. He looks now like a man who has deliberately incurred a risk, a test, and has then not had to face it. Now he does turn, to descend the little hill, but is scarcely more than a few steps away from it when he suddenly turns again, right, in the direction of the* RUNNERS, *and begins to jog after them, hands still in his pockets, moving with long, easy, powerful strides.*

SAM: Right, *stop! Ronnie!*

RONNIE BLACK *sprints.*

Suddenly IKE *takes his hands out of his pockets, and he, too, sprints, dashing past* SAM *without a glance, past* TOM BURGESS, *smiling now, while each, in turn, stands still, watching him, amazed, watching a revenant. When* IKE *is almost level with* RONNIE BLACK, BLACK *turns, his face, too, astonished, and, as he falters,* IKE *runs past him, taps him lightly on the shoulder, and stops.*

IKE: All right then, Ron?

BLACK *doesn't answer, merely gapes, and now* SAM *and* TOM, *recovering, run to join them. There is a silent confrontation,* IKE *regarding the three with a certain, expectant bravado, not unfriendly,* RONNIE BLACK *continuing to look at* IKE *with astonishment,* TOM *with recrimination,* SAM *with a strange, wry smile, nodding a little, as if to suggest that he, at least, had expected this return. The confrontation narrows, gradually, to one between* SAM *and* IKE. SAM'S *expression does not change, but* IKE'S *grows anxious, vaguely defiant, like that of a guilty and rebellious child.*

IKE (*at last*): Thought I'd come and see you.

SAM *merely nods, still grinning.*

IKE: See how you were getting on, like.

SAM *nods again, suggesting total understanding.*

SAM: I knew you'd be back, Ike.

IKE: Did you?

SAM: But you don't know whether I'll *have* you back.

IKE *opens his mouth as if to deny any such ambition, but he closes it again, without speaking.*

SAM: You've tried interval training, you've tried being on your own, and you've come back.

His voice rises steadily higher, louder.

You have come back because you need me. Because you realize now that I and I alone understand *your* needs, I alone can inspire you to surpass yourself. I alone can offer you the chance of victory in Tokyo, an Olympic vi¢tory, which must be the climax of any athlete's career. *You* have come back to *me*—

IKE (*halfheartedly*): I never said—

SAM (*inexorably*): But am *I* prepared to come back to *you?* After being deserted. After being betrayed. After being publicly criticized and denigrated.

Now, as he speaks, his words are infused by growing acrimony, a self-generating fire.

My ideas mocked. My training methods, to which you owe everything you are, held up to ridicule. To the ridicule of cranks and charlatans, impostors who *destroy* talent, while pretending to develop it.

SAM *turns to* TOM BURGESS *and* RONNIE BLACK, *who are regarding* IKE, *now, with the disdainful reproach of believers for an apostate.*

What should I tell him? Should I tell him what he deserves to be told? What I would be a thousand times justified in telling him? To go to hell. To take the consequences of what he's done: the wasting of his talent, the failure of his ambition. What should I tell him?

TOM *and* RONNIE *are silent, as if aware that these questions are rhetorical.* IKE's *expression is now strained and apprehensive. He breaks, at last, a protracted silence.*

IKE: It's up to you, Sam.

SAM: Of course, it is up to me. And I will surprise you. I will behave toward you in a Christian spirit, although in many cases I deplore the Christian spirit, the turning of the other cheek. I devoted five years of unstinting care and patience to you and your career, and you rewarded me with betrayal. But I scorn to behave in such a way. I realize that you have acted not out of malice but out of weakness, that you have been undermined and led astray by those you believed to be your friends—and closer than your friends. So I am taking you back: not despite what you have done, but *because* of what you have done. Yet I warn you now: it may be too late.

There is a hiatus. IKE *seems overwhelmed; he cannot look at* SAM. *The faces of the other two slowly relax into expressions of benign complaisance.*

Almost autonomously, IKE's *right hand rises from his side, until it is stretched toward* SAM, *who takes it in his own, looking hard into* IKE's *face, till* IKE *at last raises his eyes, to meet* SAM's.

SAM: I have told you. It may be too late.

They're together again! Miler Ike Low and coach Sam Dee, after a two-year break that both swore was forever.

Said Ike, one of Britain's hottest gold medal hopes for Tokyo, in the 1500 meters, "I realize now I made a mistake in leaving Sam. I'm glad he's prepared to coach me again."

Sixty-year-old Sam admitted, "I've missed Ike. I don't usually agree to take a runner back once he's left me, but this time I'm making an exception. I still believe in the boy."

The Hamlet-like indecisions of Ike Low, one of our few genuine hopes for Tokyo, simply go to illustrate the tremendous pressure under which an international athlete has to live, especially in an Olympic year, and the need many of them have for a friendly shoulder to lean on.

Low, who left the explosive, uncompromisingly authoritarian Dee two years ago for Professor Kurt Giesemann, a leading exponent of interval training at Nuremberg, left Giesemann, too, this season. But after only a few weeks on his own, he has now returned to Dee.

It would be irrelevant to criticize his decision on grounds of hard logic and the respective merits of the

two coaches' training systems. The fact is that when a
world class athlete reaches a certain level of achievement, what's best for him is probably what he feels to
be best. The proof of the pudding will be in the eating:
in Tokyo.

So there were two Canossas.

It was funny, being back with him. Like one of those
dreams where you think you've done it all before. His voice
again, driving you on, the whole time; just like before. Do
this, do that. Treating you like a kid, after all that time away
from him, most of it out on your own. Because that was what
he did, I could see it now: treat you like a kid.

Still it wasn't so bad being back on the old Heath again,
better than that bloody track at Nuremberg or the one at
Crystal Palace, come to that, going around and around it
till your shins ached, till you was what Sam said, like an ox
pulling a waterwheel or something.

The only thing I could have done without was the pain
barrier stuff; I wasn't used to that no more, him driving you,
yelling at you, pushing you on when you want to drop, when
there's nothing in the world but you and the pain, everything
black, the pain singing in your head. Christ, I could have
done without that. The only thing you could say is that it
don't happen that often, where with the interval stuff there's
never any end to it; you're going through these *small* barriers
lap after lap, time after time, getting whittled away. And I
knew that what he said was right, that in Tokyo I *would*
have to go through the pain barrier to beat this Keita, because to beat him, I'd have to run faster than I'd ever run
before.

He didn't let me forget about leaving him, nor any of the
things I'd said, the things I was meant to have said, in interviews and that; he'd remembered all of them; he'd keep on
throwing them up to me. Like he'd break off in the middle of
telling us where he wanted us to run, across the Heath, and
say, "But I don't allow you to think for yourselves! Ike has
said so. Ike has announced it. Sam never lets you think for
yourself. So I am only making suggestions. I would like to
know whether there is any disagreement. I am encouraging
you to be independent. No questions? No suggestions? Then

let me ask one question of Ike. Did Professor Giesemann let you think for yourself? Yes? No? I am waiting for an answer."

What did you answer him?

Jill he hardly ever talked about. He asked me once where she was. I said, "Manchester," and he nodded and smiled like he was pleased, like he'd expected it. Then, when I told him I was living at Alan's, he give me the same nod and smile; he said, "Come and live at my place. I've an extra room." So I did; I went and lived over at his gymnasium. When I told Alan I was going back to Sam, he just smiled; he said, "Naturally." I said, "You done a lot for me, Alan, really," but he said, "I've told you before, I've done nothing. It's Sam who likes to hear these things."

I'd have stayed with Alan, I honestly would, but after that race in Budapest, the one when I'd had the stomach trouble, nothing went right; I was back to where I'd been when I left Kurt. It's funny how these things can affect you. I mean, you lose a race *because* you're not fit, you know that's why you lost it, everybody else knows, but you've still lost; it still depresses you. I come home and run a lousy race in Birmingham, 4.02, I was crap over in Warsaw, though I won, and I was back in that bloody rut again, with just a few weeks to go to Tokyo.

I was desperate, I admit it, and who was there left to go to but Sam? The funny thing was that I did start feeling better; I don't think it was the training so much as it was him, the way he made you feel; even Kurt couldn't do that.

I mean, take this whole Keita thing. Where Kurt would go on and on about lap times, comparing one race with another, one lap with another, in the same race and different races, working out the averages, Sam didn't bother with none of that; he just said, "Keita has never beaten you. Keita has never *proved* that he is better than you in a race. Above all, he has never competed in an Olympiad. His world record is of *relative* importance. It proves that he is a great runner—we must give him his due—it does *not* prove he is a great competitor, which you have proved yourself time and again."

Which was exactly what I needed to hear, instead of all this stuff about the times the bloke had done, that just built him up into something bigger than what he was.

Another thing Sam said was, "Very well, Keita is the favorite. *Let* him be the favorite. It is to your advantage. Let

him come under all the pressures, while you can stand aside
and work in peace. He is welcome to be the favorite, so long
as *you* are the winner."

It was like old times, going up to Stan's place again, having his wife give me the eye. She said, "You *were* a naughty
boy," and him, "You've been a cunt. If it was me, I'd have
told you to go off and get stuffed."

The one that was really choked was old Ron Vane. We
had this Olympic get-together, over the Crystal Palace, and
he said, "I'm surprised at you, Ike, I really am. I thought
you'd grown up. I thought you were sensible now. Why
didn't you come to me if you had any problems? You know
I'm always ready to help you."

I said, "Yes, I know that, Ron."

He said, "I thought you'd seen through him. And you
know what it means? It means we'll be having him around
our necks again in Tokyo, making a nuisance of himself in
the Olympic Village. It has a very bad effect on the team,
you know."

I didn't run much between then and Tokyo, there didn't
seem no point, though I did a couple of good times in
Sweden, a 3.55.6 and 3.54.7.

Living at Sam's was okay. Normally it might have got on
my wick a bit, the way he went on, nonstop, but with how I
felt, it was what I needed; it give me my confidence back.

It was funny, really, the way he did all the cooking and a
lot of the cleaning, everything always very neat and tidy,
everything always in the right place. If you left a shoe in the
middle of the bedroom or you didn't put a barbell back, he'd
be after you. He said, "Neatness is what I acquired in the
merchant navy. The humblest dwelling can be kept bright
and tidy, just as the most luxurious can degenerate into a
slum."

Jill I didn't think a lot about, though every now and again
I got this twinge wondering about Neil: how was he; what
was he doing; what had she told him about me? It was all
Tokyo now, it had to be, and getting in touch with her would
only upset me. Afterward, well, maybe we'd work something
out. After all, she had asked for no divorce, or nothing.

And you *really* think you can do it, Ike?
I do, yes.
Bloody fool.

Because a lot of people seem to have the idea that Keita is unbeatable.

He ain't beat me yet, has he?

I knew what they thought, all right, but it didn't matter, where before it would have upset me, I would have brooded on it. But that was Sam. That was what he could do for you.

I suppose there's a certain appositeness to it, even a certain inevitability. After all, it was either Jill or Sam; she wouldn't have him, so he went to Sam. And Sam took him back. For two reasons, I think. First, because he's found no one else of that stature, no one else he could trumpet in Tokyo; second, because he's got nothing to lose.

If Ike wins, then it's thanks to him; after all, he was running badly when he forgave him. Should he lose, well, he didn't quite come back in time.

Tokyo gold medal hope Ike Low promised me today, "I'm going to give every ounce of strength I've got, I'll take all the pain and punishment my body can stand, to bring gold medal glory to Britain."

The tall, bronzed and handsome twenty-six-year-old Londoner went on, "I know that once I'm out on that Olympic track, I'm not just Ike Low from Hackney, I'm representing the hopes of fifty million people. If I fail, I don't just let myself down, I let Britain down."

Quietly he added, "They tell me world record holder Kwame Keita is a superman, that he can't be beaten. Well, we'll see about that. After all, he's only got two legs, the same as I have."

And Low flung out this warning to the prancing policeman: "Whoever wins this race, it's going to hurt him like hell."

XVI

How strange it is, how utterly unreal! Despite all their sedulous aping of all that's worst in the West, their motorways, their repugnant skyscrapers, their long, lonely, miserable American bars! How they must despise and loathe themselves! One can't account for it simply in terms of their love for us, those camera-clicking orgies for the ugliest Occidental, those television actors with their Westernized eyes.

Yet beneath the new city, the brutal parody of ourselves, it seems to me that another city lurks, the "real" Tokyo, just as a Japanese businessman, I've heard, goes home at night, takes off his city suit, and puts on a kimono. One finds it in the narrower streets, under the charming paper lanterns, in the neat little one-story houses, skulking among the skyscrapers, in the shrines beneath the spiky trees. And, more sinister, in all those mute, black banks of schoolboys, sitting in the stadia, quite subservient, waiting for orders.

I say "we," but now I'm a noncombatant, a tripper, a packaged tourist, and I take it badly, like a soldier whose regiment goes into the line without him, while he stays behind with a mosquito bite. One sees so much more; one feels so much less.

Yet some of the stadia are quite remarkable, quite different from the sordid skyscrapers; the roof of the swimming pool swoops and bucks like waves on a Cubist sea.

And heavens, how different they are from us! Our group has a delicious interpreter; last night I took her to dinner, then went home and slept with her. The shock of waking beside her, seeing that strange, infinitely foreign face on the pillow, the intensity of it, the shut, slanting eyes, the tawny color of her skin. A cat, a lion, a different species. When she's awake and smiling at me, the strangeness disappears, but in repose, asleep, she might come from another world.

How anxious to please, how frantic to be loved, the whole

city is, like a parvenu at a royal reception. And how different from Rome, where *we* were the upstarts, where the city snubbed us.

But like an old soldier, I'm not happy among civilians, once the shooting starts, and I spend hours on end in the Olympic Village. It's full of plantains, bicycles; the usual, nervy good humor. Tall Negroes tower above one in the restaurant; gigantic Russian women pedal sternly by in track suits. Sam is here, there and everywhere, holding his little seminars, cheerfully boasting and hectoring. Ike is by turns intense and remote, talkative and distracted, and when he does talk, it's always of the race or the infrastructure of the race. "I run a 1.47.8 this morning—cheerfully—or—less cheerfully—"This Keita's meant to have done 3.37.8 down the track, this afternoon." He asked me had I seen him run; what did I think of him? I said I had seen him run, that I thought he looked very fit.

"He ain't *that* fit," Ike said. "I mean, not to look at, he ain't. I'd say he looked a bit weedy, if you asked me."

I didn't disagree, any more than I'd told him what I really thought: that Keita was just as I'd expected him to be, a beautiful animal, full of a marvelous repose. An animal, that's to say, in the best, most enviable sense, explosive in movement, utterly relaxed when he's not. He has a fine, hollow-cheeked face; there's something compact and closed about him. I don't think I've ever seen him smile yet, even at his coach, the consul, a serious blond, plump man, who hovers about him as though he were guarding a favorite tribe from the corruptions of the white man.

As for his running, it's esthetically delightful, even finer than it looked on television, quite without visible effort; those thin black legs simply *devour* the ground. By comparison, even Ike's action seems mechanical and *willed*. He's still a glorious mover, of course, but if Keita is the splendid animal, then he is the imposing machine. Does this imply that the mere human athlete has no future now, no hope? Perhaps it does.

Yesterday, in Tokyo's Olympic Village, I brought Ike Low the news that 1500 meters rival Kwame Keita had run 800 meters in 1.45.6 on the training track.

"Right!" snapped the dynamic Low. "Tomorrow I'll run 1.44!"

It's in this sort of spirit that the twenty-six-year-old Cockney wonder is preparing for what he knows must be the greatest race of his sporting life. In the Olympic restaurant, he sternly waved aside a Japanese cook's smiling offer of a fillet steak.

"No meat for me!" he snapped. "Not since I've gone back to being trained by vegetarian coach Sam Dee." And I sat beside the Hackney-born, six-footer as he polished off a he-man-sized helping of peas, carrots and potatoes.

So you're still confident, Ike?
Oh, yeah, I'm confident.

Today we had the opening ceremony. How strange to watch it, instead of being part of it. And how strange the mixture of one's feelings: envy and irritation and amazement and, at the end a reluctant participation. With all its inflated silliness, its lunatic pretensions, it finished, once again, by drawing me in. Extraordinary the power of a mass ritual, however bogus and insidious. Here, the very, goggling solemnity of the Japanese made it more pompously absurd than ever.

We had the eerie beating and booming of electronic gongs, like sound effects in a Hollywood film of the mysterious East; one waited for a priestess to appear in a puff of smoke. But all we got, in the end, was a little Japanese runner with the torch, trotting into the stadium, laboring endlessly up an immense, dreamlike flight of green stairs, to light the flame— the sacred flame.

And, of course, the regimented entry of the gladiators, in straw hats and cowboy hats and pink dresses and blue blazers, the great contingents and the comically small ones, paramilitary, making one think, again, in terms of troops, the more so when the old man gave his sonorous address, with its implacable cant about youth, true amateurism and the Olympic spirit.

I think that's when I began to feel moved, seeing him there, once more addressing his cannon fodder like a Great War general, about to send them all out to die on the barbed wire. And they quite sheeplike about it all, silently attentive, listening to the dangerous platitudes, the youth of the world —which he inevitably called them—ready to sell its birthright for a medal. But had I been any better, any different?

I picked out Ike, in the British team, under his white hat. He marches well, as you'd expect, very upright, with a soldierly swing of the arms. Through my binoculars, I watched him during the old man's speech and was happy to find him paying no attention, remote again, his eyes blank and wandering, thinking perhaps of Keita.

Keita's country has only six men in its team; green blazers, white ducks. He carried the flag himself, dignified, closed, no expression. During the speech he, too, switched off, but I doubt if he was thinking about anything. He has the perfect, natural economy of a cat; when there's nothing to think about, he doesn't think.

I, too, found my mind wandering from the old man's words. There was no sense to them, anyway, only symbol: of the young's bondage to the old, the present's to the past. The real ceremony, the true ritual, should have been a public parricide—which was inconceivable.

Yet hadn't the French Army mutinied, in the very end?

At the training track, Sam went up to Keita's coach, this English bloke, and said, "Sir, I greet you as a rival and a friend," and shook hands with him. Then he got Keita over and made the two of *us* shake hands. I felt like a twot. I've got nothing against the fellow, but what do you say to him? Hope you come second?

I said, "Yeah, well, good luck then," but he didn't seem to speak no English; him and the coach chatter away in some African language.

The coach don't speak a lot either, though it's true Sam didn't give him much chance. He looked at Sam like he'd never met no one like him, which probably he hadn't, while Sam was saying, "The Olympic ideal is meaningless to me. I am interested only in the *human* ideal. The Olympic Games is not a means in itself; it is a means to an end, and that end must be brotherhood. We must compete against each other not as enemies but as brothers, not as Englishman against African, German against Russian, but brother against brother—in friendship. Through sport, we must teach the world the way to peace."

The other bloke just nodded and said he was right; he looked a bit worried; then he took Keita away with him, quick, like he was afraid Sam was mad and Keita would catch it.

Helge's here. They don't eat in our restaurant, thank God, but I knew I'd bump into her sooner or later in the village, and I did. We was both on bicycles; it was funny, really, her suddenly cycling by with another German girl, a blonde, looking great, just as good in a way as she did driving her car. Singing, she was, and when she saw me, she called out, "Hi!" with a little smile, not stopping, like she didn't know me that well, and it shook me for a second; I actually stopped; I felt so mixed up, her just going by like that. I even thought of turning around and going after her, and the funny thing was the reason I didn't, the thing that stopped me, was I was afraid how she'd be, would she just give me a brush-off? Then I thought to myself, *That's ridiculous, getting yourself tied up with her now, letting her muck up your chances.* After that, if I see her at all, I'll keep well clear.

As for Kurt, it was a bit like Sam at Perth; only the boot was on the other foot. He was down at the track a lot, of course, and Sam made a point of going up and shaking hands with him, the old bastard, saying he hoped there wasn't no resentment, that he'd always known I'd be coming back to him eventually, but in a way he was glad I'd gone to Kurt, because now I had a better perspective.

Kurt didn't say nothing, just looked upset while Sam was talking, and to me he just give a nod, not looking at me. I suppose you couldn't blame him.

Sam had everything worked out, as usual—all the tactics. The heat and the semifinal he didn't want me to go flat out, just to qualify; he said, "You are big enough now not to have to win every race to prove your superiority. Keita is a one-pace runner. He always runs the same race. He runs without strategy and without intelligence. Notice his times over both distances, the 1500 meters and the mile. They seldom vary more than two or three seconds. That is what I call a monotonous runner. You, on the other hand, are an artistic runner, a runner of temperament. You will rise to the great occasion, and will not respond to the unimportant one. The less mental and physical energy you expend on the preliminary races, the more you will have left for the final. In that race, you will allow the pace to be set by Keita, knowing in advance the race that he is certain to run.

"You will stay within ten yards of him throughout, until the back straight of the final lap, when you will overtake him. It will then be too late for him to alter his tactics, to increase his rhythm, or to recover from the psychological effect, which will be enormous."

It all sounded great while he was talking, like the stuff about letting Keita be the favorite and take all the pressure, but other times I didn't like the way people seemed to be writing me off, taking it for granted Keita was going to win. Like down at the track, the photographers and reporters, he was the bloke they was all after, taking his picture, talking to each other about him. I wasn't jealous or nothing, it just worried me, and maybe I said one or two silly things because of it.

Now here's a guy believes in himself. Name of Ike Low, who would have won the last Olympic 1500 meter final, so he'll tell you, if it hadn't just been for a little thing like a pulled muscle, that stopped him getting there.

Ike doesn't reckon there'll be any pulled muscles stopping him this time. No, sir. He's as sure of winning that gold medal as the Japanese are sure Mount Fuji's going to be there tomorrow morning. Or as sure as a whole lot of us are that a skinny African police sergeant called Kwame Keita is going to run in so far ahead that he'll have time for a quick shower before the rest of the field have made it.

Ike's got it all worked out, though. He says he's got to win because Keita's never beaten him, which is true enough. What he doesn't say is that Keita's never run against him, so maybe the best thing Ike can do is stay in bed on the day of the final and keep his unbeaten record.

Another thing he says when his coach, Sam Dee, isn't talking—it happens—is that Keita has never competed in an Olympiad before. Well, Cassius Clay had never fought a world title fight before he clobbered Sonny Liston, and come to that, John Wilkes Booth had never shot anybody before he assassinated Abe Lincoln.

Sam, who could outtalk any Southern Senator on a filibuster, says that Keita could crack under pressure, pressure meaning Ike. Uh-huh.

Keita doesn't say anything at all, he just goes right on running faster than anyone else. Which, come to think of it, speaks for itself.

Alan's another; I don't think *he* really believes I can do it. He never says so, but I just get the feeling. He smiles to himself and he keeps changing the subject.

And Helge come up to me at the training track yesterday. It was raining—it rains a lot here—and at first I didn't recognize her; she'd got this red raincoat on with a hood. Keita was running; she nodded over at him, and she said, "He runs pretty good, eh?" I said, "Yeah, he runs fine." I knew what she was at. I said, "We'll see how he runs next week."

In the village, Ronnie Black and I was sharing one of these little white hut places, and at least *he* was all right, maybe because he was another one of Sam's. He was a northern lad; he was in the 110 meters hurdles; he knew he hadn't got no chance, but he was going to have a go; everybody was. There was a very good spirit in the team, the best I'd ever known, men *and* women. Even Ron Vane hadn't been able to spoil it.

He'd say, Ronnie would, "I'd fancy me chances against this Keita. They've got no backbone, these blacks; they're all right when it's going well. Another thing, it stands to reason, doesn't it, that it's going to be stranger here for him than what it is for us?"

I reckoned he was right, because they took a bit of getting used to, the Japs, looking so different and sounding so different, the way they'd goggle at you everywhere, like you'd just walked out of a spaceship, the funny little photographers that come into the village and took your photograph, then asked you who you were, the funny, bit-off noises the announcers made over the loudspeakers in the stadium after that bloody Olympic music, noises like you'd never heard before, the crowds, and the way they'd sometimes be so quiet you'd think it was a fucking funeral.

Some of the other athletes would go into Tokyo and look around, but I didn't; there'd be time for that; I didn't want to know nothing about Tokyo till it was all over; they could keep it; it could only disturb you. So I stayed in the village, which was okay, I liked it better than Rome, at least it had a bit of green, and I liked this idea of the bicycles, picking them up when you needed one and dropping them when you didn't, though Sam was on about my not cycling too much; it was no good for the muscles.

I got quite pally with old Cooper, down the track; in a way, we was both in the same boat: It was our world record

that had gone, it was us who would have been the favorites
if it hadn't been for Keita, and now people didn't give us no
real chance. In fact, he said to me, Terry, "I'll toss you for it,
Ike, the silver or the bronze."

I told him he could have them both; there was only one
medal I was bloody interested in.

Ike's avoiding me, now. Fair enough, I suppose. He doesn't
want skeptics around him. Yet I can't find it in myself to
say, "Of course you'll win, Ike," even though I suppose it
might help him, and it would certainly make our relationship
much easier.

He's had no difficulties getting through his heat, jogging
along, full of unleashed power, in 3.39.9. Semichastny of
Russia won it, or was allowed to win it; it was clear Ike
could have passed him when he pleased. It's unusual for him
to be obviously content not to win, though I assume it must
be part of whatever convoluted plan Sam's devised for him.

As for Keita, he ran almost casually, and in a splendid
time: 3.38.5. Next morning, in the village, Ike looked very
gloomy. As soon as he saw me he said, very defensively, "I
wasn't pushing myself, Alan," and at least for once I was
able to tell him what he wanted to know, that it was perfectly
apparent.

I admit it worried me, the way he skated off with that heat;
in fact, I wish I hadn't stayed to watch him run it; it would
have been bad enough just to have heard his time. And he
didn't look pushed; that was what was worst about it. It's all
very well Sam saying he's taking it out of himself while I
ain't taking nothing out, but to me, it looked like he could
have knocked another three or four seconds off his time,
easy.

After the heats, I couldn't get to sleep; I kept wondering
how I ought to run in the semifinal, especially if I got drawn
against him; ought I to push myself or just coast? First I
thought I'd do the one, then the other, but the trouble is if I
did go all out, even if he wasn't in the same race, and I
didn't do as good a time as him, how would I feel?

When I talked to Sam, he said, "You will run as we have
planned you will run. I have told you before, he is a one-
pace runner; therefore, it is natural that he should not exert
himself to run these times. It also means that he cannot do
better than these times. I am certain he has never come to

grips with the reality of the pain barrier, and this is where you have so huge an advantage over him. Under my tuition, you have lived with pain and conquered pain. But you must not disperse your energies. In the semifinal, do enough to qualify, which you will do with ease. Do not do so much that you encroach upon your strength for the final, which is the only race that matters, the only one which will be remembered."

It was wet again the day of the semifinal, a bloody miserable day. I sat next to Sam in the bus that took us from the village to the stadium, knowing Keita was there somewhere in the back. We hadn't been drawn together, thank God. Sam said, "This is the weather that will suit you, but to which *he* is not accustomed," but as far as I was concerned, I'd still have preferred the sun; this bloody rain depressed me.

Keita's semi was first, and Cooper was in it. He'd been joking about it the night before, up the club in the village, saying things like, "Okay, now we'll see if the guy's really human." I don't mind telling you I sat there before his race with my stomach knotted up like I was in it myself. I was praying for Terry to win, because at least I'd beaten him, Terry, and if he could beat Keita, so could I; it meant I could beat both of them.

Right from the gun, Keita went off at a fantastic pace, but Terry stayed with him; the rest of the field just wasn't in it. Sam timed the first lap 52.4, Terry was still holding him well, but you could tell Keita wasn't bothered; he might have been out on a training run.

The second lap he stepped it up even more. Terry still hung on to him, but you could see he hadn't got a lot in hand, from the expression on his face, from the way his head kept lolling to one side, and I got that feeling in my guts again.

At the start of the third, Keita was a couple of yards ahead, and you just knew Terry couldn't make it up, that he'd be lucky if he kept it to that—which he didn't. It was like a nightmare, Terry pounding along, giving it everything, really driving himself, and gradually falling farther and farther behind, five yards, ten yards, nearly fifteen at the bell.

I got up on my feet yelling, "Come on, Terry, *beat* him, Terry!" knowing it was useless; you could see the poor sod was really struggling. In fact, halfway down the back straight, he cracked, and then it was only Keita, strolling it, Terry twenty-five yards behind, till a couple of the others

passed him, and he'd got all he could do to come in fourth
and qualify.

Keita did a 3.36.4, and when he'd come through the tape,
he looked like he wasn't even sweating, dead cool, as if it
hadn't meant nothing to him, while poor old Terry was staggering all over the place like a drunk, till one of those little
Jap officials in a blazer and a panama hat put a blanket
around him.

Sam said, "You see how Cooper paid for his mistake? By
the final, he will have nothing left. He was lucky even to
qualify. He ran the race that Keita wanted him to run. Now
you see how important it is to conserve your energy." But to
me it didn't look like that; to me it looked that whatever race
Terry had run, Keita would still have murdered him.

When I come onto the track, Terry was just going off;
he'd got his track suit on; I said, "Hard luck, old son," and he
pulled a face; he said, "Ike, the guy *isn't* human." Which was
the last thing I wanted to hear before my own race, and I
made a bad start. I got boxed in around the first bend, and
I was still well back until the end of the second lap. Pal of
Hungary was leading, the one that had beat me in Budapest,
and I wasn't enjoying it; I couldn't get going; it was only at
the bell that things suddenly clicked, and I was just *running*
the race instead of thinking about how I was running. I
passed a couple of them in the straight, then another, and
suddenly I felt full of power, like I said, really good.

I heard someone yelling, "Come on, Ike!" probably one
of the team, there was still twenty yards between me and Pal,
but by the back straight it was ten, and I knew I could catch
him if I wanted. He looked around, his face was so worried
that it made me want to laugh; I thought *What are you so
worried about, you silly sod? It doesn't* matter; *you'll still
qualify,* and I deliberately eased up, remembering what Sam
had said. I come in second, and I felt great, knowing I'd got
so much more, so that my time, 3.39.8, didn't mean nothing.

In fact, when I finished, I was laughing.

Tonight, in Tokyo's Olympic Village, a twenty-six-
year-old Englishman will be fighting as tough a battle
for sleep as he will fight tomorrow in the jam-packed
Olympic Stadium for a 1500 meters victory.

His name is Ike Low, and if there is one opponent

liable to keep him awake, it is Kwame Keita, red-hot favorite for this drama-packed final.

Being an outsider doesn't worry Ike. "I reckon it's an advantage," he told me. "The less people expect of you, the easier it is to surprise them." And the six-foot Londoner revealed to me that he and his controversial coach Sam Dee have a plan, a plan which they believe is capable of beating Keita.

"Obviously I can't tell you what it is," said Ike, "but we both believe it will work."

On the face of it, Ike has little chance. While Keita has been burning up the Olympic track, winning his heat and semi-finals in scorching times, Ike has been content to ease in each time in a comfortable second. Yet it has been obvious to anyone who knows the handsome, Hackney-born miler that he has been running well within his capacity.

One memory haunts him. Four years ago, in Rome, he was all set to spring one of the biggest surprises of recent Olympic history. Then, in the 1500 meters semifinal, tragedy. A pulled muscle put the twenty-two-year-old Ike out of the race and cruelly killed Britain's hopes of a gold medal.

Since then he has won and lost the world record, twice won the Empire Games mile title, and seemed all set to strike gold again in Tokyo—till Keita came on the racing scene last year.

"I'll give it everything tomorrow," he promised me. "I mean to run the race of my life. It's win or bust. You might as well come last as come second."

I don't suppose I slept more than three hours. Thinking of everything. Bloody things coming back to you. Not just the race, the way I got to run it, Keita; Jill as well, a lot about Jill and Neil. Had I done right, would I hear from her tomorrow? Because there hadn't been a bloody word, not since I'd got to Tokyo. Remembering how I'd heard from her in Perth, what a difference it had made, and then her being there at the airport, suddenly seeing her. Wondering would she do it again, send a telegram, then be at the airport if I won; be there anyway. It had to make a difference if I won; she couldn't just keep on like she was; winning would change everything, so in a way there was that on the race as well.

I thought a lot about the times I'd done and the times *he'd* done, Keita, because I'd never *done* a 1500 meter time as fast as what he'd done in Tokyo; my best ever was 3.37.8, and it was obvious he could do what he done again and better, because like I said, he'd run it without even being pushed. From that point of view you could see why they'd made him the favorite, but if he hadn't been pushed, neither had I been pushed, he was the one going to push me, and like Sam said, I was a temperamental runner, the more it mattered, the better I run, and I knew I could do a lot more than I'd ever done over 1500 meters, that I could fight my way through that fucking pain barrier; the thing was, how much more could *he* do?

All the morning I was in a daze. I don't remember a lot of it. Nothing from Jill, no cable. Sam going on and on, the usual way, but I couldn't take it in, not how I was; it was like having the radio on in the background: Now and then you'd hear a word, but mostly it was just noises:

"You will win this race. It is, as I have told you, the most important race of your life, and you will run the finest race of your life, because you will need to. Not only will you break the Olympic record, but you will break the world record. To do so, you will have to overcome the pain barrier. You are aware of this, and you are fully prepared for it. It is something you have done many times before, but this time a few seconds' pain can be rewarded with immortality.

"Your chances have been written off by those who have no understanding of athletics and still less of the relative capabilities of the human body. You will win this race because for the first time you will realize your complete potential. And I shall be there to greet you as you come through the tape."

People coming up to wish you luck, Ron Vane shaking hands with me and saying, "Good luck, Ike," like it killed him. Even Helge, that was a surprise, suddenly turning up in the restaurant, giving me a kiss, saying, "Good luck, sweetie," then going straight out again. She hadn't done too bad; she'd won a bronze.

I don't suppose I really woke up till I was actually there at the start, taking off my track suit, suddenly hearing my own name over the loudspeakers in that funny twang. It was a nice enough day, not warm, not cold, and suddenly I had this thought: *Four years and it'd all be gone in less than four minutes.*

How still Keita is, how calm! Like the eye of the hurricane or the center of the whirlpool. Jet black in a bright-green vest, he's even chromatically right. Now and again he jogs a little, but he seems to do it as a gesture, because he knows it's expected of everyone and he wouldn't be so presumptuous as to spurn it, however superfluous.

Ike jogs as though he means it and needs it. Not that he, by his own standards, or any but Keita's standards, seems tense. Even through one's binoculars, he looks surprisingly composed. Sam's brainwashing perhaps. It has its merits.

One knows so well what it feels like out there—that Calvary of waiting; that lonely expectancy. At this point I'm too involved myself to be just a spectator. One has one's own place in the ritual, one's umbilical attachment to the hero, whose every step will be one's own, his triumph our triumph, his defeat our defeat.

Where's Sam? Yes, there he is; he's managed it, bluffed his way through all the diligent gray cordons of police, right to the edge of the track. Now he leans forward toward Ike with the last, galvanizing word, Ike nodding. HMV.

Keita's coach isn't there. He doesn't need to be.

Ike Low drawn in lane four, Keita in lane six. A tremendously tough race for the British boy. He knows he'll have to run the fastest time of his career if he's to win, but in the Olympic Village this morning, he was telling me he felt sure he could do it. A great runner and a wonderful competitor. There's Keita. Very slim, as you can see. A police sergeant, holder of the world mile record, who's run two fantastic times to reach this 1500 meters final. And Terry Cooper, formerly joint record holder in the mile with Low, badly beaten by Keita in the semifinal. Low and Keita meeting for the very first time. They're going to their marks now. The whole of this gigantic stadium suddenly quiet and expectant as they await this Olympic 1500 meters final. And they're away!

Like a child playing with a puzzle. The blobs of color to be shaken and shaken again, yellow and white and red and green and blue and black, out of one pattern, into another, till the last, ineluctable pattern is formed and frozen; the tortured face looms above the tape.

Ike's away well. So's Keita, of course. I wondered what Ike's plan is? What would mine be? To survive, I suppose; but that's a spectator's view. Competing athletes don't think like that.

Cleared the bloody ruck, anyway; all them fucking elbows. Pal out there in front; he'll never stay there. Keita where I want him to be; just a couple of yards ahead.

A *very* fast lap, indeed. Pal of Hungary setting the pace, Keita just behind him, Semichastny of Russia, then Britain's Ike Low. The field's already spreading out as they complete this opening lap, and there goes Keita! My goodness, what acceleration! Passing Pal on the outside and leaving him *well* behind! And Ike Low's going after him! Ike Low, the British runner, determined not to let Keita build up an early lead. The time of that first lap, Cecil?

I made it 51.8.

51.8. This is going to be a very fast race. Keita, followed by Ike Low, then Semichastny. Britain still in with a chance in this nine-man field, in which the ninth man at the moment is Cooper. Terry Cooper of Canada, the former mile world record holder, obviously feeling the effects of that semifinal against Keita.

Stay *with* him, Ike!

Sam. What does he think I'm fucking doing?

Keita's setting a tremendous pace, yet Ike Low's keeping right there on his tail. The British boy, running very powerfully. The *only* one in this race capable of living with Keita. Now Keita is pulling away. He's definitely pulling away. They're entering the third lap, and he's opened the gap to five or six yards.

God, let me catch the cunt!

And a *wonderful* effort by Low; a marvelous recovery by the British boy! He's cut that gap to three yards, two yards. *He's nearly level with Keita!*

Is there real hope? Or is it illusory: the meaningless revival of a cancer patient? It's so obvious he's had to give everything, while Keita moves with that inexorable grace. Look at their faces: anguish and serenity.

The pain. The last lap. Now!

And there goes the bell! The final lap! Keita still in the lead, and what a burst from Low! He's two yards behind, now, one yard!

Come back, you bastard! Can't see him; nothing but the pain. My legs, my legs! Stay with it; then I'm through. Through all the blackness, then I'll see again; he won't be there, he'll be behind me. He's still there! *Fuck him, where's he get it from? Do it all again, the pain again.* Now! *My chest! I'm going to fall! All black, don't see a thing.* "Come on!" *That's Ike. Is that his face? Not running anymore. Just falling, falling.*